CHINA:

READINGS ON THE MIDDLE KINGDOM

Edited by

Leon Hellerman and Alan L. Stein

Introduction by the consulting editor

Yu-kuang Chu

This edition includes a "Supplement on Contemporary China" which covers China's admission to the U.N. as well as President Nixon's visit.

WASHINGTON SQUARE PRESS
POCKET BOOKS • NEW YORK

CHINA: READINGS ON THE MIDDLE KINGDOM

WASHINGTON SQUARE PRESS edition published March, 1971

Revised and Enlarged edition published November, 1973

L

Published by
POCKET BOOKS, a division of Simon & Schuster, Inc.,
630 Fifth Avenue, New York, N.Y.

WASHINGTON SQUARE PRESS editions are distributed in the U.S. by Simon & Schuster, Inc., 630 Fifth Avenue, New York, N.Y. 10020, and in Canada by Simon & Schuster of Canada, Ltd., Richmond Hill, Ontario, Canada.

Standard Book Number: 671-48111-8.
 Published by POCKET BOOKS, New York, and on the same day in Canada by Simon & Schuster of Canada, Ltd., Richmond Hill, Ontario.

Printed in the U.S.A.

Preface

The present work grew out of the participation by the editors in a National Defense Education Act Institute in East Asian Studies held at Queens College of the City University of New York, during the academic year 1966-1967.

We wish to express our gratitude and appreciation to Dr. Isidore Starr, Director of the Institute, for his encouragement and for bringing our work to the attention of the publisher. We also wish to thank Dr. Helen Storen, Professor of Education of the NDEA Institute, and Mrs. Sharon Kanon of Washington Square Press.

We are indebted to Dr. Yu-kuang Chu of Skidmore College, a scholar and educator, for his many suggestions and insights. Without his assistance and patience, this work would not have been possible.

We also thank the many publishers for permission to reprint materials.

For whatever shortcomings, errors of commission and omission, we, naturally, take full responsibility.

L.H.
A.L.S.

Alan L. Stein has received several grants for research in the field of East Asian studies. Leon Hellerman is the author of Polk and Mexico *and the co-editor of* Voices of the Past. *Consulting Editor Yu-kuang Chu is Chairman of the Program of Asian Studies at Skidmore College.*

Table of Contents

CONTENTS

List of Illustrations

Maps

Introduction

The compilers and editors of this book have made a collection of significant readings on China, past and present. Of course, no collection can please everybody. Although some important material may have been omitted, most, if not all, of what is included will be found very useful. An advantage of a book of readings is that it permits flexible approaches in teaching as well as in student discussion.

No matter what approach is employed, it is not sufficient for students merely to learn certain specific facts about China, however important they may be. They must, in a sense, transcend the study of China and see it as an illustrative example of a more general attempt to view a foreign society and culture as a sociocultural whole. They must perceive the interrelationships among (1) the geographical and economic foundations of life; (2) the social institutions, especially the family and the government, and their historical development; and (3) the attitudes, beliefs, and values of the people as reflected in their religion, philosophy, literature, and art. Only when they see how these several aspects hang together do they achieve a meaningful understanding of China or any other foreign culture.

Let us take the Chinese family as an example. The family is important in any society, but perhaps more especially so in China. Why? The traditional family in China was linear, emphasizing continuity of generations on the basis of the father-son relationship. It was also joint, since married sons and their own families stayed with their parents. In spite of the joint character of the family, its average size was only five to six persons. However, large families were the ideal, and well-to-do families were usually larger than poor ones.

Members of the family were organized on the principle of seniority. Seniority was determined first by generation and then within the same generation by age. A married woman derived her status from her spouse, ranking next to him. So each person in the family had a definite status and knew exactly who were his seniors and who were junior to him. The more senior a person was, the more privileges and power he had. This normally worked out so that the oldest male in the highest generation became the head of the family. It also meant, generally, the old controlled the young and women were subordinate to men.

Each relationship between members of the family was precisely named. For example, there were different words for older or younger brothers or sisters, and if there were more than one of each kind, they were numbered. Instead of the general term "uncle," different names were used to differentiate paternal uncles from maternal ones, and among paternal uncles, an uncle older than one's father was named differently from one younger than one's father. They were also numbered. Members of the family called one another not by their personal names, but by their relationship names with numbers. The significance of exact kinship names lay in the fact that they fixed the moral obligations of various members of the family toward one another.

Family welfare took precedence over individual welfare. The group was more important than the individual. For example, marriage was not a personal affair to be decided by personal choice, but a family matter to be arranged by parents. Normally, the young couple to be married did not meet each other until the wedding ceremony. Ancestor worship was an important ritual, because it strengthened a sense of linear continuity and a respect for age. Members of the family performed the ritual in strict order of seniority.

Since in old China there were few social agencies besides the family and the government and since the government rendered few social services, the family had to perform many functions. It not only had the biological functions of reproduction and of caring for the young and the old, but also produced and consumed as an economic unit and was treated by the government as a political unit in taxation, draft, and legal responsibility. Social, religious, educational, and even recreational activities were conducted on a family or interfamily basis. The family was a self-sufficient unit answering practically all basic human needs.

Such were the characteristics of the traditional family

system in China, which persisted for many centuries. It will not do to say that its durability was due to the powerful influence of Confucius or the conservatism of the Chinese. The true explanation, at least in part, lies in its geographical and economic background. In spite of China's large size (third largest country in the world), less than 15 percent of its land is arable because so much of it is mountainous, or too high, or too dry. A perennial problem has been and still is the scarcity of arable land in relation to an expanding population. The average-size farm in pre-Communist China was only about four acres as compared with the over-350-acre farms in the United States. As a result, farming in China has been extremely intensive, in the effort to make every square foot of land produce the most. Lacking capital and modern technology, the farmer has found that about the only way he can increase per-acre yield is to put in more labor. Hence, the importance of the joint family and the emphasis on having sons.

The feudalistic practice of primogeniture (the passing on of land from father to the eldest son only) was abandoned in Han times (ca. 200 B.C.–A.D. 200) in favor of equal division of land among sons. The latter practice, though more democratic, would have quickly created millions of tiny farms too small to be efficient in production. The joint family counteracted this by having married sons stay together and work cooperatively on the family farm. Thus, it tended to preserve the family farm intact or at least slowed down the division process.

There were other environmental factors that supported the joint family system. Transportation was undeveloped. People stayed put and were attached to their land though they were not serfs. The government relied on family and clan heads to control the people and so backed up the authority of these heads. The legal doctrine that the group could be held responsible for the conduct of any of its members placed special responsibility on family heads and acted as a deterrent to crime. Naturally, joint families simplified the task of government.

However, men do not live by bread alone, or by environmental or political necessity only. Life would have been miserable if members of a joint family had felt they had to stick together purely out of practical necessity. Herein lay the contribution of Confucianism. It provided an ethical code based on the natural human feelings among kin, which stressed parental love for children, children's filiality toward parents, fraternal affection between brothers, etc. The ideal was to achieve family harmony and welfare by each member of the family fulfilling his moral obligations according to his status. Confucianism gave joint family life an ethical meaning and inspired it with a noble ideal. It was not so much a matter of necessity to live together as it was natural and human and, therefore, morally right to do so. The attitudes and values inculcated by Confucianism fitted into the joint family system, which in turn fitted into the geographical and economic background.

Given the set of circumstances in old China, if a social engineer were asked to design a family system to best serve human needs under those conditions, his creation would probably come very close to the historic family system of China. The question may be asked: If the system worked so well for so long, why doesn't it continue to work in modern times? The answer, of course, is that objective conditions have changed. As China's economy becomes diversified and as transportation is developed, more and more people leave their village farms and go elsewhere to take up nonagricultural work. Those who remain together are the nuclear family. In Communist China individual small farms have been combined to form large communes and thus the economic basis of the joint family has been removed.

Modern government therefore no longer acts through the heads of joint families. Participation in the numerous social agencies which have appeared is also on an individual basis. In Communist China the young are deliberately freed from control by the old, and women are liberated from male domination. Even in Nationalist China on Taiwan, the same tendencies have developed, though more mildly and more gradually. The joint family is yielding to the nuclear family. The influence of Western ideas of individual development and freedom has eroded, if not replaced, the Confucianist attitudes and values of solidarity and cooperation within the joint family. The truth of the matter is that the nuclear family is more viable in a modern industrial economy, whether socialistic or capitalistic, and the individual has become the unit of action whether in a democracy or under an authoritarian government. Given these circumstances, not even a resurrected Confucius could restore the traditional joint family system of China to its former position of preeminence.

Bearing constantly in mind the problem of discovering the interrelationships among the geographical and material foundations of life, the social institutions of the people, their attitudes, beliefs, and values will lead the student to a rational and penetrative understanding of an unfamiliar society, of which the study of China may well serve as an interesting example.

YU-KUANG CHU

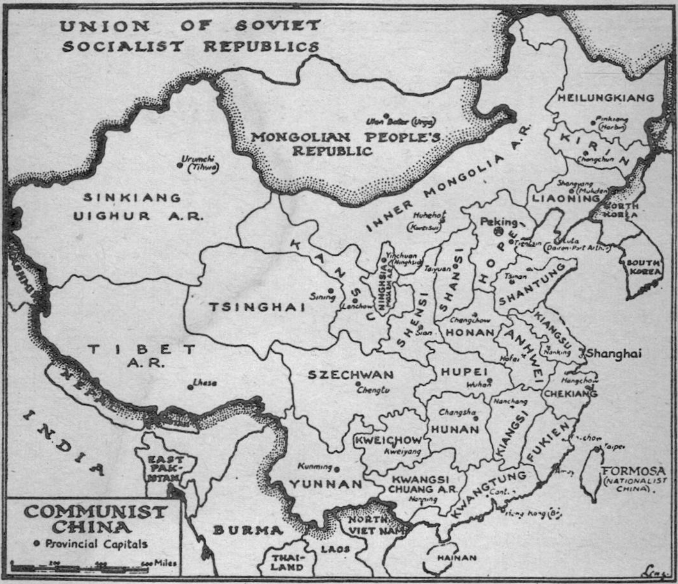
UNION OF SOVIET SOCIALIST REPUBLICS
MONGOLIAN PEOPLE'S REPUBLIC
HEILUNGKIANG
KIRIN
LIAONING
INNER MONGOLIA A.R.
SINKIANG UIGHUR A.R.
Urumchi (Tihwa)
Peking
HOPEI
SHANSI
SHANTUNG
KANSU
NINGHSIA
TSINGHAI
SHENSI
HONAN
KIANGSU
ANHWEI
Shanghai
TIBET A.R.
Lhasa
SZECHWAN
Chengtu
HUPEI
Wuhan
CHEKIANG
Changsha
HUNAN
KIANGSI
FUKIEN
KWEICHOW
Kweiyang
Kunming
YUNNAN
KWANGSI CHUANG A.R.
KWANGTUNG
FORMOSA (NATIONALIST CHINA)
INDIA
EAST PAKISTAN
BURMA
NORTH VIET NAM
LAOS
THAILAND
HAINAN
SOUTH KOREA
COMMUNIST CHINA
Provincial Capitals
Miles

PART ONE

UNDERSTANDING CHINA

We all come to the study of China with certain preconceived notions, impressions, and assumptions. It is best to be aware of these preconceptions so we can attempt to look at China objectively. It is important also to realize that the Chinese have their own self-image. The geography and the language of China have been instrumental in laying the foundations of traditional Chinese civilization. To understand China or any other civilization, all these factors should be considered.

• 1 •

A General Technique for Studying a Foreign Culture

All people tend to be ethnocentric—that is, they see the world revolving around themselves at the center. As we shall see, this is no less true of the Chinese than it is of Americans. As a result of this ethnocentricity, we tend to judge another culture and its people in terms of our own standards and values. Hence we conclude that our way of life is superior and are often surprised when others do not agree with us. This kind of thinking can lead to arrogance; it may force us to think in stereotypes and prevent us from appreciating and understanding the uniqueness and diversity—as well as the commonality—of the peoples of the world. It can also prevent us from understanding what is most unique and worthwhile in ourselves. Finally, ethnocentricity can threaten the peace of the world.

Professor Yu-Kuang Chu of Skidmore College offers some suggestions for developing a technique for studying non-Western cultures. Why should we study non-Western peoples and cultures if Western civilization is conquering the globe?

YU-KUANG CHU

(1) How do the people make a living (the material foundation of life)? (2) How do they live together (their social organizations and processes)? and (3) How do they think of themselves and of other people in the world and the universe (their images as reflected in religion, philosophy, literature, and art)? These three questions are deceptively simple but they indicate a valid approach to the study of any country or culture. . . .

Reprinted with permission, from Yu-kuang Chu, "The Liberal Values of Non-Western Studies," *Topic: A Journal of the Liberal Arts* (Spring 1962). Copyright by Washington & Jefferson College.

Of the three basic questions about a society, it is the third one about images which puts a distinctive stamp upon a culture. Preindustrial societies in different parts of the world tend to be more alike than different in their modes of living and social organization, but their most distinctive differences are generally traceable to their different ways of seeing life and formulating their life ideals. The Hindu belief that truth is seen in many manifestations and that a person progresses in his understanding of truth through a series of rebirths has strengthened their ability to live peaceably with diverse alien groups and to reconcile extremes whether in economic programs or in foreign policy. The Chinese emphasis on mundane life seems congenial to the present fascination with material construction and the impatient speed with which it is done. To probe the images of a foreign people through a study of their religion, philosophy, literature, and art as well as their social institutions is to understand the roots of a culture. . . .

In the course of a study of a non-Western culture there are at least six necessary attitudes or abilities:

1. *Beware of stereotyped notions about foreign peoples.*

Stereotypes are shortcuts in thinking and abbreviated guides to action. As such they are natural to the human mind, and a residual amount of stereotyping is perhaps unavoidable. However, students should be led to see that some popular notions are entirely false and that others, though having an element of truth, are sweeping oversimplifications. The chief trouble with even valid stereotypes is that they may not apply to a particular individual.

Examples of some common stereotypes about Asians are: Japanese are good imitators but not very creative. All Chinese eat rice as a staple food. If an Indian is an "untouchable," you may be quite sure he is destitute and illiterate. The first notion is false. The second one has partial validity but needs qualification. The third statement illustrates the danger of applying a sweeping generalization to a particular individual. Although the Japanese have adopted many elements from diverse cultures, they have shown great ingenuity in modifying and fitting them into their own cultural pattern. Also, they have demonstrated inventiveness in modern science and industrial technology as well as creativeness in art and other fields. It is true that southern Chinese eat rice as a staple food, but northern Chinese eat wheat bread or millet and only occasionally eat rice, because north China is wheat- and millet-growing. While "untouchables" in India are, generally speaking, in abject poverty and illiterate, this generalization certainly did not apply to B. R. Ambedkhar, who was an "untouchable" but not poor or illiterate. With a Ph.D. degree from Columbia University he joined the first cabinet of the Republic of India and wrote the draft of the Indian Constitution, which outlawed "untouchability"! . . .

2. *See the common humanity of man amidst cultural diversities in the world.*

Non-Western studies must constantly avoid two extreme emphases. One is to overemphasize the differences between the West and the non-West to such an extent that it strengthens the popular notion that Easterners are mysterious, inscrutable, and somehow not naturally and reasonably human as we are. The other extreme is to assume that all other peoples are exactly like us so that any Western institution such as democracy can be transplanted on any foreign soil provided the willful obstructionists would simply give way. . . .

There are many curious reversals of customs between the West and the Far East. The family name comes before the personal name in Chinese and Japanese. A letter is addressed to the country, province, city, street, house number, and lastly the recipient. The title of a person comes after his name instead of before. There the left is the honored side, while in this country right has the higher priority. At mixed parties in the home of the writer, Occidental friends are seated on the right and Orientals on the left. Everybody is happy. An American child sticks out his tongue to show defiance, a Tibetan to show courtesy to a stranger, a Chinese to express wonderment, and before World War II a Japanese put his tongue between his teeth and sucked in his breath, producing a hissing sound, to show extreme respect to the emperor. In all of these bewildering and amusing reversals, there is no question of superiority of one custom over another; but the establishment of a definite custom giving orderliness to life is the same. . . .

3. *Recognize a different scale of values in a non-Western society.*

Although many values are universals cutting across cultural differences, yet there are differences in value systems. Students should see that in societies characterized by the absence of strong government or by the presence of precariousness or danger, social stability is much more highly prized than social change, and group solidarity is much more valued than individual freedom. A cornerstone of social stability is family solidarity. Once this value system is accepted, then many corollaries follow: respect for the aged, because in a stable society wisdom comes from accumulation of experience; marriages arranged by parents, because marriage is not the personal affair of the couple involved but a family matter profoundly affecting its welfare and integrity; . . .

4. *Develop human empathy and active concern for other peoples.*

Education is a process continuously extending human sympathy and understanding in time and in space—from one's immediate family through the community and nation to the world and from the present backwards to the remote past and forward into the future. Students should be led to see human problems on a world scale and feel ethical obligations on the international level. . . .

5. *Discern the interrelationships between language and culture.*

This discernment can never be acquired if one is limited to one's own language and culture. Here non-Western studies and languages have the special advantage of affording a sharper contrast to Western counterparts, thus bringing out the problem more clearly. As is well known, language is intimately related to thinking, feeling, and acting. When one hears somebody say "Pardon me" for having made a *faux pas,* a Westerner says "Certainly," but a Chinese would say "Not at all." Both are being courteous, but the Westerner is the more frank and direct and seems to say, "Yes, you have made a slip, but since you have asked my pardon, there is no question at all about my being willing to pardon you." The Easterner, on the other hand, is the more circuitous, tries to overlook the *faux pas,* and sounds as if he is saying, "What is there to pardon? Nothing at all!" . . .

6. *Finally, study non-Western cultures for their intrinsic worth and thus see the richness of human thought and life.*

This better acquaintance with mankind will naturally reduce ethnocentrism or academic provincialism. An art student seeing how Chinese painters use blank space as a structural element or how Japanese craftsmen create beauty out of simplicity has a fuller understanding of art. A student in philosophy exposed to the variety of Indian philosophies and religions will have a much richer view of life and reality. A student of literature will delight in discovering "new" (to Westerners) forms and techniques of literary expression in Asian writings. . . .

• 2 •

From Marco Polo to Pearl Buck: American Images of China

Few Americans have made any serious effort to understand China or its people. Even so, almost every American has an image of China and the Chinese that determines his opinions and attitudes. About a decade ago Harold R. Isaacs of the Massachusetts Institute of Technology conducted a survey among Americans of varying classes and backgrounds in order to find out what they thought about China and the Chinese. Here are some of the results of that survey. Do you think that Americans still think of China in the same way as did Americans ten years ago? How does a person develop a set of images of a foreign land if he has not traveled there or studied about it? How can you account for the fact that contrary images seem to be held simultaneously?

HAROLD R. ISAACS

Like China's great rivers, flooding and receding and shift-

Reprinted with permission of The John Day Company, Inc., from Harold R. Isaacs, *Scratches on Our Minds*. Copyright 1958 by Massachusetts Institute of Technology.

ing their courses to the sea, American images of the Chinese have traveled a long and changing way, from Marco Polo to Pearl Buck, from Genghiz Khan to Mao Tse-tung.

The name of Marco Polo is scratched onto the mind of almost every American school child. Attached to it are powerful images of China's ancient greatness, civilization, art, hoary wisdom. With it in time comes a heavy cluster of admirable qualities widely attributed to the Chinese as people: high intelligence, persistent industry, filial piety, peaceableness, stoicism. These were attributes identified in our own generation with the people of Pearl Buck's novels, solid, simple, courageous folk staunchly coping with the blows of fate and adverse circumstances.

Genghiz Khan and his Mongol hordes are the non-Chinese ancestors of quite another set of images also strongly associated with the Chinese; cruelty, barbarism, inhumanity; a faceless, impenetrable, overwhelming mass, irresistible if once loosened. Along this way we discover the devious and difficult heathen, the killers of girl infants, the binders of women's feet, the torturers of a thousand cuts, the headsmen, the Boxer Rebellion and the Yellow Peril, the nerveless indifference to pain, death, or to human disaster, the whole set of lurid, strange, and fearful images clustered around the notion of the awakening giant and brought vividly to life again by Mao Tse-tung's "human sea" seen flooding down across the Yalu, massed barbarians now armed not with broadswords but with artillery, tanks, and jet planes.

In the long history of our associations with China, these two sets of images rise and fall, move in and out of the center of people's minds over time, never wholly displacing each other, always coexisting, each ready to emerge at the fresh call of circumstance. . . .

Our notions of Chinese traits have included sage wisdom and superstitious ignorance, great strength and contemptible weakness, immovable conservatism and unpredictable extremism, philosophic calm and explosive violence. Our emotions about the Chinese have ranged between sympathy and rejection, parental benevolence and parental exasperation, affection and hostility, love and a fear close to hate.

Today these contending views and emotions jostle each other at close quarters, for we are in the midst of a great passage from one set to the other. The dominant impressions of the 181 Americans interviewed for this study were acquired in the past on which the gates clanged so abruptly in 1949. . . .

The images of the Chinese that still so largely exist in the minds of most of these Americans are for the most part the product of the experience of the first four decades of this century. This experience is framed in a characteristic and meaningful paradox. The beginning of this experience included the powerful prejudice and contempt and violent rejection which had marked American attitudes and behavior toward the Chinese who had come to the United States. Out of this came the exclusion laws and all the mythology and synthetic villainy attached in popular folklore to the Chinatowns and the Chinese laundries right across the country, a pattern which persists in some measure right down to the present time. But these also became the years of the full flowering of the most sympathetic images of the great qualities and great virtues of the Chinese who had sensibly remained in China. . . . It was common to find in our interviews that even the scantiest notions about China and the Chinese acquired in this time were likely to be in some way, however slight, favorably disposed, kindly, or admiring of the Chinese, or at least vaguely sympathetic to their needs and travails. The Chinese —on their own ground—were a people Americans had always helped, a nation that somehow evoked a special and unique benevolence and even a sense of obligation, a people of sterling qualities who deservedly held our high regard.

These impressions are not likely to be reproduced in any similar form in the minds of today's children or to reappear in their thinking when they grow into maturity. Their images of the Chinese are being shaped by the new circumstances. . . .

• 3 •

The Center of the Earth: The Middle Kingdom

The Chinese have been more ethnocentric than most other peoples and cultures. The Chinese have the longest continuous history of any nation—a history punctuated by invasion and disorder, but one in which the invaders adopted the superior culture of the conquered.

Developing in isolation, China's evolution was slow and gradual and only occasionally influenced directly by outside forces. The attitudes of her people concerning her relations with other cultures were shaped early.

Hugo Portisch, a recent German visitor to China, comments on the prevalence of these attitudes in the past—and perhaps also in the present. Was there (and is there) any justification for the Chinese self-image? Does Chinese ethnocentrism have any effects on the contemporary world? Do Americans today think of the United States as the dynamic center of the world? If so, is there any justification for this attitude?

HUGO PORTISCH

During my first weekend in Peking, I visited a most singular and impressive building dating from the time of the empire. In the official *Guide Through Peking* this building is listed as the "Temple of Heaven." Here the emperor gave thanks to God and the gods for rich harvests and held dialogues with the celestial powers. . . .

On reaching the topmost terrace, one is struck by a curious geometric arrangement. The ground is covered with large stone slabs, arranged in bands around the center point. Each band

---

Reprinted with permission of Quadrangle Books, Inc., from Hugo Portisch, *Red China Today*. Copyright 1965 by Verlag Kremayr & Scheriau, Vienna. English translation copyright 1966 by Quadrangle Books, Inc.

is made of nine slabs, diminishing in size toward the center. (The number nine has always played an important role in Chinese mysticism.) In the exact center lies a round stone.

"This is the center of the earth," said my guide, pointing to the stone. Feeling somewhat peculiar, I did what many visitors have undoubtedly done, though it would have been an outrage even a hundred years ago. I stepped onto that round stone. . . .

The round stone on which I stood reveals more about the history of China, the attitudes of its rulers, and the mentality of its populace than many of the other things I subsequently heard and saw in China. It was neither accident nor conscious presumption that led the Chinese to place the midpoint of the earth in their realm, thus elevating their country to the central position on earth.

"In this world, there have been only two truly great cultures and civilizations, the Occidental and the Chinese," the Chinese professor told me. "Everything else, magnificent as it might be in its own way—the realms of the Aztecs and the Incas, the cultures of the Middle East and of India—all pale beside the achievements of these two spheres of culture and civilization. Above all, these are the only two cultures that have survived in the stormy history of humanity until this very day, and that are still effective." . . .

It is estimated that Chinese culture had its beginning about four thousand years ago, that is, two thousand years before the birth of Christ. In that remote period, thoughts were first recorded in written characters, Chinese political organization began to develop, legal decrees were issued that established order in the country. By 1500 B.C. the Chinese had a highly developed political organization. It gave the country a comprehensive administration: property and labor were regulated, commerce was channeled, art and science were cultivated, and philosophy was exalted.

"However, Chinese culture developed mainly in isolation, unlike the European," the Chinese historian said. "China had no contact with other highly cultivated peoples. . . . As long as 3,500 years ago, the Chinese had already put large sections of the country in order and were trying to live in harmony with the gods and the universe. Europe, if I may say so in all modesty, was still shrouded in the fogs of prehistory."

I suggested that individual Chinese tribes, under advantageous climatic conditions, had developed their culture at about the same time as other people living under similarly favorable, geographical circumstances. "Yes," replied the professor, "but Chinese culture has remained intact and continues to this day. It has suffered no interruptions. In Europe one culture is replaced by another; peoples spring up and disappear. Remember, China has been one country and has remained one country, except for periods of dismemberment, in contrast with what has happened in Europe. Further, this realm has been settled principally by one ethnic group, the Han; the non-Chinese minorities have played hardly any role in Chinese history. Moreover, this nation belongs to one single race, the Chinese, which is different from other races. Let me try to explain how strongly this has influenced our thinking, our opinions about the world. We Chinese call our country the 'Middle Kingdom' (Chung Kuo) to this day, have done so for 3,500 years, and don't recognize any other name for it. Today, on the postage stamps of the People's Republic, you'll see the same written characters, 'Middle Kingdom.' This, too, is no accident. Because, again in contrast with Europe, the Chinese for centuries knew no other world than China, for thousands of years no other highly developed culture than their own. Even our greatest thinkers assumed that nothing outside of China was worth knowing, nothing was worth striving for, nothing was worthy of emulation, except what we had known for a long time. The realm of the Han was the center of civilization, the center of the earth."

On modern maps of the world we can see that China borders on other large nations inhabited by large numbers of peoples. To the north is the Soviet Union. But even a century ago this northern region was sparsely populated, and the Chinese came upon nothing but nomadic tribes in the inhospitable reaches of Mongolia and Siberia. True, they were often warlike men who fell upon China in its moments of weakness, and at times even usurped its sovereign throne—as for instance the Huns, Genghis Khan, and the Manchus. But in the eyes of the Chinese they were barbarians who had hardly any culture of their own worthy of the name.

In the west, China bordered on Tibet, on the Himalayas. There the mountains were too high and the terrain too inhospitable to make explorations in that direction worthwhile. Although there is historical evidence of caravan routes at a very early time from China to Afghanistan and Persia, and also of some contacts between Chinese and Indians, the fact remains that the tales of traders could not convince the Chinese court and the sages of the existence of nations and peoples that could compare with the greatness of China and with its cultural development.

In the south and southeast, where Korea, Viet Nam, Laos, Cambodia, and Burma are located today, the Chinese met nothing but insignificant peoples, barbarians in their eyes, who were soon persuaded or forced to accept Chinese culture and Chinese domination.

The same was true of the insular realm to the east of China, Japan. The tribes inhabiting these islands had not yet developed much of a culture or civilization when the first Chinese seafarers and, later, armies brought them news about the Son of Heaven and of the Middle Kingdom, taught them the Chinese written characters and Chinese customs, and in this way laid the foundation for a future Japanese culture.

"Weren't there really sufficient grounds to believe that nothing in the world outside China counted for anything, or even that the world consisted of China?" the professor continued. "When we suffered a military defeat, when barbarians usurped the sovereign throne, they could survive only by adopting our culture, by submitting to our customs, by surrounding themselves with Chinese advisers, philosophers, and administrators. Barbarian chieftains sent embassies from afar to the Chinese throne to plead for a highly cultivated Chinese princess whom they could marry, for Chinese scribes and organizers so that they too could share in the achievements of Chinese culture. And if they occasionally had something worthwhile to offer, we were flexible enough to adopt their ideas, to enlarge upon and to transform them, and often within one generation to make them an integral part of the Chinese cultural heritage."

• 4 •

The Shape of the Land: Too Many Want Too Much From Too Little

Every civilization's institutions and basic assumptions about itself are shaped to a large degree by the relationship between the people and the land. In China another major influence on its civilization has been its relative isolation from the other great civilizations of mankind. Even so, contact with other regions never entirely disappeared. Archaeological evidence indicates that the early culture was influenced by migrations over Central Asian routes from the Near East. However, as in later times when Mongols and Manchus entered and conquered China, these influences were quickly absorbed and assimilated into the Chinese scene. Thus a distinct life emerged in East Asia.

A study of China's geography will help to give insight into her history. A look at the physical environment of China will help make clear why certain distinctive characteristics of Chinese life—system of agriculture, system of government, family patterns, beliefs about the nature of the universe—evolved. Finally, China's natural features, when studied, should help us to make some reasonable projections concerning China's future role in world affairs.

In this selection, G. Etzel Pearcy, geographer of the United States Department of State, explores the strengths and weaknesses of China's geography.

G. ETZEL PEARCY

Greater China was never an outward-looking area. . . . A few trade caravans pushed westward through the Jade Gate or over desolate trails. Along the seaward margin to the east a few junks ventured into the narrow seas to trade or skirmish

From G. Etzel Pearcy, *Mainland China—Geographic Strengths and Weaknesses*, U.S. Department of State Publication 8135 (Washington, D.C.: Government Printing Office, September 1966).

with little-known maritime peoples. But beyond such meager contacts with the outside world, the Chinese Empire was largely self-contained. . . .

With but few exceptions the international boundaries of China traverse areas which are sparsely populated or completely empty of settlement. Thus, the outer periphery of the country generally has a barrier effect accounting for a certain degree of isolation characteristic of the Chinese people on the mainland. . . .

THE LANDSCAPE

High land, whether rugged or in the form of high plain or plateau, prevails in China. It has been estimated that 60 percent of the total area is a mile or more above sea level. True lowlands, either coastal plains or river valleys, make up a relatively small proportion of the country. The three most important lowland areas are the North China Plains, the heart of Northeast China (Manchuria), and the valley of the Yangtze. These areas, the most favorable to human settlement, amount to less than 10 percent of China's total land surface. By adding the remaining lowland areas the total does not exceed more than about 11 percent. Thus, over about eight-ninths of China, the terrain limits or completely excludes human endeavors.

Two rivers hold the power of life or death for more than one-half of the Chinese, a number approaching 15 percent of the world's population. The basins of the Yellow River (or Hwang Ho or Huang) and the Yangtze (or Yangtze Kiang or Ch'ang) provide life-giving waters which sustain nearly half a billion people. At the same time, their intermittent flooding causes havoc at a scale unknown in most parts of the world.

The Yellow River, aptly nicknamed "River of Sorrow," has broken out of its banks with deadly regularity, at times drowning hundreds of thousands of people during a single flood season. . . .

THE CLIMATE

That the climate of China's regions is not too cold, too hot, too wet, or too dry for sustaining the lives of so many hundreds of millions unquestionably classifies it as favorable to human existence. . . .

Actually, the potentialities of China's climate in relation to the number of people living there leaves but little margin for irregularities. Any departure from a normal climatic regime brings disaster. While temperatures seldom deviate sharply enough from the expected to jeopardize human life or productive activities, the variation and unreliability of precipitation constitute a constant threat to well-being throughout China.

Overabundance of rainfall may be as serious as too little. Areas of heavy rainfall are subject to violent atmospheric disturbances which release undue amounts of water onto the landscape. This phenomenon is especially prevalent in the southeast, where typhoons bring torrential rains along with winds of destructive force, wreaking havoc in densely populated areas from Hainan Island in the south to as far north as Shanghai. . . .

A greater, though less spectacular, handicap is the lower precipitation to the north and west. From the Yangtze Valley southward, rainfall generally increases from 40 to 80 inches, sufficient for almost any type of agricultural growth. But to the north the annual rainfall drops to 25 inches or less in the North China Plain and in the northeast. To the west the drop is far greater. Here rainfall measures less than 10 inches and sometimes less than 4 inches. Unfortunately, rainfall in these areas is undependable. Occasionally there may be heavy rains, causing great floods, but more frequently droughts plague the hard-pressed farmers.

Climatic catastrophes, whether physically destructive or in the form of a long, grinding drought, mark the economy of China.

CHINA'S POPULATION PROBLEMS

Population problems in China may be summarized by a fact terrifying in its implications: too many people demanding too much from too little land. In short, any assets which the country may possess must be divided to the extent that per capita values cannot be impressive in any field and in most are ridiculously low.

The United States Bureau of the Census recently released statistics giving the total population of mainland China as of January 1, 1966: 760,300,000. . . . About 90 percent of the total population lives in the eastern third of the country. . . .

MINERAL RESOURCES

Recent data . . . suggest that China is one of the richest coal nations in the world. Reserves, largely of good quality, reach 1,500 billion tons. The heaviest prewar production, in the early 1940s, amounted to 62 million tons, which was one-sixth that of Japan and one-thirty-first that of the United States. In 1960 production was given at 425 million tons, roughly as much as for the United States or the Soviet Union in that year. But when regarded on a per capita basis, such huge amounts are not too impressive.

Iron ore and petroleum show about the same record, reflecting discovery of more accurate appraisals which indicate potential reserves of promise. . . . Alloy metals, too, appear in abundant supply, especially tungsten, manganese, and antimony, which rank high in world statistics. Other deposits in appreciable quantities include tin, copper, aluminum ores, mercury, molybdenum, graphite, talc, magnesite, sulfur, bismuth, mica, lead, and zinc. . . .

FROM G. ETZEL PEARCY, **MAINLAND CHINA-GEOGRAPHIC STRENGTHS AND WEAKNESSES**, U.S. DEPARTMENT OF STATE PUBLICATION 8135 (WASHINGTON, D.C.: GOVERNMENT PRINTING OFFICE, SEPTEMBER, 1966).

TRANSPORTATION

Transportation and communications from China proper to the peripheral areas of the north, northwest, and west even today are reminiscent of the last century's pioneer conditions in North America.

Travel other than by air must be reckoned in days; not so long ago weeks and months were the units of time for measurement. . . .

China's inadequate transportation pattern is one of the greatest handicaps to any plans for industrialization. Before 1949, rail lines were concentrated in the eastern segment of the country and roads were largely for primitive means of travel, if they existed at all. Rivers and canals formed a semblance of an inland waterway in the lowlands, extending well inland only in the valley of the Yangtze. A great drive has taken place to build railroads and roads into the western reaches of the country. . . .

• 5 •

The Chinese Language

Language is the major means by which we learn to express ourselves. It is the medium of thought in all civilizations. The words and phrases we use to write and speak what is on our minds ultimately shape the way we think, and either help or hinder us in communicating our ideas to others.

Unlike most languages, written Chinese is not a phonetic system, but one which developed from simple pictures to a highly sophisticated use of symbols, called ideographs, rather than sounds for words. There are more than fifty thousand characters in the language, although today, as a result of language reform, a Chinese can read popular material by mastering as few as two thousand characters.

All of the basic principles of the language were present in the ancient Shang (1765–1123 B.C.) writing system. As a result it is not surprising that even today's Chinese feel a cultural affinity with the ancient Shang, one that often eludes us if we seek identification with the Greeks and Romans.

In this selection, Professor Derk Bodde of the University of Pennsylvania gives some idea of those features of the Chinese language that make it so different from our own. Some questions that you might consider while reading this piece are: How might this language influence the thought of the people? What effects do you think this language would have on the development of political and social institutions? Will this language help or hinder the people in developing modern technology? Do Arabic numerals function in the same way as Chinese characters?

DERK BODDE

Major Principles of Chinese

Language is an important factor in any cultural tradition. That is why, when studying a civilization other than our own, it is always pertinent to ask ourselves such questions as, To what extent can the distinctive ideas and institutions of the civilization in question be attributed to the influence of its language? In what ways has that language either aided or hindered the interchange of ideas with the outside world? . . .

Much has been written about the Chinese language apropos the questions we have raised, but before these differing opinions can be intelligently considered, it is essential to have at least a minimal understanding of what the language itself is like. . . .

1. *Lack of Inflection*

"Lack of inflection" means, for example, that the Chinese third personal pronoun *t'a* can mean "he, him, she, her, it"; the noun *ma* can mean either "horse" or "horses"; the verb *tsou* can mean "go, went, will go." And this in turn means that *context* is all important. Only by prefixing words like "one," "two" or "some" to *ma,* and "yesterday," "today," or "tomorrow" to *tsou,* can we know whether one or more horses are involved, and when the action takes place.

---

2. *Word Order*

Word order, as well as context, is very important because, in the absence of inflection, it is often only through grammatical position, as well as ideological context, that we can know how a word functions in a given sentence: as a noun, verb, or other part of speech. The single word *shang,* for example, can, depending on its position and context, variously function as a preposition (on, above, upon), an adverb (up, upward, above), an adjective (upper, high, superior, excellent), a noun (top, summit, a superior), or a verb (to mount, ascend, esteem). *Ma shang,* literally "horse-above," signifies "on horseback," whereas the reverse combination, *shang ma,* ordinarily means "to mount a horse." By putting the phrase into a different context, however, in which *shang* becomes an adjective instead of a verb, *shang ma* can equally well mean "superior or excellent horse(s)."

3. *Primary and Secondary Meanings*

Chinese words (as well as phrases) commonly have a primary meaning (which tends to be concrete), and, deriving from this, a series of secondary meanings which are often increasingly abstract or metaphorical. *Shang* as a verb, for example, primarily means "to ascend," but it also has the secondary meaning of "to esteem." *Ma shang,* primarily "on horseback," has a secondary but even more common idiomatic connotation of "immediately, at once". . . . One of the many problems in reading Chinese is to determine which of several possible meanings best fits a given word or phrase in a given sentence.

4. *Chinese Characters*

Chinese characters, as is well known, consist of nonalphabetic graphs or symbols, each used to designate a single idea and a single spoken syllable, the pronunciation of which, however, can vary according to the particular Chinese dialect in which it is being read. They are thus similar to our numerals 1, 2, 3, 4, which always retain the same meaning irrespective of how they are pronounced in different languages. The Chinese characters have been created according to several different principles, all of which, however, go back originally to simple pictographs or combinations of such pictographs; these in the course of time have become conventionalized or simplified into the forms current today. The character 木, for example, is pronounced *mu* (in the standard northern dialect) and means "tree or wood"; it is the modern form of a pictograph showing a tree with roots and branches. By combining one such tree with another 林, we obtain an entirely new character, *lin,* meaning "grove or forest"; by tripling the trees we obtain 森, pronounced *sen* and meaning "luxuriant vegetation, jungle growth, overgrown." . . .

5. *The Spoken and Written Languages*

Chinese contains an abundance of homonyms (syllables pronounced identically but having different meanings, such as English "to, too, two," "meat, meet, mete"). Were these to be used individually, they would, of course, create many verbal ambiguities. The spoken language avoids such ambiguities, however, by combining two syllables, similar in meaning, into a dissyllabic compound, and letting this compound stand for the idea which is common to both its components. The two syllables *yi* and *fu,* for example, both mean "clothing" (in addition to many other things); hence the spoken word for "clothing" becomes *yi-fu,* a compound which will not readily be confused by the ear for any other compound. When expressing the same idea in writing, however, this device is no longer needed, since every individual written character, regardless of its pronunciation, is *visually* distinct from every other character; hence it is necessary only to write the single character *yi,* meaning "clothing," or the single character *fu,* meaning the same, but not both of them put together. . . .

Because of the above and other factors, too complex to be discussed here, a distinction early arose between Chinese as it is spoken and Chinese as it is written. Spoken Chinese, precisely because it was a spoken and therefore living language, underwent continuous evolution in the course of which it discarded old words, adopted new ones, and changed significantly in syntax. The more concise written medium, on the other hand, because of its separation from the living colloquial, froze at an early date into a relatively fixed form, stylistically and syntactically sharply different from the colloquial. So far apart, indeed, did the two become that even a native Chinese requires years of study to master the written language (also commonly known as literary or classical Chinese). And yet so great was the prestige of the literary language that until recently almost everything was written in it, aside from fiction and drama (which, for the very reason that they followed the colloquial idiom, were looked down on in traditional China).

EARLY	MODERN	MEANING AND EXPLANATION
	厂	Cliff
	口	Mouth
	囗	Enclosure
	夕	Evening, dusk (*crescent moon*)
	大	Large (*frontal view of "large" man*)
	子	Child, boy (*child with upraised arms*)
	廾	To lift, greet (*joined hands*)
	弓	Bow (*Chinese reflex bow*)
	心 忄 ⺗	Heart, mind (*picture of physical heart*)
	户	Door, house (*left leaf of double door*)
	手 扌	Hand (*showing five fingers*)
	攴 攵	To beat, tap (*hand holding stick*)
	日	Sun
	曰	To speak (*mouth with protruding tongue?*)
	月	Moon, month

EARLY	MODERN	MEANING AND EXPLANATION
	木	Tree, wood (*tree with roots and branches*)
	比	To compare (*file of 2 men*)
	毛	Hair, feathers (*piece of fur or down*)
	艸 艹	Grass (*growing plants*)
	虫	Insect, reptile (*snake or worm*)
	見	To see (*exaggerated eye on legs*)
	言	Speech (*vapor or tongue leaving mouth*)
	豆	Eating vessel (*vessel on pedestal*)
	豸	Feline, reptile (*cat-like animal*)
	魚	Fish
	鳥	Birds
	麻	Hemp (*hemp plants drying under shed*)
	黽	Toad
	鼎	Sacrificial urn (*two-handled tripod vessel*)
	鼓	Drum (*drum on stand; hand with stick*)

Early and Modern Forms of Chinese Pictographs. Other Chinese characters can be much more complex than these. The "early" forms are in many cases not the earliest known. The "modern" ones became current around the first century A.D. (Adapted from Raymond D. Blakney, *A Course in the Analysis of Chinese Characters*, Peiping, 1948)

己 Self

所 That which

不 Not

欲 Want

勿 Don't

施 Do

於 To

人 People

What you don't want, don't do to others.

PART TWO

TRADITIONAL CHINA

Chinese civilization originated in the Yellow River Valley basin and the North China Plain some four thousand years ago. The history of the Chinese is the story of their expansion from this base. The creation of the Chinese empire and imperial system was accomplished by the dynasties that ruled throughout Chinese history.

Early in the course of Chinese history there emerged the major ideas and institutions of Chinese civilization as expressed and recorded in its philosophy, arts, government, and economic and social institutions. In this section we will take a look at some of these features of Chinese thought and life, and try to understand why the Chinese achieved one of the great civilizations.

TIME CHART

	China	Western World
4000 B.C.		Origins of River Valley civilizations in Mesopotamia and Egypt
3000 B.C.	Neolithic Period: Legendary emperors established patterns of culture in Yellow River Valley and North China Plain (Hsia dynasty)	Invention of writing; use of metals; peak of Sumerian and Egyptian civilizations
2000 B.C.	Feudal Age: Shang dynasty (1765-1123 B.C.) Chou dynasty (1122-221 B.C.) Hereditary military lords control territory Use of writing Oracle bones testify to highly complex civilization	Indo-European Invasions (Persia, Greece, Italy) Babylonia Israel Phoenicia Aegean civilization (c. 1000 B.C.)
1000 B.C.	Later Chou dynasty Period of Warring States Breakup of feudalism Philosophic speculation Confucius (551 B.C.) Taoism Legalism	Age of Homer (c. 800 B.C.) Founding of Roman Republic (509 B.C.) Persian Wars
500 B.C.	Ch'in dynasty (221-206 B.C.) Unification of China under strong central government through use of legalist methods	Golden Age of Greece (5th century B.C.) Alexander (325 B.C.) Hellenistic Age (3rd-1st centuries) Punic Wars (264-146 B.C.)

	China	Western World
500 B.C. (Continued)		
	Han dynasty (206 B.C.-A.D. 220)	Expansion of Rome
	Expansion of empire	
	Acceptance of Confucianism as model for government and society	Julius Caesar (44 B.C.)
A.D.		
	Han dynasty	Pax Romana
	Introduction of civil service	Origins of Christianity
	Introduction of Buddhism	Silk trade with China
	Silk trade with Rome	
	Collapse of Han dynasty	
	Period of Six Dynasties (220-589)	Collapse of Roman Empire
	Disintegration	Disintegration in West
	Spread and acceptance of Buddhism	Spread and acceptance of Christianity
500		
		Dark Ages
	T'ang dynasty (618-907)	Muhammad (622)
	Golden Age of Empire	Byzantine civilization
	Consolidation of government	Charlemagne (800)
	Commercial expansion into Indian Ocean	Muslim Empire
		Feudal Age
	Contact with Arabs	
1000		
	Disintegration of Empire	
	Sung dynasty (960-1127)	Crusades (1096-1291)
	Creativity and scholarship in spite of barbarian invasions	Introduction of Asian ideas, culture, products via Arabs, Turks, Mongols
	Great age of painting	
	Conquest by central Asian invaders	
	Yuan (Mongol) dynasty (1278-1368)	Beginnings of breakup of feudal society
	China part of Mongol Empire stretching from Pacific Ocean to central Europe	
	Overland trade with Europe	Overland trade with Asia
	Marco Polo serves the Khan	
	Ming dynasty (1368-1644)	Italian Renaissance
	Reassertion of Chinese control	Growth of strong nation-states
		Commercial expansion
	Bureaucratic stability	Search for new trade routes
	Imitation of previous culture	
	Suspension of maritime explorations	Discovery of New World

	China	Western World
1500	Ming dynasty (1368-1644)	Protestant Reformation
	Limited commercial contact with West	Commercial and colonial expansion into New World and Asia
	Admission of Jesuits who adhere to Chinese culture and customs	
1700	Ching (Manchu) dynasty (1644-1912)	
	Manchus conquer China and attempt to maintain identity	Age of Enlightenment
	Borders extended to greatest extent	
	Self-sufficiency	Chinese ideas, culture, and products flood Europe
	European traders tolerated in few southern ports as part of tribute system	
	Jesuits act as advisers to emperors sending books on China to Europe	American Revolution
	Jesuits expelled as result of Papal Rites controversy	French Revolution
1800	Collapse and disintegration of Ching dynasty	Industrial Revolution
		Napoleonic Wars
	Failure to solve land and population problem	Congress of Vienna
		Dissolution of colonial empires in New World
	Economic exploitation by West leads to unfavorable balance of trade	Growth of democracy
		New imperialism
	Opium Wars (1842)	Commercial and colonial expansion into Africa and Asia
	Taiping Rebellion (1851-1864)	West divides China into spheres of influence and stakes out concessions
	Unequal Treaties (1842-1895)	
	Sino-Japanese War (1895)	
	Failure of reforms	Unification of Italy and Germany
1900	Boxer Rebellion (1900)	Great Power rivalries
		Alliances
	Russo-Japanese War (1904)	Colonial conflicts
	Chinese Revolution (1911-1912)	
	Warlordism	
	World War I	World War I
	Growth of Chinese Nationalism	Russian Revolution
	May 4th Movement (1910)	
	Kuomintang attempts to unify China and drive out foreigners with aid of U.S.S.R.	

	China	Western World
1900	(Continued)	
	Founding of Chinese Communist Party (1921)	Italian Fascism
	Great Depression	Great Depression
	Civil War: Kuomintang vs. Chinese Communists	German Nazism
	War with Japan	
	Truce between CCP and KMT	Munich
	World War II	World War II
	Triumph of Communism	Cold War
	Problems of development	

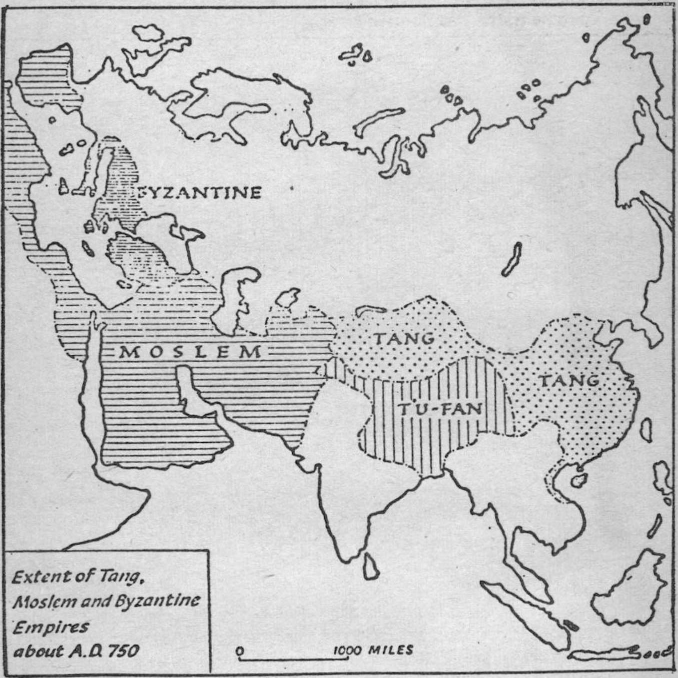

REPRINTED WITH PERMISSION, FROM T. R. TREGEAR, A GEOGRAPHY OF CHINA (LONDON: UNIVERSITY OF LONDON PRESS, LTD., 1965).

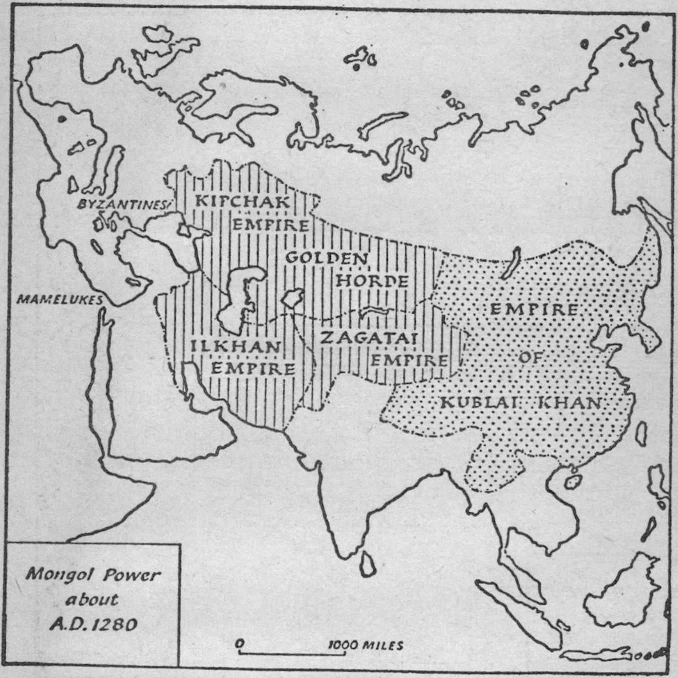

REPRINTED WITH PERMISSION, FROM T. R. TREGEAR, A GEOGRAPHY OF CHINA (LONDON: UNIVERSITY OF LONDON PRESS, LTD., 1965).

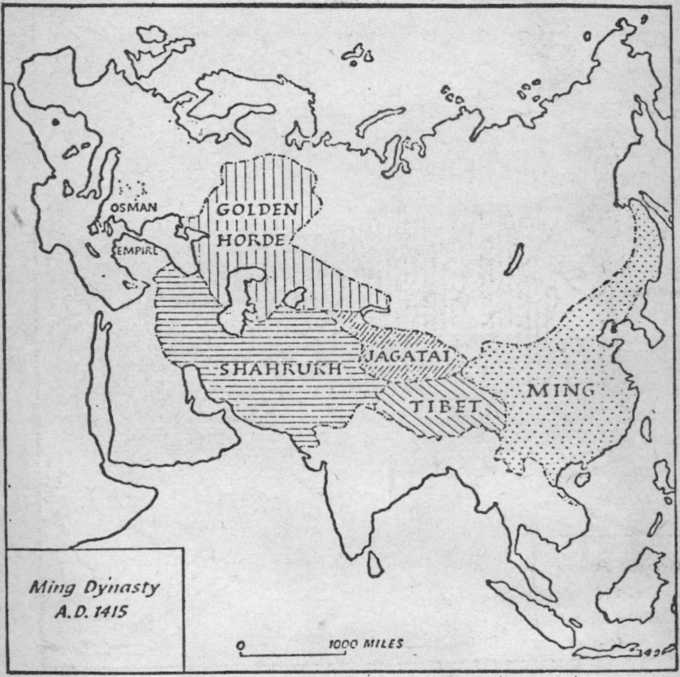

REPRINTED WITH PERMISSION, FROM T. R. TREGEAR, A GEOGRAPHY OF CHINA (LONDON: UNIVERSITY OF LONDON PRESS, LTD., 1965).

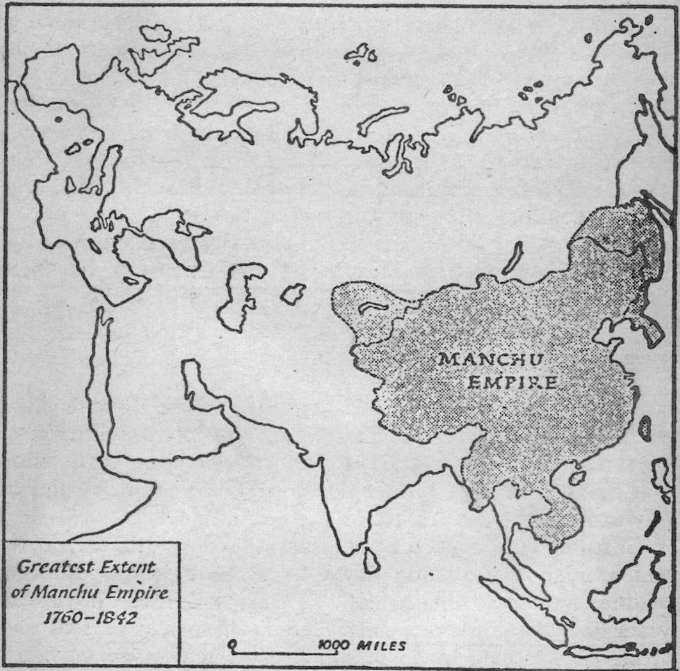

REPRINTED WITH PERMISSION, FROM T. R. TREGEAR, A GEOGRAPHY OF CHINA (LONDON: UNIVERSITY OF LONDON PRESS, LTD., 1965).

• 1 •

The Oracle Bones

How old is Chinese civilization? Until this century much of ancient Chinese history was thought by Westerners to be largely the fabric of myth and prehistory. But, with the discovery of the oracle bones, it is now known that a literate, highly developed culture—traditionally known as the Shang—existed in China as early as the second millennium B.C. The complexity of this culture, as revealed by the artifacts, suggests a considerable history in earlier times.

Professor Herrlee G. Creel, an authority on Chinese antiquity, discusses the significance of the discovery of these bones and the light they shed on the history of China.

HERRLEE G. CREEL

More than three thousand years ago, there flourished on the plains of North China one of the most interesting and important peoples the world has ever known. Their civilization was equal in many respects, and superior in some, to that of any other people in the world of their time. . . .

Unfortunately most of the things used by these people, which might have come down to us as evidence of their culture, were very perishable. . . . Only within the last seven years have we come to possess definite historical records and actual objects used by them which make it possible now, for the first time, to give a reasonably detailed picture of their life and some connected account of their history, based on fact rather than conjecture. . . .

All of the new evidence for this ancient civilization comes from the site of one city. . . .

The site of this ancient city includes the tiny modern village of Hsiao T'un, in the district of Anyang in northern

---

Honan Province. It is some eighty miles north of the Yellow River, three hundred miles west from the sea. Its latitude is approximately that of Gibraltar. Farmers noticed that in their fields on the bank of the Huan River, directly north of the village, after a rain or after ploughing, bones of a very peculiar sort came to the surface. Most of them were broken pieces, yet some of their edges showed an uncommon smoothness and finish. The surfaces of some were polished until they gleamed like glass. Most of them had queer oval notches on their backs, and T-shaped cracks. . . .

A few of the bones, about one out of ten, had even more mystifying markings—rows of geometric designs and small pictures. . . . In 1899 some of these bones still bearing their markings came into the hands of Chinese antiquaries skilled in the most ancient known forms of Chinese writing, who recognized that this must be a still older form.

With this event an entirely new epoch in our understanding of the history of man in the Far East was begun. These fragments of bone are at present our sole remnant of the written records of most ancient eastern Asia. There is much talk of the four thousand years of Chinese history, but actually we knew virtually nothing of the period before 1122 B.C. until they were discovered. . . .

. . . The longest inscriptions barely exceed sixty words, and most of them contain not more than ten or twelve. If they were ordinary documents, such as records of trading or memoranda of debts, they might tell us very little of the people who produced them. . . .

These bone fragments contain records of questions which the people of that time put to their ancestors and their gods. . . . There was good reason for them to do this. The spirits they consulted were believed to be able to help men powerfully if they wished, but they also harmed them most terribly if they were displeased. They might send swift-raiding enemies, who fell upon their victims without warning and carried off as many as they could capture to slavery or death. They might send plagues of disease. They might appear in one's dreams, as ghosts, and frighten one almost out of one's senses. For all of these reasons it was better to take no action of any possible importance without first asking what they thought about it. And it was better to take care to give them sacrifices regularly, and sacrifices of just the things they preferred; to know what would please them most—this was divined about, too.

To learn the will of the spirits they used the scapula or leg bones of cattle, or the shell of the tortoise. The leg bones were split, so as to make flat or slightly rounded pieces of bone. The tortoise-shells, at least, were probably prepared with much ceremony and laid away carefully until they were needed. The divination itself probably took place in the ancestral temple. The diviner asked a question, such as "So-and-so is ill; if this fact is announced to the spirit of Grandfather Ting (will he aid him to recover)?" Heat was applied to the back of the shell or bone, and this caused a T-shaped crack to appear on its face. From this crack the diviner decided whether the answer of the spirits was favourable or unfavourable, and announced the result to the king or other person for whom he was divining.

In many cases, though not always, the diviner wrote the question, inscribing it with some sort of stylus, on the bone beside the cracks which answered it. These questions, covering a wide range of subjects, give us archaeological material of a sort not often found. They make it possible to form a picture of the men who asked them such as no materials less intimate could possibly do. And it must be noted that these inscriptions have a reliability which history, and many inscriptions, do not have. For they are not history, and they were not written for posterity or for anyone save the writer and perhaps his colleagues to read. To exaggerate, then, would have been without point. For this reason it is highly probable that when we read "It is asked, 'Shall an army of five thousand men be raised?' " for a certain campaign, there actually were just about that number of men involved. In contrast to this we find an inscription on a bronze of a few centuries later which tells us that a general who conducted an expedition against some barbarians in the West captured thirteen thousand and eighty-one living men, in addition to the number slain. This figure seems quite unbelievable. His whole army could hardly have been so large, to say nothing of its being able to take so many captives. But this bronze was cast as a souvenir of his prowess, to be left to his admiring posterity. We should expect him to boast in such an inscription. It cannot possibly have the same value, as historical evidence, as is possessed by the oracle bone inscriptions. . . .

• 2 •

The Mandate of Heaven

Legend tells us that the Hsia was China's first dynasty. Even if the Hsia did not in fact exist, the relics of the Shang do indicate the prior existence of an advanced people conquered by the Shang. The Shang, in turn, were conquered by the Chou, a martial, perhaps semibarbaric people, who lived on the fringes of the Shang civilization and probably shared their language and basic culture.

The chief deity of the Chou was Heaven *(T'ien)*, an impersonal force of nature, unlike our concept of Supreme Being. The Chou justified their conquest in a way that later was to become incorporated into the political philosophy of the Confucianists. The Mandate of Heaven became a fundamental principle of Chinese government.

The following selection—the first statement of what Heaven meant to the Chinese—explains that the ruler was to be guided by this force. Given this justification for rule, what kind of relationship would exist between the people and the government? Does the Chinese ruler govern with the authority of divine right? Can his power be taken away from him?

SHU CHING

(Book of History)

God sent down correction on Hsia,* but the sovereign *only* increased his luxury and sloth, and would not speak kindly to the people. . . . He kept reckoning on the decree of God *in his favour,* and would not promote the means of the people's support. By great inflictions of punish-

Reprinted with permission of Hong Kong University Press, from James Legge (ed.), "The Shoo King," *The Chinese Classics*, Vol. III.

* [Spellings changed to Wade-Giles system: Shoo King—Shu Ching; Hea—Hsia; Yih—Yi; Chow—Chou.—Ed.]

ment also, he increased the disorder of the States of Hsia. The first cause *of his evil course* was the internal misrule, which made him unfit to deal well with the multitudes. Nor did he seek at all to employ men whom he could respect, and who might display a generous kindness to the people, but he daily honoured the covetous and cruel, who were guilty of cruel tortures in the cities of Hsia. Heaven on this sought *a true* lord for the people, and made its distinguishing and favouring decree light on T'ang the Successful, who punished and destroyed the sovereign of Hsia. . . .

In the case indeed of T'ang the Successful, it was because he was the choice of your many regions that he superseded Hsia and became the lord of the people. He paid careful attention to the essential virtues *of a sovereign,* in order to stimulate the people, and they on their part imitated him, and were stimulated. From him down to the emperor Yi,* the sovereigns all made their virtue illustrious, and were cautious in the use of punishments;—thus also exercising a stimulating influence *over the people.* . . .

. . . It was the case that the last sovereign of your Shang was luxurious to the extreme of luxury, while his schemes of government showed neither purity nor progress, so that Heaven sent down such ruin on him.

The wise, not thinking, become foolish, and the foolish, by thinking, become wise. Heaven for five years waited kindly, and forbore with the descendant *of T'ang, to see if* he would indeed prove himself the true ruler of the people, but there was nothing in him deserving to be regarded. Heaven then sought among your many regions, making a great impression by its terrors to stir up one who might look *reverently* to it; but in all your regions, there was not one deserving of its regard. There were, however, our kings of Chou,* who treated well the multitudes of the people, and were able to sustain the burden of virtuous *government,* and to preside over all services to spirits and to Heaven. Heaven thereupon instructed them, and increased their excellence, made choice of them, and gave them the decree of Yin,† to rule over your many regions.

* [Spellings changed to Wade-Giles system: Shoo King—Shu Ching; Hea—Hsia; Yih—Yi; Chow—Chou.—Ed.]

† [The latter part of Shang dynasty.—Ed.]

• 3 •

The Foundations of Chinese Thought

The Chou dynasty (1122-221 B.C.) was never a centralized unit but rather a loose confederation of more or less independent states, somewhat akin to a feudal system. The middle and late Chou periods were times of great political and social upheaval as the various states struggled among themselves and with newly arrived semibarbarian peoples for mastery of China. Eventually the state of Ch'in became supreme, and though its rule was brief—221–206 B.C.— it provided the model for the unified centralized state in China.

This period of great instability and turmoil was an age of great creativity. The major influence was in thought—thought about the universe, about government, about man. Given the failure and collapse of the old ways, the philosophers were seeking answers to the age-old problem of social order and stability.

A. The Great Teacher

Confucius was a teacher from the state of Lu whose aspirations for high political office were never achieved. Thus, he considered himself a failure in life. Yet his answers to the problem of social order provided the chief rationale and justification for Chinese government down to the twentieth century. Although Confucianism did not remain constant and static (it underwent considerable revitalization with the Neo-Confucianist school in the twelfth and thirteenth centuries), its broad principles on the relationship between man, government, and society, became fundamental.

As you read these selections attributed to Confucius, try to keep the following questions in mind: What does Confucius think of man? What answer does Confucius provide for maintaining order and stability? Is Confucianism a conservative or radical philosophy? Does it provide for an aristocratic or democratic system of government? Why do you think the Chinese accepted the principles of Confucianism? Are there any similarities or differences between Confucianism and Western political thought?

CONFUCIUS (551-479 B.C.)

CONFUCIUS AS A TEACHER

15. Confucius said: "Sometimes I have gone a whole day without food and a whole night without sleep, giving myself to thought. It was no use. It is better to learn."

22. Confucius said: "In education there are no class distinctions."

23. Confucius said: "By nature men are pretty much alike; it is learning and practice that set them apart."

26. Confucius said: "Those who are born wise are the highest type of people; those who become wise through learning come next; those who learn by overcoming dullness come after that. Those who are dull but still won't learn are the lowest type of people."

28. Confucius said: "Learning without thinking is labor lost; thinking without learning is perilous."

29. Confucius said: "Yu, shall I teach you what knowledge is? When you know a thing, say that you know it; when you do not know a thing, admit that you do not know it. That is knowledge."

30. Confucius said: "Worthy indeed was Hui! A single bamboo bowl of millet to eat, a gourdful of water to drink, living in a back alley—others would have found it unendurably depressing, but Hui's cheerfulness was not affected at all. Worthy indeed was Hui!"

32. Confucius said: "A young man's duty is to be filial to his parents at home and respectful to his elders abroad, to be circumspect and truthful, and, while overflowing with love for all men, to associate himself with humanity *(jen)*. If, when all

---

Reprinted with permission of Columbia University Press, from Wm. Theodore de Bary, Wing-tsit Chan and Burton Watson, *Sources of Chinese Tradition* (New York, 1964), Vol. I.

that is done, he has any energy to spare, then let him study the polite arts."

THE TEACHINGS OF CONFUCIUS

39. Confucius said: "Shen! My teaching contains one principle that runs through it all." "Yes," replied Tseng Tzu. When Confucius had left the room the disciples asked: "What did he mean?" Tseng Tzu replied: "Our Master's teaching is simply this: loyalty and reciprocity."

45. Fan Ch'ih asked about humanity. Confucius said: "Love men."

46. Tzu Chang asked Confucius about humanity. Confucius said: "To be able to practice five virtues everywhere in the world constitutes humanity." Tzu Chang begged to know what these were. Confucius said: "Courtesy, magnanimity, good faith, diligence, and kindness. He who is courteous is not humiliated, he who is magnanimous wins the multitude, he who is of good faith is trusted by the people, he who is diligent attains his objective, and he who is kind can get service from the people."

53. Confucius said: "Riches and honor are what every man desires, but if they can be obtained only by transgressing the right way, they must not be held. Poverty and lowliness are what every man detests, but if they can be avoided only by transgressing the right way, they must not be evaded. If a gentleman departs from humanity, how can he bear the name? Not even for the lapse of a single meal does a gentleman ignore humanity. In moments of haste he cleaves to it: in seasons of peril he cleaves to it."

56. Tzu Yu asked about filial piety. Confucius said: "Nowadays a filial son is just a man who keeps his parents in food. But even dogs or horses are given food. If there is no feeling of reverence, wherein lies the difference?"

58. Confucius said: "In serving his parents, a son may gently remonstrate with them. If he sees that they are not inclined to follow his suggestion, he should resume his reverential attitude but not abandon his purpose. If he is belabored, he will not complain."

62. Confucius said: "Courtesy without decorum becomes tiresome. Cautiousness without decorum becomes timidity, daring becomes insubordination, frankness becomes effrontery."

64. Confucius said: "A man who is not humane, what has he to do with rites? A man who is not humane, what has he to do with music?"

67. Tzu Lu asked about the worship of ghosts and spirits. Confucius said: "We don't know yet how to serve men, how can we know about serving the spirits?" "What about death?" was the next question. Confucius said: "We don't know yet about life, how can we know about death?"

84. Tzu Kung asked about the gentleman. Confucius said: "The gentleman first practices what he preaches and then preaches what he practices."

86. Confucius said: "The gentleman is always calm and at ease; the inferior man is always worried and full of distress."

87. Confucius said: "The gentleman understands what is right; the inferior man understands what is profitable."

88. Confucius said: "The gentleman cherishes virtue; the inferior man cherishes possessions. The gentleman thinks of sanctions; the inferior man thinks of personal favors."

95. Confucius said: "If a ruler himself is upright, all will go well without orders. But if he himself is not upright, even though he gives orders they will not be obeyed."

97. Confucius said: "Lead the people by laws and regulate them by penalties, and the people will try to keep out of jail, but will have no sense of shame. Lead the people by virtue and restrain them by the rules of decorum, and the people will have a sense of shame, and moreover will become good."

98. Chi K'ang Tzu asked Confucius about government, saying: "Suppose I were to kill the lawless for the good of the law-abiding, how would that do?" Confucius answered: "Sir, why should it be necessary to employ capital punishment in your government? Just so you genuinely desire the good, the people will be good. The virtue of the gentleman may be compared to the wind and that of the commoner to the weeds. The weeds under the force of the wind cannot but bend."

100. When Confucius was traveling to Wei, Jan Yu drove him. Confucius observed: "What a dense population!" Jan Yu said: "The people having grown so numerous, what next should be done for them?" "Enrich them," was the reply. "And when one has enriched them, what next should be done?" Confucius said: "Educate them."

101. Tzu Kung asked about government. Confucius said: "The essentials are sufficient food, sufficient troops, and the confidence of the people." Tzu Kung said: "Suppose you were forced to give up one of these three, which would you let go first?" Confucius said: "The troops." Tzu Kung asked again: "If you are forced to give up one of the two remaining, which would you let go?" Confucius said: "Food. For from of old, death has been the lot of all men, but a people without faith cannot survive."

102. Duke Ching of Ch'i asked Confucius about government. Confucius replied: "Let the prince be prince, the minister be minister, the father father and the son son." "Excellent!" said the duke. "Indeed if the prince is not prince, the minister not minister, the father not father, and the son not son, then with all the grain in my possession shall I ever get to eat any?"

B. Taoism

Taoism was originally a reaction to the strict social controls espoused by the Confucianists. Taoism provides a set of beliefs about the nature of man and of the universe completely different from Confucianism. But the Chinese regard Taoism as a complement to the principles of Confucius rather than rejection of them. It has often been said that the Chinese official is a Confucian in office, and a Taoist upon retirement.

Lao Tzu, the presumed author of the *Tao Tê Ching,* one of the major works of Taoism, was most likely a figure of legend. His followers fixed the dates of his life so that he should precede Confucius. How does Taoism differ from Confucianism? What do the Taoists think of man? What kind of government would the Taoists establish if they got into power? Why does the Taoist delight in paradoxes? How can there be action without acting? Why do you think Taoism has been the major influence on Chinese art? How could a Chinese accept both Confucianism and Taoism? Which part of a doughnut is Taoism and which part is Confucianism?

LAO TZU (?)

I.

The Way that can be told of is not an Unvarying Way;
The names that can be named are not unvarying names.
It was from the Nameless that Heaven and Earth sprang;
The named is but the mother that rears the ten thousand creatures, each after its kind.
Truly, "Only he that rids himself of desire can see the Secret Essences";
He that has never rid himself of desire can see only the Outcomes. . . .

IV.

The Way is like an empty vessel
That yet may be drawn from
Without ever needing to be filled.
It is bottomless; the very progenitor of all things in the world.
In it all sharpness is blunted,
All tangles untied,
All glare tempered,
All dust smoothed.
It is like a deep pool that never dries. . . .

IX.

Stretch a bow to the very full,
And you will wish you had stopped in time;
Temper a sword-edge to its very sharpest,
And you will find it soon grows dull.
When bronze and jade fill your hall
It can no longer be guarded.
Wealth and place breed insolence
That brings ruin in its train.
When your work is done, then withdraw!
Such is Heaven's Way.

Reprinted with permission of Houghton Mifflin Company, from Arthur Waley (ed.), *The Way and Its Power, A Study of the Tao Tê Ching and Its Place in Chinese Thought* (Boston, 1935).

XIX.

Banish wisdom, discard knowledge,
And the people will be benefited a hundredfold.
Banish human kindness, discard morality,
And the people will be dutiful and compassionate.
Banish skill, discard profit,
And thieves and robbers will disappear. . . .

XXII.

"To remain whole, be twisted!"
To become straight, let yourself be bent.
To become full, be hollow.
Be tattered, that you may be renewed.
Those that have little, may get more,
Those that have much, are but perplexed.
Therefore the Sage
Clasps the Primal Unity,
  Testing by it everything under Heaven.
He does not show himself; therefore he is seen everywhere.
He does not define himself, therefore he is distinct.
He does not boast of what he will do, therefore he succeeds.
He is not proud of his work, and therefore it endures.
He does not contend,
And for that very reason no one under Heaven can contend with him. . . .

XLIII.

What is of all things most yielding
Can overwhelm that which is of all things most hard.
Being substanceless it can enter even where there is no space;
This is how I know the value of action that is actionless.
But that there can be teaching without words,
Value in action that is actionless,
Few indeed can understand.

LVI.

Those who know do not speak;
Those who speak do not know. . . .

LVII.

The more prohibitions there are, the more ritual avoidances,
The poorer the people will be.
The more "sharp weapons" there are,
The more pernicious contrivances will be invented.
The more laws are promulgated,
The more thieves and bandits there will be.
Therefore a sage has said:
So long as I "do nothing" the people will of themselves be transformed.
So long as I love quietude, the people will of themselves go straight.
So long as I act only by inactivity the people will of themselves become prosperous.
So long as I have no wants the people will of themselves return to the "state of the Uncarved Block."

C. The Rights of the People

Mencius was the major disciple and chief interpreter of Confucius. His emphasis on the natural goodness of men and on humane government added new ideas that became assimilated into the general body of Confucian thought.

Here Mencius talks about the relationship between a ruler and his people. How does Mencius expand upon the concept of the Mandate of Heaven? Does Mencius think the people have the right to revolution? If so, under what conditions?

MENCIUS (372-289 B.C.)

Mencius said: "An overlord is he who employs force under a cloak of humanity. To be an overlord one has to be in possession of a large state. A king, on the other hand, is he who gives expression to his humanity through virtuous conduct. . . . When men are subdued by force, it is not that they submit from their hearts but only that their strength is unavailing. When men are won by virtue, then their hearts are gladdened and their submission is sincere. . . ."

Mencius said: ". . . Here is the way to win the empire: win the people and you win the empire. Here is the way to win the people: win their hearts and you win the people. Here is the way to win their hearts: give them and share with them what they like, and do not do to them what they do not like. The people turn to a humane ruler as water flows downward or beasts take to wilderness. . . ."

Mencius said: "Men are in the habit of speaking of the world, the state. As a matter of fact, the foundation of the world lies in the state, the foundation of the state lies in the family, and the foundation of the family lies in the individual."

Mencius said: "[In the constitution of a state] the people rank the highest, the spirits of land and grain come next, and the ruler counts the least."

King Hsüan of Ch'i asked: "Is it not true that T'ang banished Chieh and that King Wu smote Chou?" Mencius replied: "It is so stated in the records." The king asked: "May a subject, then, slay his sovereign?" Mencius replied: "He who outrages humanity is a scoundrel; he who outrages righteousness is a scourge. A scourge or a scoundrel is a despised creature [and no longer a king]. I have heard that a despised creature called Chou was put to death, but I have not heard anything about the murdering of a sovereign."

Reprinted with permission of Columbia University Press, from Wm. Theodore de Bary, Wing-tsit Chan and Burton Watson, *Sources of Chinese Tradition* (New York, 1964), Vol. I.

D. Legalism

The ideas of the Legalists represented a total rejection of the Confucian political and social order. They were accepted and put into practice by the Ch'in in their unification of China. The rulers who came after the Ch'in preferred to rule by Confucian principles once they had achieved power. Why?

Although the Legalists were condemned and discredited, what do you think would be their permanent influence on Chinese civilization? Would you agree with Professors John K. Fairbank and Edwin O. Reischauer, two eminent scholars, that "the Legalist spirit is more obviously alive in Communist China today than either Confucian morality or Taoistic nature mysticism?"

HAN FEI TZU (died 233 B.C.)

When the sage rules the state, he does not count on people doing good of themselves, but employs such measures as will keep them from doing any evil. If he counts on people doing good of themselves, there will not be enough such people to be numbered by the tens in the whole country. But if he employs such measures as will keep them from doing evil, then the entire state can be brought up to a uniform standard. Inasmuch as the administrator has to consider the many but disregard the few, he does not busy himself with morals but with laws. . . .

. . . when the Confucianists of the present day counsel the rulers they do not discuss the way to bring about order now, but exalt the achievement of good order in the past. They neither study affairs pertaining to law and government nor observe the realities of vice and wickedness, but all exalt the reputed glories of remote antiquity and the achievements of the ancient kings. Sugar-coating their speech, the Confucianists say: "If you listen to our words, you will be able to become the leader of all feudal lords." . . . Therefore, the intelligent ruler upholds solid facts and discards useless frills. He does

---

Reprinted with permission of Columbia University Press, from Wm. Theodore de Bary, Wing-tsit Chan and Burton Watson, *Sources of Chinese Tradition* (New York, 1964), Vol. I.

not speak about deeds of humanity and righteousness, and he does not listen to the words of learned men.

Those who are ignorant about government insistently say: "Win the hearts of the people." . . . For all that the ruler would need to do would be just to listen to the people. Actually, the intelligence of the people is not to be relied upon any more than the mind of a baby. If the baby does not have his head shaved, his sores will recur; if he does not have his boil cut open, his illness will go from bad to worse. However, in order to shave his head or open the boil someone has to hold the baby while the affectionate mother is performing the work, and yet he keeps crying and yelling incessantly. The baby does not understand that suffering a small pain is the way to obtain a great benefit.

Now, the sovereign urges the tillage of land and the cultivation of pastures for the purpose of increasing production for the people, but they think the sovereign is cruel. The sovereign regulates penalties and increases punishments for the purpose of repressing the wicked, but the people think the sovereign is severe. Again, he levies taxes in cash and in grain to fill up the granaries and treasuries in order to relieve famine and provide for the army, but they think the sovereign is greedy. Finally, he insists upon universal military training without personal favoritism, and urges his forces to fight hard in order to take the enemy captive, but the people think the sovereign is violent. These four measures are methods for attaining order and maintaining peace, but the people are too ignorant to appreciate them.

• 4 •

Understanding Chinese Philosophy

It would be a mistake to compare Chinese thought to Western religion. Confucianism, Taoism, and Legalism are systems of thought—philosophies—rather than religions. Fung Yu-lan, one of the leading contemporary interpreters of

Confucian thought, sums up some of the major principles that lie behind most Chinese philosophy.

FUNG YU-LAN

. . . [The] craving for something beyond the present actual world is one of the innate desires of mankind, and the Chinese people are no exception to this rule. They have not had much concern with religion because they have had so much concern with philosophy. They are not religious because they are philosophical. In philosophy they satisfy their craving for what is beyond the present actual world. In philosophy also they have the super-moral values expressed and appreciated, and in living according to philosophy these super-moral values are experienced.

According to the tradition of Chinese philosophy, its function is not the increase of positive knowledge (by positive knowledge I mean information regarding matters of fact), but the elevation of the mind—a reaching out for what is beyond the present actual world, and for the values that are higher than the moral ones. . . .

There are many people who say that Chinese philosophy is a this-world philosophy. It is difficult to state that these people are entirely right or entirely wrong. Taking a merely superficial view, people who hold this opinion cannot be said to be wrong, because according to their view, Chinese philosophy, regardless of its different schools of thought, is directly or indirectly concerned with government and ethics. On the surface, therefore, it is concerned chiefly with society, and not with the universe; with the daily functions of human relations, not hell and heaven; with man's present life, but not his life in a world to come. When he was once asked by a disciple about the meaning of death, Confucius replied: "Not yet understanding life, how can you understand death?" And Mencius said: "The sage is the acme of human relations," which, taken literally, means that the sage is the morally perfect man in society. . . .

This, however, is only a surface view of the matter. Chinese

Reprinted with permission from Fung Yu-lan, *A Short History of Chinese Philosophy*, Derk Bodde (ed.). Copyright 1948 by The Macmillan Company.

philosophy cannot be understood by oversimplification of this kind. So far as the main tenet of its tradition is concerned, if we understand it aright, it cannot be said to be wholly this-worldly, just as, of course, it cannot be said to be wholly other-worldly. It is both of this world *and* of the other world. . . .

According to Chinese philosophy, the man who accomplishes this synthesis, not only in theory but also in deed, is the sage. He is both this-worldly and other-worldly. The spiritual achievement of the Chinese sage corresponds to the saint's achievement in Buddhism, and in Western religion. But the Chinese sage is not one who does not concern himself with the business of the world. His character is described as one of "sageliness within and kingliness without." That is to say, in his inner sageliness, he accomplishes spiritual cultivation; in his kingliness without, he functions in society. It is not necessary that the sage should be the actual head of the government in his society. From the standpoint of practical politics, for the most part, the sage certainly has no chance of being the head of the state. The saying "sageliness within and kingliness without" means only that he who has the noblest spirit should, theoretically, be king. As to whether he actually has or has not the chance of being king, that is immaterial.

Since the character of the sage is, according to Chinese tradition, one of sageliness within and kingliness without, the task of philosophy is to enable man to develop this kind of character. Therefore, what philosophy discusses is what the Chinese philosophers describe as the *Tao* (Way, or basic principles) of sageliness within and kingliness without. . . .

Since what is discussed in philosophy is the *Tao* (Way) of sageliness within and kingliness without, it follows that philosophy must be inseparable from political thought. Regardless of the differences between the schools of Chinese philosophy, the philosophy of every school represents, at the same time, its political thought. . . .

• 5 •

Chinese Buddhism

Of all foreign religions and influences that came to China, until modern times only Buddhism from India gained widespread acceptance and became a major influence on Chinese life and thought. The Han dynasty (206 B.C.–A.D. 220) had succeeded the Ch'in and proceeded to rule on the basis of Confucian principles while expanding the empire. The downfall of the Han brought about another period of disunity and social disorder that was to last until the sixth century. Although the first Buddhist missionaries had entered China as early as the first century, it was during this period of upheaval, when the people were looking for some new message to sustain them, that Buddhism was accepted and spread throughout China.

Buddhism reached its greatest height under the T'ang dynasty which had reunified China during the seventh and eighth centuries. Many different schools of Buddhism flourished and many monasteries became very wealthy. At that time there was considerable travel between India and China. For a variety of reasons Buddhism began to decline as a major force during the ninth century, and never again reached the peak of prestige or influence it had enjoyed under the T'ang. Its effects, however, were permanent and lasting.

First, Professor Herrlee G. Creel describes some of the basic doctrines of Buddhism that appealed to the Chinese. Then, Professor Kenneth K.S. Ch'en of Princeton explains how Buddhism from India became Chinese.

HERRLEE G. CREEL

Buddhism in China

Around the beginning of the Christian Era, Buddhism spread to China from India. This meant far more than the mere coming of a religion. For some Chinese it meant a new way of life. For all Chinese, whether they accepted Buddhism or rejected it, it meant that henceforward the world would be looked at in new ways, and the universe conceived to be quite a different thing from what it had been. The whole Chinese manner of thinking was to some extent changed, so gradually and so universally that very few people knew what was happening. For roughly a thousand years the Chinese mind was largely dominated by Buddhism. . . .

His doctrine, as it is set forth in various scriptures, is based on the law of causation. Existence is an evil to be got rid of. What causes existence? Desire, the clinging to life and the things of sense. Exterminate this desire and clinging, and one will be free from the round of existence. To the end of one's life, then, one is simply to practice celibacy, good deeds, and contemplation, and at death (if not before) one will enter nirvana. Those who embarked upon such a life and became members of the order were monks; Gautama later permitted women to become nuns, though he did this with great reluctance. The laity were not members of the order but acquired merit by supporting monks and nuns. Laymen had a much simpler code of conduct to follow; they must not take life, drink intoxicants, lie, steal, or be unchaste. While the layman may hope for nirvana, it is also right for him to aim at rebirth in a temporary heaven. . . .

. . . early Buddhism is sometimes called "Hinayana Buddhism." This name was given to it by the advocates of a variety of Buddhism developed later, which they called "Mahayana." This means "great vehicle"; they patronizingly called the earlier form "Hinayana," "lesser vehicle," to distinguish it. The Mahayana was developed in India, possibly

---

Reprinted with permission of The University of Chicago Press, Eyre & Spottiswoode (Publishers), Ltd., London, and Curtis Brown, Ltd., New York and London, from Herrlee G. Creel, *Chinese Thought: From Confucius to Mao Tse-tung* (New York: A Mentor Book, The New American Library, 1963).

around the beginning of the Christian Era. Its most essential difference is the place it gives to the *bodhisattva,* literally, "being of enlightenment." A bodhisattva is a being who has qualified to enter nirvana and become a Buddha, but who voluntarily renounces this privilege in order to remain among the still unenlightened beings of the universe and work for their salvation. He is a heroic figure, reverenced and even worshiped for his suffering, toil, and compassion for others. The Mahayana Buddhists consider the striving for personal attainment of nirvana that characterized the Hinayana to be selfish.

In general, Mahayana Buddhism caters to the popular tastes, developing to the highest degree those superstitious and mythological elements which were not pronounced in early Buddhism. . . .

It is not mere coincidence that the period of the tremendous growth of Chinese Buddhism was one in which the Chinese world was exceedingly troubled. . . . the later days of the Han dynasty, in the second century A.D., were anything but placid. Intellectuals took refuge in a sort of nihilism or in Taoist mysticism. The common people, ground between the oppression of the officials and that of the great landed proprietors, fell more and more into the ranks of the landless proletariat, if not of slaves. . . .

Only a few could become monks or nuns, but everybody could be a lay Buddhist. This was rather a new thing. To get much satisfaction from Confucianism one needed to be able to read fairly well. In Taoism the goal was to become an immortal, but only a few rare spirits could attain this. In Buddhism, however, and especially in its Mahayana aspects, absolutely everybody could win a very satisfying degree of salvation. Of course, one would have to wait until after death for it, but traditional Chinese thought had been almost silent on life after death. Buddhism offered at least a hope, and at times when men were living in a hell on earth it was much to be able to hope for heaven after death. In any case, it was something that even the humblest individual could hope to win *for himself.* . . .

Buddhism in China has not only offered salvation to the good and the faithful but has also portrayed in graphic terms the tortures that await the wicked in the multiplicity of Buddhist hells. But here again it offers a way out. These torments are not permanent, but only a series of purgatories; by an elaborate series of ceremonies it is possible to help those one loves to pass through them quickly. Services for the dead have been important in China from time immemorial; Buddhism succeeded in making for itself a large place in the performance of this age-old function. . . .

The Chinese are tolerant. They see nothing wrong in taking part in ceremonies in a Buddhist, a Taoist, and a Confucian temple on the same day. . . .

KENNETH K.S. CH'EN

Mahayana Buddhism and Chinese Culture

Of all the foreign religions introduced into China, why is it that only Buddhism managed to gain such widespread acceptance among the Chinese? It is probably safe to say that one of the primary reasons was that after its introduction it rapidly adjusted itself to the Chinese environment, and by so doing ceased to be Indian and became Chinese. Hence the frequent use of the term Chinese Buddhism. . . .

. . . Various features of Indian Buddhism were modified on Chinese soil. Bodhisattvas took on definite Chinese appearances. For instance, Maitreya, the future Buddha, was transformed into the Laughing Buddha, and in almost all Chinese Buddhist temples the image of this jovial figure with heavy jowls and a very pronounced belly greets the visitor as soon as he enters the temple. In this jolly pot-bellied figure one is able to see the representation of a number of Chinese life ideals. The huge protruding stomach denotes prosperity and a wealth of material goods. Only the rich can afford to eat and be fat. The reclining figure denotes spiritual contentment and relaxation. He appears to be at peace with himself and the world. The large number of children usually seen climbing all over him is indicative of yet another Chinese life ideal, a large family consisting of many children. In such a figure one sees Buddhism absorbing some of the popular beliefs of the Chinese people. . . .

Buddhism was accepted by the Chinese because it accom-

Reprinted with permission, from Kenneth K.S. Ch'en, "Mahayana Buddhism and Chinese Culture," *Asia*, No. 10 (Winter 1968). Copyright 1968 by the Asia Society, Inc.

modated itself to the dominant Confucian virtue of filial piety. Buddhism as a religion in India aimed at individual salvation in nirvana, a goal attained by leaving the household life and entering the houseless stage, which meant the life of celibacy and mendicancy. Upon assuming the monastic garb the monk terminated his ties with family and society; his wife became a widow and his children orphans. When this religion was introduced into the country where filial piety and family life were the dominant features, conflict was inevitable. . . .

How did the Buddhists proceed to adjust and accommodate themselves to the ethical atmosphere in China so as to present a better image of their religion as far as filial piety was concerned? Briefly they sought to make Buddhism palatable by three methods: by pointing to the numerous sutras in the Buddhist canon which stress filial piety; second, by forging a body of literature which emphasized piety as its central theme, and third, by contending that the Buddhist concept of piety was nobler and superior to that of the Confucians because it aimed at universal salvation for all living creatures, while the Confucian piety was limited to just one family. This last point is the most important of all. It was an original idea of the Buddhists, and it merits some further remarks.

The Buddhists contend that when a person is converted to Buddhism and takes up the monastic vow he becomes a vehicle for the conversion of his own parents, so that they attain salvation and escape from the endless cycles of rebirth. Surely this is the greatest boon that a filial son can convey to his parents. The Chinese Buddhists pursued this argument further and contended that the Buddhist monk was not merely aiming at salvation for his parents, but at universal salvation for all living creatures. In this role he was fulfilling what the Buddhists call the *ta-hsiao,* the great filial piety.

• 6 •

The World of the Spirits: Death and Funerals

Buddhism and Taoism were the major institutional religions in China. Each influenced and borrowed from the other. Both religions, however, assimilated many ancient, perhaps primitive Chinese beliefs about the world of the spirits and ghosts. Chinese folk religion is basically an amalgam of nature worship, animism, ancestor worship, combined with elements of Confucianism, Taoism, and Buddhism that filtered down to the populace.

Dr. Francis L.K. Hsu, an anthropologist from Northwestern University, studied the folk religion of the Chinese in a semirural community in southwest China in the early 1940s. Though the particular customs and beliefs that he records may be unique to that area of China, these selections should give the reader an idea of the social relationships and values that are reflected in the folk religion of the people.

FRANCIS L.K. HSU

Man's Relation with Spiritual Worlds

Each person has a body and a *huei,* or spirit. When a person has died an ordinary death from old age or sickness, he becomes a *huei* and goes to the spirit world. If a person has died in expiation of some crime, such as banditry, his spirit will become a *gur,* or ghost. The body of a person who has died an ordinary death is usually buried properly. The body of a person who has been executed is usually left exposed; such exposure as a rule produces a *gur,* or ghost.

Huei is not harmful or malicious to human beings, but *gur* is. *Gur* can be uplifted (transformed) through prayers and scripture reading by hired priests. It then becomes a

---

Reprinted with permission of the author, from Francis L.K. Hsu, *Under the Ancestors' Shadow* (London: Routledge and Kegan Paul, Ltd., 1949).

huei and therefore harmless. Only *huei* can reincarnate. The spirit of a person who has been killed by bandits or by accident does not, as a matter of course, turn into *gur*. But if the spirit of a dead person is dissatisfied, it will become *gur* and create trouble.

"*Gur*" is applied to males only. The female equivalent is *yao*. . . .

The duration and the degree of prosperity or misery of a person's life depend chiefly upon two things: the preordained fate and the person's behavior in life. The first refers to the duration of life prescribed for the person when he or she was born; the second refers to whether the person has been a good or a bad person. "Good" and "bad" are defined by tradition and will be made clear shortly. These records are kept by *cheng huangs* and the assistants of the Ten Judges according to reports given them by various gods including: Kitchen God, Day Inspecting and Night Inspecting Gods. The *cheng huangs* normally dispatch emissaries to call for or to arrest the spirits of human beings whose time is up either because it was preordained or because it was precipitated by his or her bad behavior. Good behavior will prolong the preordained duration of life; bad behavior will shorten it or cause it to be miserable or disease-bound.

When the *huei* of a person leaves his or her body, it has entered the World of Spirits. As soon as it passes the boundary line, it will see two roads; the broad and nice one leads to the Higher World, or the Western World, and the other, not so broad and pleasant, leads to the Lower World. If the deceased was widely known for his or her good deeds in life, the spirit will be received with pomp and led to the broad road. If the spirit is of someone who was not so well known, it will be sent through the Gate of Ghosts before the first judge. The spirits of people notorious for their bad behavior and whose lives were shortened as a result by special decree, will be put in chains.

However, before reaching the first judge all spirits must cross a river by a *nai ho* bridge. This bridge seems to be a precarious structure. The spirit that crosses it is in danger of falling from it and being swallowed by the monsters underneath.

By each judge in succession, the spirits who have committed the worst behavior in life will be submitted to many forms of torture, such as being cut to pieces, ground to cream in a mill, roasted, disemboweled, etc. The severity of the torture depends upon the extent to which they had misbehaved in life. At the court of the tenth judge they may be allowed to reincarnate. Many of the worst ones may be kept in hells permanently and never get such a chance at all. Those who reincarnate may be allowed to become only a lower animal. The somewhat better behaved ones will be made into human beings, but kept in poverty and misery.

The spirits who did not misbehave in human form will be sorted out, on the basis of the records of the ten judges. Most of them are quickly dispatched to the tenth judge and then born into families with means. Those who are more deserving will be entertained for a longer or shorter time in special guest palaces in the headquarters of one of the judges. A few of these will be offered official positions in the spiritual hierarchy. The usual position offered is *cheng huang,* the spiritual figure corresponding to the magistrate. A very few will become permanent higher gods and go to reside in the Higher World or the Western World. Should such a figure reincarnate, it will become at least a high official in the government.

The punishment suffered by a spirit in the Lower World may be mitigated or increased, respectively, by the good deeds or misdoings of its descendants. Prayer services at which hired priests officiate are part of the good deeds. Its destination in the next reincarnation may also be improved or prejudiced, respectively, in the same way.

Death and Funerals

Death is the event which marks the passage of an individual from the world of man to the world of spirit. All rites in West Town funerals aim at one of four things: (1) expediting the spirit's safe entry into that world; (2) its comfort in that world; (3) expressing sorrowful feelings on the part of the living and their reluctance to let the dead go; and (4) making sure that the death has not created conditions for future disaster through circumstances which are beyond his or her control.

The elaboration of a funeral is in direct proportion to the economic condition of the family and the social station of the dead. It also varies according to age. Dead children are not entitled to any funeral at all. An unmarried adolescent boy or girl may be given a small funeral. . . .

When a member has died, the first thing for the family to do is to find out whether death occurred on a "double death" date. There are eight months in which such dates occur. . . . In the lunar calendar, a copy of which every family possesses, each day is represented by two words which are one of the combinations of two sets of symbols, the *t'ien kan*, or zodiac symbols, and the *ti chih*, or earth symbols. Any day on which one of the six words *(keng, chia, yi, hsin, wu*, and *chi)* occurs is a "double death" date. As there are only ten earth symbols used cyclically, there are bound to be about sixteen or seventeen "double death" dates in every month. . . .

[On such occasions] a red date and a white date, the latter tied with colored thread, are put in the mouth of the corpse. An ordinary hat will be put on the head of a male, and a piece of black cloth will be placed on that of a female. Then the whole body is covered with red cloth after having been dressed in the best clothes, which have been prepared for the purpose. Under and covering the corpse are "blessing quilts," made of cotton and red cloth. After the corpse is lowered into the coffin, the latter will be filled with wicks or more cotton quilts to keep the corpse from shifting when the coffin is being carried in the funeral procession. A small jar covered by red cloth and containing two small fish and some water will be buried in the pit underneath the coffin. These measures are to ensure the prosperity of the family. The hour when the coffin lid will be nailed on the coffin, the hour when the coffin will be removed from the house, and the day when the coffin will be lowered into the pit for burial must be decided by diviners or by referring to the Lunar Almanac. This is to ensure that the God of Earth (T'u Ti) will not be offended, and therefore that the dead may not be uncomfortable in the tomb. . . .

Certain years and certain months of each year are more propitious for certain burial locations with reference to the family dwelling. There are eight directions: south, north, west, east, southeast, southwest, northeast, and northwest, and a diviner must decide which direction is auspicious. If the family graveyard is located on a slope southwest of the house and if the diviner says that this location is not good for the family in that particular year, the coffin will be taken out of the house and deposited elsewhere temporarily. The coffin will not be buried in a pit, but will be laid on the surface of the ground and then covered with slabs or pebbles until the year and month propitious for the southwest location. If a family should fail to follow this rule, the good effects of the family graveyard may be totally annulled. . . .

As soon as death has occurred, an elderly woman of the household will take some incense and food and report to the local patron god or *cheng huang* at the nearest temple. This is to ensure the good will of the first major god which the spirit of the dead will encounter. Quantities of paper money, but not paper horses, carriages, or houses, as in other parts of China, are burned for the spirit of the dead in anticipation of its expenses in the other world. Paper horses, carriages, and houses are burned only in order to send away undesirable ghosts in connection with sickness.

• 7 •

The Imperial System: The Bureaucracy

One way the Chinese look at their history is to view the past as a series of cycles embodying the rise and fall of the great dynasties. The histories that the Chinese scholars have written have been dynastic histories, the chronicles of the ruling families. There seems to be a similar pattern to the rise and fall of each dynasty, representing a kind of cosmic rhythm. Periods of disorder were followed by the founding of a new ruling house (in two cases by men from peasant stock) whose successful rule in achievement of unity, control of floods, and expansion of the empire, indicated they had received the Mandate of Heaven. Inevitably, after years of successful rule, corruption and inefficiency would set in, and the accumulation of land by government officials would increase the burden of taxation upon the peasantry who farmed the least amount of land. Thus revenue would decline, flood control would collapse, and disorder and rebellion would result. The scholars would withdraw their support of the ruling house, and the dynasty would collapse, having lost Heaven's Mandate to rule for the common good. (Within the context of this Chinese view of their own past, what would the present period represent in the cycle?)

While this is somewhat of an oversimplification of the cyclical process, it does represent a view that fits into the Chinese concept of the rhythm of the forces at work in the world—yin and yang. (How does this view of history differ from the way we in the West look at history?) On the surface this is a rather static view of the past, but a closer examination of Chinese history does reveal that considerable change and evolution of institutions had taken place from one dynasty to another. Alterations, though gradual, were great. However, the fact that one dynasty ultimately succeeded another indicates that unity was the desired goal—a unity and a harmony that had been achieved in the days of the Sage Kings of myth and legend. The political institutions that the Chinese developed were geared toward achieving and maintaining that goal.

In this reading, Professor John K. Fairbank describes the role and function of the bureaucracy. Though it changed over the centuries, it remained as the major link between the ruling dynasty and the people. Professor Fairbank points out the weaknesses inherent in the system. What strengths do you think enabled the bureaucracy to survive, dynasty after dynasty?

JOHN K. FAIRBANK

The Capital.

The old government centered in the capital. Without question the vast symmetrical plan of Peking makes it the most magnificent of all capital cities. . . .

At Peking, for the greater part of thirteen centuries the civil administration of China was divided among the famous Six Ministries (or Boards), namely those of civil office (ap-

---

Reprinted with permission of Harvard University Press, from John King Fairbank, *The United States and China*. Copyright 1948, 1958 by the President and Fellows of Harvard College.

pointment of officials), revenue, ceremonies, war, punishments, and public works (such as flood control). . . . In addition to the Six Ministries there were two other independent hierarchies of administration—the military establishment and the Censorate, as well as a number of minor offices—the imperial academy of literature, a court to review criminal cases, a historiographer's office, the imperial stud, and offices in charge of banquets and sacrificial worship. At the apex of everything the Ming had created the Grand Secretariat, in which high officials assisted the Emperor in his personal administration of affairs. One of the few Manchu innovations was to add in 1729 a less formal body, the Grand Council, which handled military and other important matters and so became the real top of the administration.

The Provinces.

Spread out over the eighteen provinces of China under the Manchu dynasty was a network of territorial divisions. Each province was divided into several circuits *(tao)* and below them into prefectures, departments, and *hsien* (districts or counties) in descending order. The mandarins in charge of these divisions with their ubiquitous assistants and subordinates formed the main body of the territorial magistracy. Like civil servants trained in the classics at Oxford, they were supposedly omnicompetent, responsible for the collection of revenue, maintenance of order, dispensing of justice, conduct of literary examinations, superintendence of the postal service, and in general for all public events within their areas. . . .

Intervening between the hierarchy of local officials and the government at the capital stood the higher administration in each province. This consisted of a governor-general who was in most cases responsible for two provinces and, as his junior colleague, a governor responsible for a single province. These two officials were of course so placed as to check each other, for they were expected to act and report jointly on important matters. Under the Ch'ing (Manchu) dynasty, frequently the governor-general was a Manchu and the governor Chinese. Beneath them were four provincial officers who exercised province-wide functions—a treasurer, judge, salt comptroller, and grain intendant (who supervised the collection of grain for the capital). . . .

The flow of paper work was maintained by an official post

which reached to all corners of the empire but was limited to the transportation of official mail, official shipments (as of funds), and persons traveling on official business. This postal system was made up of some two thousand stations stretched out along five main and many subsidiary routes which ran into Manchuria, across Mongolia, westward to Turkestan and Tibet, southeastward through the coastal provinces, and southward through the interior of Central China. . . . In time of crisis couriers could cover 250 miles a day.

Such speed was achieved by the use of horses in relays a system which the Mongols had developed to cover the distances of Central Asia.

Central Controls.

Given this network of officials, connected by a flow of documents and persons along the postal routes, it was the problem to stimulate the local bureaucrats to perform their functions and yet prevent them from getting out of hand. . . .

Among these techniques the first was the appointment of all officers down to the rank of district magistrate by the Emperor himself. This made them all aware of their dependence upon the Son of Heaven and their duty of personal loyalty to him. Circulation in office was another device. No official was left in one post for more than three years or at most six years. Ordinarily when moving from one post to another the official passed through the capital and participated in an imperial audience to renew his contact with the ruler. . . .

The evils inherent in bureaucracy were all too evident. All business was in form originated at the bottom and passed upward to the Emperor for decision at the top, memorials from the provinces being addressed to the Emperor at the capital. The higher authority was thus left to choose alternatives of action proposed, and yet the proposal of novel or unprecedented action was both difficult and dangerous for the lower official. The greater safety of conformity tended to kill initiative at the bottom. On the other hand the efficiency of the one man at the top was constantly impaired by his becoming a bottleneck. All business of importance was expected to receive his approval. All legislation and precedent were established by his edict. Modern China still suffers from this tradition.

• 8 •

The Scholars and the Civil Service

It is often pointed out that one of the great contributions of Chinese civilization has been the concept of a government run by the most capable of its citizens, chosen not by birth or wealth, but by merit on the basis of objective examination. These citizens did not serve within their own province. This is what we know as the civil service—a most Confucian concept.

The origins of the examinations can be traced back to the Han dynasty, but the system evolved and changed during each successive dynasty. Each dynasty, if it so chose, could ignore the system by the practice of nepotism, and the system itself was often criticized as being corrupt, ineffective, and inefficient. Yet the institution—a remarkably impersonal one in a society that placed so much value on personal relations—itself survived until the twentieth century, being most dynamic and effective in those periods when the dynasties themselves were at their greatest. It has been described as the major institution, next to the family, that held Chinese society together.

Wang An-shih, an important Sung reformer, points out weaknesses in the system. Yeh Shih, a Ming bureaucrat, looks at the weaknesses during his time. As will be seen, a major controversy centers around the question of the degree to which the civil service acts as an avenue of social mobility. (This raises the question as to what role myth can play within a culture.) Professors Herrlee G. Creel and Dun J. Li offer differing views on this question.

Why do you think the Chinese gave the greatest amount of prestige and status to the scholars?

Do you think the examination system was capable of choosing the most meritorious candidates? Was the system generally an effective and efficient one? How did the examination system foster cultural unity? Compare the Chinese examination system with the civil service examinations of the West.

WANG AN-SHIH

Condemns Scholar Officials

What is the way to select officials? The ancient kings selected men only from the local villages and through the local schools. The people were asked to recommend those they considered virtuous and able, sending up their nominations to the court, which investigated each one. Only if the men recommended proved truly virtuous and able, would they be appointed to official posts commensurate with their individual virtue and ability. Investigation of them did not mean that a ruler relied only upon his own keenness of sight and hearing or that he took the word of one man alone. If they wanted to ascertain a man's virtue, they inquired into his conduct; if they wanted to ascertain his ability, they inquired into his utterances. Having inquired into his actions and utterances, they then tested him in government affairs. What was meant by "investigation" was just that—to test them in government affairs. . . .

Today, although we have schools in each prefecture and district, they amount to no more than school buildings. There are no officers of instruction and guidance; nothing is done to train and develop human talent. . . .

That, however, was not the way men were taught in ancient times. In recent years, teaching has been based on the essays required for the civil service examinations, but this kind of essay cannot be learned without resorting to extensive memorization and strenuous study, upon which students must spend their efforts the whole day long. Such proficiency as they attain is at best of no use in the government of the empire, and at most the empire can make no use of them. Therefore, even if students remained in school until their hair turned gray, and spent their efforts the whole day long pursuing the instruction given them, when finally appointed to office, they would not have even the faintest idea of what to do. . . .

Reprinted with permission of Columbia University Press, from Wm. Theodore de Bary, Wing-tsit Chan and Burton Watson, *Sources of Chinese Tradition* (New York, 1960).

In the present system for electing officials, those who memorize assiduously, recite extensively, and have some knowledge of literary composition, are called "splendid talents of extraordinary accomplishment" or "men of virtue, wise, square, and upright." These are the categories from which the ministers of state are chosen. . . .

Candidates are examined in such fields as: the Nine Classics, the Five Classics, Specialization [in one Classic], and the Study of Law. The court has already become concerned over the uselessness of this type of knowledge, and has stressed the need for an understanding of general principles [as set forth in the Classics]. Nevertheless, those obtained by emphasizing general principles are no better qualified than under the old system. Now the court has also opened up another field of examination, "Understanding of the Classics," in order to promote those proficient in classical studies. However, when we consider the men selected through "Understanding of the Classics," it is still those who memorize, recite, and have some knowledge of literary composition who are able to pass the examination, while those who can apply them to the government of the empire are not always brought in through this kind of selection. . . .

YEH SHIH

Civil Service Examinations

A father urges his son to study not because he believes that books are important in themselves but because they are keys whereby his son can open the door to officialdom. While the government attaches great importance to the examination system, the people view it as merely a means to a worldly end. What they like about a successful candidate is not the character of the candidate as a person; rather, it is his writings that they appreciate. In fact, they know nothing about the candidate himself because a man's writings are not necessarily indicative of his person. It is not surprising that our examination system today does not produce men who command esteem, since it has become a vehicle whereby men

---

of dubious motives ride to officialdom. Yet it is the major instrument whereby scholars are transformed into officials from whom ministers of great responsibilities will eventually emerge. Is it not contradictory that a man who is despised on account of his selfish motives when entering the civil service examinations will be relied upon by the nation to shoulder great responsibilities?

A harmful corollary of using the examination to select governmental personnel is to convert all scholars to aspirants of governmental positions. A healthy society cannot come about when people study not for the purpose of gaining wisdom and knowledge but for the purpose of becoming government officials. A person who seeks knowledge will know what "righteousness" means, and a man of righteousness does not need a salary to become rich and a title to become honorable. The outward things that other people envy and seek after will not in any way affect his determination to preserve his own integrity.

Nowadays the situation is different. Beginning with childhood, all of a man's study is centered on one aim alone: to emerge successfully from the three days' examinations, and all he has in his mind is what success can bring to him in terms of power, influence, and prestige. . . . The old concept of studying for the refinement of one's character and for the acquirement of the sense of righteousness is painfully noteworthy because of its absence. How can one sincerely believe that a system which produces persons of this type as government officials can also generate men of talent eager and able to shoulder great responsibilities? . . .

Scholars are the source from which men of talents are drawn and are in fact the very foundation upon which the nation's destiny rests. They cannot live up to their expected usefulness if the government, instead of cultivating them as true scholars, chooses to corrupt and demoralize them. . . .

HERRLEE G. CREEL

Evaluation of Exam System

The insistence of Confucius that the administration should be placed in the hands of the most capable men in the land, selected solely on the basis of their virtue and education, resulted in the examination system, which was gradually elaborated from Han times onward. Its specific organization differed from period to period. During the Manchu dynasty it consisted of three kinds of examinations—local, provincial, and national—held every two or three years. The candidates competed, at each level, for three successively higher degrees. The competition was intense; in each examination, only a small proportion of the candidates could hope to pass. Naturally there was corruption, but elaborate precautions were taken to prevent it, and during the better periods under Chinese rulers they seem to have been remarkably successful.

Even the lowest degree gave its possessor, though he might be the son of the poorest peasant, great social distinction. In some cases those who held it were given government stipends, or minor posts in the local administration, which meant that in effect they received state assistance in continuing their education. Possession of the highest degree did not always assure that its holder would be appointed to office, but under Chinese dynasties a large proportion of the most responsible posts were normally filled by men who had excelled in the examinations. Although office might be attained in other ways, it appears that, in many periods at least, the man who had passed the examinations had the best prospect of reaching the top of the official hierarchy.

An important exception must be noted, however, in the case of dynasties established by foreign invaders; they naturally gave many of the highest offices to their own people, without subjecting them to the competition of the examinations. Nevertheless, after all of the necessary qualifications have been made, it remains true that in large measure China has been ruled by a bureaucracy imbued by education with

---

Confucian ideals, and recruited through the examinations from the people in general. This does not mean, of course, that all of the highest posts were filled by the sons of farmers. Entirely aside from favoritism, which did operate, the son of a member of the bureaucracy had natural advantages; his family could afford to give him a good education, and he grew up in a learned and professional atmosphere. It is not remarkable that a great many of the principal ministers were the sons or grandsons of officials, but it is surprising that some of them were able to rise from the ranks of the people without such advantages. Although our information is incomplete, it appears that at least in some periods the lower ranks of the bureaucracy, in particular, were infused through the examinations with fresh blood from the masses in considerable volume. . . .

Despite its shortcomings, the examination system gave China a unique kind of government which had many advantages. It brought many of the ablest men in the country into government service. In so far as it was effective, it assured that officials were men of culture, not mere wasters who had inherited their positions. Because its very basis was the philosophy and the ethics of Confucianism, it inculcated a body of shared ideals which produced a very unusual *esprit de corps.* Although it fell short of what we today consider political democracy, it gave to the common people a kind of representation in the government, since in each generation some of their number normally won official posts. It did not make a classless society since education automatically raised the status of its possessors, but it did bring about a degree of social democracy that has probably never been equaled in so great a country over such a long period.

DUN J. LI

Exam System Evaluated

Like all other systems, the examination system had its advantages and disadvantages. On the positive side, it might be said that it had broadened the government's base by

---

drawing officials from all levels of society and thus introduced a democratic element into an otherwise oligarchic society. Theoretically at least, it was entirely possible for a man of the humblest origin, by passing the specified examinations, to rise in power, wealth, and prestige. More than anything else, the examination system accounted for the absence of a caste system in China and the large degree of social mobility denied to many other authoritarian societies. Second, to find the right man for the right task, nothing could be more objective than a test impartially administered, and the civil service examination system was adopted precisely for that purpose. Many great statesmen in China were a product of this system. Third, the examination system brought to mind the importance of education and learning and thus indirectly raised the cultural level of the country as a whole. While in other countries landlords, merchants, or industrialists might be men of the greatest prestige, in China the most respected had always been the scholars.

However, those who criticized this system could point out that the examination which at best was a test of literary learning should not be used as the sole criterion to judge a man's true ability, since a good administrator was more often a man of the world than a man learned in Confucian classics or skillful in writing poetry. Moreover, while the examination system might have increased social mobility, it did not end social stratification. A barber's son might pass the examination and thus be accepted as one of the social elite, but this did not help the rest of the barbers who were still regarded as the "mean" people. Furthermore, except for the wealthy few, who could afford to spend years of study just to prepare for the examinations? The so-called democratic outlook of the examination system was perhaps more apparent than real. Critics of this system were anxious to point out that the overemphasis on literary learning at the expense of other intellectual pursuits had done great damage to other areas of learning of equal importance. This accounted for, at least in part, China's lag behind some other countries in the field of science and technology, despite its achievement in the humanities. Individual scientific talents did occur from time to time, but as society did not attach much importance to the study of natural science and offered no reward for its development, and as people generally looked down upon manual work, there was no intellectual tradition outside the study of humanities. Last, perhaps the most serious indictment against the examination system was its contribution to the development of despotism. After this system was adopted, a man could no longer attain political authority or social recognition through any channel but one, which was controlled by the government. Forever looking for favor and patronage from the central government, the country's educated lost their political initiative and independence and became the ardent defenders of the status quo. As the educated class went, so went the country as a whole.

• 9 •

Economic Conditions: Land and Agriculture

Since Han times, the Chinese economy has been based on a system of intensive agriculture—rice in the south, wheat in the north. Because of the necessity of providing irrigation and other public works, the central government began early to play a major role in regulating the Chinese economy. Even when extensive trade developed between town and countryside, or between China and foreign nations, the government remained dominant. Land taxes were the major source of income for the state, and human labor was the major source of power.

The Chinese never developed a genuine capitalist economy like that which evolved in the West during the seventeenth and eighteenth centuries. There was plenty of commercial capital available, but merchants preferred to get licenses to sell those products which were under government monopoly, such as salt and tea. Moneylending was more lucrative than speculative investment. The accumulation of money *per se* was never valued as highly as patronage of the arts or membership in the ruling scholar-gentry class. Thus, wealthy merchants, rather than reinvesting their profits, used them to provide their sons with education so that they could compete in the exams, or actually to purchase offices and titles in the bureaucracy. Literary achievement was valued over technological innovation. The absence of a system of primogeniture led to a more even distribution and sharing of wealth than in other traditional societies—a factor that accounts for the high degree of social mobility (especially downward) found in China.

The merchant, in fact, was considered to be the parasite of the community. At the very heart of the Confucian system was concern for the well-being of the people, the overwhelming majority of whom were peasants. Thus the peasants ranked directly below the scholars in the Confucian social scale. It was their labor that enabled the system to function. The contentment of the people would be the sign that would indicate that the ruler enjoyed the Mandate of Heaven, and that the bureaucracy was ruling by virtue of its moral authority. There was one fundamental weakness in this system: there was no constitutional or legal mechanism to ensure that the rulers maintained their virtue. All too often they succumbed to their human frailties, and the corruption and inefficiency that accompany unchecked power set in. This, combined with certain inherent flaws in the economic system, made the peasants' lot too often resemble the classical image of the suffering Chinese farmer.

The following group of readings offers a broad picture of economic conditions in traditional Chinese society. The first four selections are from the work of a Chinese historian of the first century, Pan Ku, and present a historical picture of the evolving economy, including certain recurrent features. The next reading is from a first century memorial to the emperor by the Han statesman Ch'ao Ts'o, offering suggestions on how to curb the greed of merchants. In the sixth selection, Ch'eng Hao, eleventh-century adviser to the Sung emperor, details the evils of his day (and of other eras) and suggests a remedy. In the seventh selection, Wang An-shih, the famous Sung reformer, outlines a plan for famine prevention and control that sounds strikingly modern. (The proposal was adopted.) The final reading is from a memorial by the seventeenth-century statesman Ma Mao-ts'ai, addressed to the Ming emperor. It describes conditions that ultimately led to a rebellion that overthrew the Ming dynasty.

How would you describe the major economic problems of China? How did the Chinese attempt to deal with these problems? Why did the traditional Chinese economic system ultimately break down?

PAN KU

Budget of a Farming Family of Five Persons: ca. 400 B.C.

Now [at that time] if a man supporting a family of five persons [including himself] cultivated one hundred mou* of [arable] land, each year from each acre he would harvest one picul and a half [of grain], making [a total of] one hundred and fifty piculs† of unhusked grain. Out of this would be taken one tenth for taxes-in-kind [that is] fifteen piculs, and there would remain one hundred and thirty-five piculs. For food per person for one moon [he would require] one picul and a half, and for five persons for an entire year ninety piculs, leaving a residue of forty-five piculs, which at thirty coins a picul would be worth one thousand three hundred fifty [coins]. Deducting expenses which cost three hundred [coins], for offerings of new [grains] at the [Earth] local shrines, and for spring and autumn sacrifices at the village altars, there would remain [only] one thousand and fifty [coins]. For clothing usually each person required three hundred coins and five persons through the whole year would use one thousand five hundred, [so there would be] a deficit of four hundred and fifty [coins]. [Moreover] expenses in times of afflictions, illnesses both slight and grave, deaths, burials, as well as [military] taxes and other government levies were not included [here]. That is why farmers were constantly in want, and had not the heart to exert themselves in plowing. Instead the price of grain was made excessively dear.

Reprinted with permission of Princeton University Press, from Nancy Lee Swann (ed.), *Food and Money in Ancient China* (Princeton, N.J., 1950).

* [About 4.75 English acres.—Ed.]

† [About 161 U.S. wheat bushels.—Ed.]

Government Measures to Control Price of Grain in Times of Plenty and of Want: ca. 400 B.C.

[In a year] of best harvest the government then purchased three parts of it, leaving one part [for use of the people]. [In a year of] medial harvest [the government] then bought two parts, [while in a year of] good harvest it bought one part (that is, one half). This caused the people to have just a sufficiency for all needs; and when the price returned to its ordinary level [purchase] would be stopped. [In a year of] first degree failure [the government] then put on sale [fifty piculs of grain] which had been bought [in a year of good harvest]; [in a year of] second degree failure it then put on sale [two hundred piculs of grain] which had been bought [in a year of medial harvest]; and [in a year of] great failure it then put on sale [three hundred piculs of grain] which had been bought [in a year of best harvest].

Therefore, though there occurred famines from failures of grain crops and dearth of vegetables, or floods, or drought, the price of grain was not high and the people did not emigrate, [because of the government policy] of collecting when there was an oversupply in order to supplement when there was a deficiency. When this policy was practiced in Wei, the feudatory thereupon became replete [in resources], and was strong.

Oppressive Measures of Ch'in: Compulsory Military and Labor Services; people revolt: 246-207 B.C.

When it came to the time of the first emperor [of Ch'in], he united [into one political unit] all the then known world. Within the empire he started meritorious enterprises (public works) and on its borders he drove back the I and the Ti (that is, the unassimilated peoples of the east and north). He collected (ca. 212 B.C.) much more than a half [that is,

---

two thirds of the products of the people as military] tax and mobilized [men from families living on] the left side of the [village] gateways to guard the frontiers. [As a result] the men [remaining on the land] did their best to plow it, [yet] there were not enough provisions for food [even for men on military and labor services, nor for lunches of laborers in the fields; and though] the women spun [and wove yet] there was not enough for clothing. Although the wealth of the whole empire had been exhausted to support his government, still there was not enough to satisfy his desires. All within the seas were brought to grief and became embittered; and then consequently [the people either] ran away or revolted.

Rise of Han: War, Famine, High-Priced Grain, Cannibalism, Death, Sale of Children: 206 B.C.

When the House of Han arose, it inherited the evils [left] by the Ch'in. [Former] feudal lords all at the same time started [rebellions], and the people lost their means of livelihood. Hence, there was a widespread dearth of supplies in both grains and vegetables. . . . People ate human flesh; and more than half [of the population] died. . . . When the empire was stabilized, the people lacked [supplies] either to conceal or to store. From the Son of Heaven, who was unable to equip himself with a team of four horses of the same color [for the imperial equipage], down to generals of the army and first ministers [of the empire and the fiefs all] at times had to ride in the oxen-drawn carts [used customarily by the poor].

Reprinted with permission of Princeton University Press, from Nancy Lee Swann (ed.), *Food and Money in Ancient China* (Princeton, N.J., 1950).

CH'AO TS'O (178 B.C.)

Among the traders and merchants, . . . the larger ones hoard goods and exact a hundred percent profit, while the smaller ones sit lined up in the markets selling their wares.

Reprinted with permission of Columbia University Press, from Wm. Theodore de Bary, Wing-tsit Chan and Burton Watson, *Sources of Chinese Tradition* (New York, 1964), Vol. I.

Those who deal in luxury goods daily disport themselves in the cities and market towns; taking advantage of the ruler's wants, they are able to sell at double price. Thus though their men neither plow nor weed, though their women neither tend silkworms nor spin, yet their clothes are brightly patterned and colored, and they eat only choice grain and meat. They have none of the hardships of the farmer, yet their gain is ten to one hundredfold. With their wealth they may consort with nobles, and their power exceeds the authority of government officials. . . .

At present, although the laws degrade the merchants, the merchants have become wealthy and honored, and although they honor the farmers, the farmers have grown poor and lowly. Thus what common practice honors the ruler degrades, and what the officials scorn the law exalts. With ruler and ruled thus at variance and their desires in conflict, it is impossible to hope that the nation will become rich and the law be upheld.

CH'ENG HAO (1068)

The lands of the rich extend on and on, from this prefecture to that subprefecture, and there is nothing to stop them. Day by day the poor scatter and die from starvation, and there is no one to take pity on them. Although many people are more fortunate, still there are countless persons without sufficient food and clothing. The population grows day by day, and if nothing is done to control the situation, food and clothing will become more and more scarce, and more people will scatter and die. This is the key to order and disorder. How can we not devise some way to control it? . . .

In ancient times, the people had to have [a reserve of] nine years' food supply. A state was not considered a state if it did not have a reserve of at least three years food. Your servant observes that there are few in the land who grow food and many who consume it. The productivity of the earth is not fully utilized and human labor is not fully employed. Even the rich and powerful families rarely have a surplus; how much worse off are the poor and weak! If in one locality

---

their luck is bad and crops fail just one year, banditry becomes uncontrollable and the roads are full of the faint and starving. . . . Certainly we should gradually return to the ancient system—with the land distributed equally so as to encourage agriculture, and with steps taken by both individuals and the government to store up grain so as to provide against any contingency. In this, too, there is no difference between past and present. . . .

But now in the capital region there are thousands upon thousands of men without settled occupations—idlers and beggars who cannot earn a living. . . .

WANG AN-SHIH (1069)

In the second year of Hsi-ning [1069], the Commission to Coordinate Fiscal Administration presented a memorial as follows:

. . . Now we propose that the present amount of grain in storage should be sold at a price lower than the market price when the latter is high; and that when the market price is low, the grain in the market should be purchased at a rate higher than the market price. . . .

Now we propose to survey the situation in regard to surpluses and shortages in each circuit as a whole, to sell when grain is dear and buy when it is cheap, in order to increase the accumulation in government storage and to stabilize the prices of commodities. This will make it possible for the farmers to go ahead with their work at the proper season, while the monopolists will no longer be able to take advantage of their temporary stringency. All this is proposed in the interests of the people, and the government derives no advantage therefrom. Moreover, it accords with the idea of the ancient kings who bestowed blessings upon all impartially and promoted whatever was of benefit by way of encouraging the cultivation and accumulation of grain.

Reprinted with permission of Columbia University Press, from Wm. Theodore de Bary, Wing-tsit Chan and Burton Watson, *Sources of Chinese Tradition* (New York, 1964), Vol. I.

MA MAO-TS'AI (1629)

An Eyewitness' Report on Famine Conditions

Yenan, the prefecture from which your humble servant comes, has not had any rain for more than a year. Trees and grass are all dried up. During the eighth and ninth months of last year people went to the mountains to collect raspberries which were called grain but actually were no better than chaff. They tasted bitter and could only postpone death for the time being. By the tenth month all the raspberries were gone, and people peeled off tree bark as food. Among tree bark the best was that of the elm. This was so precious that in order to conserve it, people mixed it with the bark of other trees to feed themselves. Somehow they were able to prolong their lives. Toward the end of the year the supply of tree bark was exhausted, and they had to go to the mountains to dig up stones for food. Stones were cold and tasted musty. A little taken in would fill up the stomach. Those who took stones found their stomachs swollen and they dropped and died in a few days. Others who had no wish to eat stones gathered as bandits. They robbed the few who had some savings, and when they robbed, they took everything and left nothing behind. Their idea was that since they had to die either one way or another it was preferable to die as a bandit than to die from hunger and that to die as a bandit would enable them to enter the next world with a full stomach. . . .

There were situations even more pathetic than those described above. For instance, there was a dumping ground to the west of Anse, to which two or three infants were abandoned by their parents each morning. Some of these infants cried aloud; others merely whimpered because they had lost all strength to cry. . . .

What seemed strange at the beginning was the sudden disappearance of children or single persons once they wandered outside of the city gates. Later it was discovered that some people in the suburb had been eating human flesh and using human bones as fuel for cooking. By then people knew that those who had disappeared were actually killed and eaten. . . .

. . . The people that have not left or died are forced to flee

---

Reprinted with permission of D. Van Nostrand Company, Inc., from Dun J. Li (ed.), *The Essence of Chinese Civilization* (Princeton, N.J., 1967).

from their home, reluctant and unhappy as they are. With their roots cut off from the land which once they tilled, they wander from place to place until eventually they lose all the money they originally carried with them. By then they can only dream about their home, while facing the reality of death. Under circumstances like these, it is no wonder that they should choose to become bandits.

• 10 •

The Mind of China: The Search for Harmony

Is there such a thing as the "mind of China"? The following article tries to extract some basic beliefs common to all Chinese which shape their view of themselves and of the world. Can you draw any conclusions concerning the Chinese character? Does this article give any clue to the continuity and relative stability of Chinese history and society?

TIME MAGAZINE

. . . Western man, in the image of Prometheus or Faust, seeks to dominate nature; the Chinese seeks to live in harmony with it. The ideal of harmony—with the universe, with the past, within society—helps to explain China's durability, its long resistance to change, the subordination of the individual to the overall design. Above all, it helps to account for the periodic outbursts of violence in a land that values nonviolence. When society is repressed, when forms are meticulously observed, when balance is sought above all, sooner or later the strain can become too much. The reaction is then apt to be more violent than in a society that is psychologically accustomed to struggle, and considers it a law of life.

The apparent serenity of China has often hidden the recurring tensions between central government and regions, between Emperor and officialdom or ambitious war lords—and,

---

above all, the sometimes intolerable inner tensions of trying to maintain harmony. . . .

. . . The traditional Chinese view of the universe does not, as in the West, see a struggle between good and evil. The famous principles of Yin and Yang imply an alternate cosmic rhythm but not a struggle. Nor is there a relationship of struggle—or love or dialogue—between man and God. China is agnostic and scarcely knows a religion in the Western sense. Confucian teaching is not concerned with metaphysics. As the Master once told his disciples: "Till you have learned to serve men, how can you serve spirits?" In the Confucian view, man is essentially good—which is why the Chinese have a sense of shame but not of sin. To stay good, he needs moral guidance, and to provide it is the essence of Confucianism.

The well-being of the state and people depends on the proper conduct of proprieties and rites, or *li*—which one scholar calls "the politeness of the heart." . . .

This practical, moralistic code has encountered many rival teachings, chief among them mystical Taoism, which holds that Tao, or the Way, knows no distinction between big and small, high and low, good and bad. . . .

These comforting paradoxes provided mental escape for the Chinese in times of stress. Thanks to the unique Chinese gift for blending all manner of faiths, Taoism managed to coexist with Confucianism over the centuries. A Chinese in power, it has been said, is a Confucian: out of power, he is a Taoist, and when about to die, a Buddhist. China absorbed Buddhism, too; in China, somehow, the evanescent idea of nirvana became transmuted into a far earthier notion.

While the Chinese mind is earthbound, it is strongly drawn to magic. It sees the world inhabited by a multitude of spirits. Before a house or a temple is built, its location must be carefully considered in relation to mountain or water spirits. Children sometimes dress in striped tiger clothing to ward off evil influences. It is unlucky to meet a bald-headed man on the way to a mah-jongg party and dangerous to help a drowning man, because evil spirits might drag the rescuer down too. The aggregate of thousands of such superstitions is not transcendental or spiritual. It is not an attempt to commune with the unseen forces but to constrain them. . . .

At the center of reality is the family. Until recently,

worshiping one's ancestors was the highest spiritual duty; to be loyal to one's kinsmen is still for most the highest social duty. Legend abounds with stories of filial devotion, including the boy Meng who lured the mosquitoes to bite him so that they would leave his mother and father alone. Chinese tradition tells of a son who reported his father for stealing a sheep; the judge decided that the son should be put to death because he had shown greater loyalty toward the authorities than toward his own father. This extreme devotion to family explains why the traditional Chinese has no social conscience in the Western sense, for the community outside family or clan is an abstraction. One looks after one's own, not others: this is at the root of much Chinese corruption.

The Western notion of individualism, which insists on its own rights but respects the rights of others, is hard for the Chinese to understand. . . .

In China, anything resembling nationhood was understood only in terms of a kind of superfamily, with the Emperor as the patriarch. Ultimately, in the Confucian view, all government was based on virtue. So long as the head of the great Chinese family was virtuous, all was well with the land; but if the country fared ill, it must be because the Emperor had fallen into evil ways and the "Mandate of Heaven" had been withdrawn. . . .

The distaste for force in the Confucian order is profound, one indication being the low social status of the soldier. Men who know how to employ ruse, the traditional weapon of the weak against the strong, are particularly admired. A famous Chinese story describes how a poet wrote a novel considered dangerous by the Emperor and was summoned to court to be punished. He bribed the boatman to travel as slowly as possible, and by the time he arrived, he had written a new novel so fantastic that the Emperor decided he must be insane and spared his life. . . .

It was the lack of science, the absence of intellectual equipment or desire to accept change that proved so disastrous when, in the 19th century, the West broke through the Great Wall of Chinese isolation. The Mandarins, that elite corps of scholar-officials who had so long governed under the Emperors—in the words of one Western scholar, as "managers before their time"—finally lost their power to manage. Always opposed to specialization, in the belief that the really wise man can know and do everything, they were unable and unwilling to cope with modern knowledge. Suddenly, the old formulas no longer worked. Numbers, concepts, labels could not prevail against modern guns and machines. So long unshaken in its sense of superiority, China in the last years of the Manchu rule suffered military defeat and economic exploitation. A social order based on harmony with nature was shattered by the West's promethean energy. Suddenly, it was devastatingly clear that the Middle Kingdom was not really at the center of the universe.

• 11 •

The Chinese Character

Confucius once said that men are pretty much alike by nature, but that environment—learning and practice—is what makes them different. Thus, the peoples of the world, though having similar needs and wants, are nonetheless different. These differences are the qualities usually ascribed to national character.

Lin Yutang, a major interpreter of China to the West, and Professors Dun J. Li and Herrlee G. Creel describe some of these traits of Chinese character. Do you think the characteristics described are really unique to the Chinese? Would these characteristics apply to all Chinese? How can you explain the development of these characteristics? Are these traits valid or merely stereotypes? Can you point out traits of national character among other peoples?

LIN YUTANG

Chinese Patience

The quality of patience is the result of racial adjustment to a condition where overpopulation and economic pressure

---

Reprinted with permission of the author, from Lin Yutang, *My Country and My People* (New York: A John Day Book, Reynal & Hitchcock, 1935). Copyright by Lin Yutang.

leave very little elbow room for people to move about and is, in particular, a result of the family system, which is a miniature of Chinese society. . . .

That patience is a noble virtue of the Chinese people no one who knows them will gainsay. There is so much of this virtue that it has almost become a vice with them. The Chinese people have put up with more tyranny, anarchy and misrule than any Western people will ever put up with, and seem to have regarded them as part of the laws of nature. . . . As it is, this capacity for putting up with insults has been ennobled by the name of patience, and deliberately inculcated as a cardinal virtue by Confucian ethics. I am not saying that this patience is not a great quality of the Chinese people. Jesus said, "Blessed are the meek, for they shall inherit the earth," and I am not sure but that Chinese patience has enabled us to inherit half a continent and keep it. The Chinese also inculcate it consciously as a high moral virtue. As our saying goes, "A man who cannot tolerate small ills can never accomplish great things."

The training school for developing this virtue is, however, the big family, where a large number of daughters-in-law, brothers-in-law, fathers and sons daily learn this virtue by trying to endure one another. In the big family, where a closed door is an offense, and where there is very little elbow room for the individuals, one learns by necessity and by parental instruction from early childhood the need for mutual toleration and adjustments in human relationships. The deep, slow, everyday wearing effect on character can scarcely be overestimated.

There was once a prime minister, Chang Kungni, who was much envied for his earthly blessedness of having nine generations living together under the same roof. Once the emperor, T'ang Kaochung, asked him the secret of his success, and the minister asked for a brush and paper, on which he wrote a hundred times the character "patience" or "endurance." Instead of taking that as a sad commentary on the family system, the Chinese people have ever after envied his example, and the phrase "hundred patience" *(po-jen)* has passed into current moral proverbs which are written on red paper and pasted on all house-doors on New Year's Day: *"peaceableness brings good luck"; "patience is the best family heritage,"* etc. But so long as the family system exists and so long as society is built on the principle that a man is not an individual but attains his full being only in living in harmonious social relationships, it is easy to see how patience must be regarded as a supreme virtue and must grow naturally out of the social system. For in such a society, patience has a reason for existence.

Chinese Humanism

To understand the Chinese ideal of life one must try to understand Chinese humanism. The term "humanism" is ambiguous. Chinese humanism, however, has a very definite meaning. It implies, first, a just conception of the ends of human life; secondly, a complete devotion to these ends; and thirdly, the attainment of these ends by the spirit of human reasonableness or the Doctrine of the Golden Mean, which may also be called the Religion of Common Sense. . . .

The Chinese humanists believe they have found the true end of life and are conscious of it. For the Chinese the end of life lies not in life after death, for the idea that we live in order to die, as taught by Christianity, is incomprehensible; nor in nirvana, for that is too metaphysical; nor in the satisfaction of accomplishment, for that is too vainglorious; nor yet in progress for progress' sake, for that is meaningless. The true end, the Chinese have decided in a singularly clear manner, lies in the enjoyment of a simple life, especially the family life, and in harmonious social relationships. . . .

The difference between China and the West seems to be that the Westerners have a greater capacity for getting and making more things and a lesser ability to enjoy them, while the Chinese have a greater determination and capacity to enjoy the few things they have. This trait, our concentration on earthly happiness, is as much a result as a cause of the absence of religion. For if one cannot believe in the life hereafter as the consummation of the present life, one is forced to make the most of this life before the farce is over. The absence of religion makes this concentration possible.

From this a humanism has developed which frankly proclaims a man-centered universe, and lays down the rule that the end of all knowledge is to serve human happiness. . . .

Reprinted with permission of the author, from Lin Yutang, *My Country and My People* (New York: A John Day Book, Reynal & Hitchcock, 1935). Copyright by Lin Yutang.

Humanism occupies, for instance, a mean position between the other-worldliness of religion and the materialism of the modern world. Buddhism may have captured popular fancy in China, but against its influence the true Confucianist was always inwardly resentful, for it was, in the eyes of humanism, only an escape from life, or a negation of the truly human life.

On the other hand, the modern world, with its overdevelopment of machinery, has not taken time to ensure that man enjoys what he makes. . . . There needs to be a religion which will transcribe Jesus' famous dictum about the Sabbath and constantly preach that the machine is made for man and not man made for the machine. For after all, the sum of all human wisdom and the problem of all human knowledge is how man shall remain a man and how he shall best enjoy his life.

DUN J. LI

Thrift

Unable to escape the limitations imposed by nature, the Chinese incorporated into their custom and tradition many safeguards against economic hazards. Even social and moral values reflected the same concern. The Chinese, for instance, glorified thrift and condemned waste in unequivocal terms. Though thrift has been a virtue in practically every culture, the Chinese carried it to an almost unbelievable degree. Two stories might suffice to elaborate this point. A man [described in *An Unofficial History of the Literati* (Chapter X)] continued to raise his two fingers while lying on his deathbed speechless, and his relatives were at a loss to understand his last instruction in connection with the two fingers. Finally someone grasped what he meant and removed one of the two wicks in the oil lamp, and the man nodded his head and died in peace. The other story is in connection with the Ch'ing statesman Tseng Kuo-fan who turned down an applicant for a position despite high recommendations because in an interview over a dinner table the applicant had carefully picked up the unpolished rice in his rice bowl and set it aside on the table,

---

instead of eating it indiscriminately with the good, polished rice. In Tseng's eyes a man so wasteful could not be trusted to rule the people. In this matter of thrift, the emperor and his officials were supposed to set the example. . . .

HERRLEE G. CREEL

The Gods of Shang

Those who generalize have labelled the Chinese as "ancestor-worshippers." While this cannot be taken without qualification, it strikes closer to the mark than do many such statements. It is true, of course, that China has the "three religions" of Confucianism, Taoism, and Buddhism, but it is also true that the cult of ancestors had found a considerable place for itself in connection with each of these. . . . The farther back we go in our investigation of Chinese religion, the greater is the part played by ancestors.

Foreigners commenting on Chinese ancestor-worship sometimes go too far in either of two directions. On the one hand, they may depict it as a weird, mysterious, "Oriental" practice which Occidentals can never understand. Again they tell us that it is nothing more than a form of paying respect to the dead, exactly as we hold funerals and put flowers and tombstones on our graves. The latter may be true for a few Chinese at the present day, but it is in no sense true of the attitude of the ancient Chinese nor of that of the great majority of the people today.

If we think of it as a mere putting of food instead of flowers on the grave, or before a tablet representing the ancestor in a temple, we shall quite fail to understand the vital motivation of ancestor-worship—the greatest force which has held the Chinese people to traditional ways. The ancestor was no powerless corpse lying supine in the grave waiting for his descendant to pay respect to him or not, according to the descendant's whim. On the contrary, the ancestor's real power began when he died. For then he was transformed into a spirit, of power undefined but vast. He was more or less vaguely dependent on his descendants for food, in the form

---

of sacrifices, but he could very well see that these were forthcoming, or make his descendants wish that they had been. . . .

Success in hunting, agriculture, war and other activities was theirs to give or to withhold. Famine, defeat, sickness and death were the penalties which they could and did hurl at any who had the temerity to displease them.

But we must not suppose that the attitude of the ancient Chinese toward their dead was wholly one of awe and fear. Nor can we accept the interpretation of sacrifice which would make it a simple "bargain" with the spirits, to deliver so much in sacrifices in return for the delivery of so much in prosperity and other blessings. To be sure there was this aspect of the matter, just as there are those who contribute money to the religious enterprises of Christendom for the same reason. But there was also not a little of real devotion to the departed, and real grief at their death. Among the evidence for this is the Shang word meaning "death," 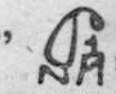, a pictograph of a mourner kneeling with bowed head beside a corpse. . . .

• 12 •

Family Patterns and Land Distribution

The family was the cement that held the fabric of Chinese society together. The family system shaped and, in turn, was shaped by other institutions. The following group of readings offers some insight into the structure of Chinese society. Professor John K. Fairbank of Harvard University writes on the family as a social system. T. R. Jernigan, who studied Chinese society firsthand, describes how mutual responsibility became the core of China's legal system. Dun J. Li, Professor at Princeton, discusses patterns of land distribution and their relationship to the family system. Why did this particular kind of family system evolve in China? How did this system reveal the values held dear by the Chinese? How did the family system influence the legal system and land distribution (and vice versa)? What effects do you think this kind of social structure had on the history of China?

JOHN K. FAIRBANK

The family, not the individual, has been the social unit and the responsible element in the political life of its locality. The filial piety and obedience inculcated in family life have been the training ground for loyalty to the ruler and obedience to constituted authority in the state.

This function of the family to raise filial sons who would become loyal subjects can be seen by a glance at the pattern of authority within the traditional family group. The father was a supreme autocrat, with control over the use of all family property and income and a decisive voice in arranging the marriages of the children. The mixed love, fear, and awe of children for their father was strengthened by the great respect paid to age. An old man's loss of vigor was more than offset by his growth in wisdom. As long as he lived in possession of his faculties the patriarch possessed every sanction to enable him to dominate the family scene. He could even sell his children into slavery. In fact, of course, parents were also bound by a reciprocal code of responsibility for their children as family members. But law and custom provided little check on parental tyranny if they chose to exercise it.

The domination of age over youth within the old-style family was matched by the domination of male over female. Chinese baby girls in the old days were more likely than baby boys to suffer infanticide. A girl's marriage was, of course, arranged and not for love. The trembling bride became at once a daughter-in-law under the tyranny of her husband's mother. . . . Until the present century their subjection was demonstrated and reinforced by the custom of footbinding. . . .

Within the family every child from birth was involved in a highly ordered system of kinship relations with elder brothers, sisters, maternal elder brothers' wives, and other kinds of aunts, uncles, and cousins, grandparents, and in-laws too

---

numerous for a Westerner to keep in mind. These relationships were not only more clearly named and differentiated than in the West but also carried with them more compelling rights and duties dependent upon status. A first son, for example, could not long remain unaware of the Confucian teaching as to his duties toward the family line and his precedence over his younger brothers and his sisters.

Chinese well habituated to the family system have been prepared to accept similar patterns of status in other institutions, including the official hierarchy of the government. One advantage of a system of status (as opposed to our individualist system of contractual relations) is that a man knows automatically where he stands in his family or society. He can have security in the knowledge that if he does his prescribed part he may expect reciprocal action from others in the system. . . .

Socially, the Chinese in the village are organized primarily in their kinship system and only secondarily as a neighborhood community. The village has ordinarily consisted of a group of family or kinship units (clans) which are permanently settled from one generation to the next and continuously dependent upon the use of certain landholdings. Each family household is both a social and an economic unit. Its members derive their sustenance from working its fields and their social status from membership in it.

The Chinese kinship system is patrilineal, the family headship passing in the male line from father to eldest son. . . . Until recently a Chinese boy and girl did not choose each other as life mates, nor did they set up an independent household together after marriage. Instead, they entered the husband's father's household and assumed responsibilities for its maintenance, subordinating married life to family life in a way that modern Americans would consider insupportable.

From the time of the first imperial unification, before Christ, the Chinese abandoned the institution of primogeniture by which the eldest son would have retained all the father's property while the younger sons sought their fortunes elsewhere. . . . By the abolition of primogeniture the Chinese created a system of equal division of the land among the sons of the family. They left the eldest son only certain ceremonial duties, to acknowledge his position, and sometimes an extra share of property; otherwise the land was divided. . . . Under this system the prime duty of each married couple has been to produce a son who can maintain the family line, and yet the birth of more than one son may mean impoverishment.

Contrary to a common myth, a large family with several children has not been the peasant norm. The scarcity of land, as well as disease and famine, has set a limit to the number of people likely to survive in each family unit. The large joint family of several married sons with many children all within one compound, which has usually been regarded as typical of China, appears to have been the ideal exception, a luxury which only the well-to-do could afford. The average peasant family was limited to four, five, or six persons. Division of the land among the sons has constantly checked the accumulation of property and savings and the typical family has had little opportunity to rise in the social scale. The peasantry have been bound to the soil not by law and custom so much as by their own numbers.

T.R. JERNIGAN

Mutual Responsibility

No correct understanding of either the criminal or civil branch of the law can be arrived at without constantly bearing in mind the doctrine of mutual responsibility. This doctrine is the keynote of the entire system and gives to the system its penal and relentless character. . . . The relentless feature of the doctrine is so strongly drawn, in connection with the doctrine of mutual responsibility, that I quote the very language. After stating that when several persons are parties to one offence, the original contriver of it shall be held to be the principal and the rest who follow as accessories, the language of the Code is as follows: "When the parties to an offence are members of one family, the senior and chief member of that family shall alone be punishable, but if he be upward of eighty years of age, or totally disabled by infirmities, the punishment shall fall upon the next in succession."

The members of a Chinese family are those who live as

From T.R. Jernigan, *China in Law and Commerce* (New York: The Macmillan Company, 1905).

members of the same household, which includes all who enter by marriage or adoption as well as slaves and servants. . . .

Next to family responsibility comes the mutual responsibility of neighbour for neighbour, and the question whether the neighbours are related does not count in fixing the responsibility. The deciding principle is that good neighbours make good neighbours, and when a neighbour commits an offence, it is no defense for another neighbour to say, "I did not know anything about it," for the answer is, "You are the neighbour of the offender and should have known." It is reported that the mother of Mencius removed three times in order to live in a desirable neighbourhood. . . .

From the neighbour to the village is another step in the doctrine of mutual responsibility. It has already been pointed out what important functions are exercised by the head-man of a village, and that these functions are of a most miscellaneous nature. Although the head-man may be first held responsible for the conduct of the inhabitants of the village, responsibility attaches more or less to every inhabitant and makes it the interest of each one to aid in preserving peace and order. . . .

DUN J. LI

Land Distribution

. . . by the second century B.C. practically all land suitable for agriculture had been brought under Chinese control. The frontier of agriculture had virtually disappeared.

The importance of the disappearance of the agricultural frontier cannot be overemphasized. It means that subsequent increases in population had to be accommodated within the limited amount of arable land in China. . . . It is no coincidence that after the unification of China by Ch'in, major dynasties usually lasted two or three hundred years, enough time to reduce food production per capita to a dangerously low level. With the exception of Ch'in Shih-huang who in an enthusiastic mood predicted that his regime would last "thousands of emperors," no Chinese ruler ever believed that his

---

dynasty would continue indefinitely. Sooner or later, there would be famine, rebellion, and war, and his dynasty, like so many before, would collapse in a mass social upheaval.

Since the amount of arable land was limited, the logical solution to the production problem seemed to be the increase of yield per unit area. Unfamiliar with the Chinese situation, many people blame the lack of technological advances for the Chinese inability to raise total production. While it is true that no major technological advance has occurred since the invention of the iron-shod plow in the sixth or fifth century B.C., the result would not have been materially different even if there had been such improvements. The fact is, the manual farming as conducted by the Chinese has been and still is one of the most efficient in the world, as far as yield per acre is concerned. For instance, in the production of rice or wheat, a Chinese farm produces more per acre than a mechanized European or American farm. The introduction of machinery would have aggravated rather than alleviated the Chinese problem. The same farming method, highly efficient and suited particularly well to the Chinese situation, has not been changed for more than two thousand years. The prospect of reduced yield would have discouraged any prospective inventor of labor-saving devices. This might account for, partially at least, the lack of technological advances in Chinese agriculture. In short, the Chinese problem has been and still is the problem of land shortage.

All factors considered, it seems that there only could be two solutions to this problem: to reduce population pressure by practicing birth control and to make equally available to all what the land produced. Birth control was out of the question because, in addition to social and cultural considerations (such as the glorification of large families), the Chinese had no such knowledge and could not practice birth control even if they wished to. The second solution was not a true solution, but it was the best available to the Chinese. Because of the lack of a better term, we shall call it the principle of equalitarianism. The spirit of this principle was: no man should have too much at the expense of others.

Though it was difficult to translate the principle of equalitarianism into the equalization of land ownership, the principle was nevertheless built into Chinese customs. Contrary to many European countries where primogeniture was the rule, in China the property of the deceased was divided equally among his male children. However large the original size of a landholding, it would be eventually fragmented among a number of owners. . . . Those who have visited rural China must have noticed the crisscrossing footpaths that separate small, garden-like plots, most of which are a fraction of an acre in size. An old Chinese proverb says, "No family can be rich or poor consecutively for three generations." Though to become rich in three generations was more an expression of hope than a statement of fact, for a wealthy family eventually to become poor was in fact a commonplace.

Within a family the application of the equalitarian principle meant that all family members should have the same standard of living despite differences in earning power. A Chinese family was more like a clan in the Western sense, consisting of three or four generations and including brothers, cousins, and their wives and children. It was not merely a biological relationship; it was an economic unit, the members of which protected one another in financial matters. Men being unequal in natural endowment, their achievements in society (and in earning power) were bound to be different, and the Chinese believed that the strong had a moral obligation to help and protect the weak. Since the family came into being through a natural, biological relationship, it seemed to a Chinese that it was the most logical place to fulfill such moral obligations. . . . If the family prospered, all members benefited; if the family fortune declined, all suffered the same. Thus, a Chinese family served the same purpose as many of our social inventions put together—the insurance company, the Social Security Act, the unemployment compensation. . . .

From the point of view of a modern society, the equalitarian principle had its obvious shortcomings. The implementation of such a principle necessitated an authoritarian organization, on the family as well as at the national level, because only an unchallenged authority could enforce it. Moreover, the principle discouraged individual incentive and enterprise, especially in connection with economic and financial matters. It took away a man's independence and made him a silent conformist to the status quo. These, of course, are all justifiable criticisms. However, it should be pointed out that individualism and independence are modern Western values and that they did not apply to historical China. In historical China conformity was a virtue and individualism was denounced in unequivocal terms. . . .

• 13 •

Filial Piety

Chinese myth and legend abound with stories of the sacrifices children made for their parents. This particular story was written down by a scholar-official, Hou Fang-yü, during the seventeenth century. What do you think he is trying to communicate to his audience? Why do you think he chooses this particular legend?

HOU FANG-YÜ

Wan, the Dutiful Son

Wan the Dutiful Son cut a piece of flesh from his thigh to feed his mother and was consequently able to cure her illness. People say that this honorable occurrence should be reported to higher authorities so that his virtuous conduct could be exemplified in testimonials, to be remembered by posterity for years to come. Others say that this cannot be done because it is explicitly prohibited under the present law. . . .

Many years ago there was in Ch'üanchou a dutiful son named T'ang Yen who cut a piece of flesh from his right arm to feed his father. His motive was the same as that of Wan. Commenting on this incident, the historian Yao Lai* maintained that to mutilate one's own body, for whatever

---

Reprinted with permission of D. Van Nostrand Company, Inc., from Dun J. Li (ed.), *The Essence of Chinese Civilization* (Princeton, N.J., 1967).

* [A Ming historian of the sixteenth century.—Ed.]

purpose, is incompatible with the concept of righteous conduct and should not be regarded as a good example to follow. Since then people have considered this statement the final word on this subject.

That we should not mutilate our own body, including its hair and skin, has been an ancient adage handed down by our sages. . . . Han Yü maintained that self-inflicted death can be justified only under extraordinary circumstances, and that this principle is equally applicable in cases wherein a person's loyalty towards his sovereign or parents is involved. Only then, he continued, should the dead man be exemplified as a model to follow.

What does Han Yü mean by "extraordinary circumstances"? He means a situation in which the prevention of disaster or the seeking of revenge has become a compelling necessity. What situation could be more compelling than the suffering of unbearable pain by one's parents as a result of injury or illness? If a person decides to mutilate his own body so that his parents can live, I cannot see any reason why he should not be allowed to do so. Furthermore, a man who mutilates himself will be on the verge of death; unless he is absolutely sincere, he would not have taken such a step in the first place. It is wrong to compare him with those hypocrites who take drastic actions for the sole purpose of earning an undeserved reputation. His example will inspire others to show the same boundless love for their parents. . . .

Filial piety was one of the cardinal virtues of ancient times. During a period of moral decline such as we experience today, our leaders no longer encourage or promote the cultivation of good customs. Our scholars, who neglect their duties towards their parents in normal times, are indifferent during the time of crisis. They ignore the sufferings of their parents as if they were the sufferings of strangers, while quoting ancient classics to cover up their cowardliness. In fact, they defend their lack of action as the normal course to follow, a course which they claim is becoming to a virtuous person. They regard a man as impulsive or hypocritical and criticize him severely if he chooses to sacrifice his own life for the benefit of his king or parents. If this line of thinking goes unchallenged, how can our customs be improved and our people be led to a righteous path?

• 14 •

Chinese Women

The subordinate role of women fit in well with Chinese ideas on natural forces in the universe—the complementary and interacting forces of yang and yin. Yang was the active force representing masculinity, strength, light. Yin was the passive force representing femininity, weakness, darkness. Both were necessary, but one by nature was passive toward the other. Confucian ideology stressed the passive role of women, and of the five basic relationships, only one—that of husband and wife—included women. Thus, from birth, the role of the Chinese girl was ordained.

The first three selections, written during the Ch'ing dynasty (1644–1912), cast light on the role of women, and the traditional Chinese attitude toward them. Are arranged marriages necessarily bad? Why did the widow's position have little to be envied? Do you think these women led unhappy lives? Did Chinese women have any authority? What virtues in women were praised by Chinese men?

The fourth selection presents another kind of woman—one who ruled an empire. The Lady Wu was by no means an exception. The story of the Lady Wu, as told by René Grousset, a French authority on China, suggests another kind of role that Chinese women have played. How can you account for this apparent paradox?

CHU CH'EN-YING

A Testimonial in Memory of My Wife

My wife was born with high intelligence and learned to sew at an early age. Whenever she had time in the even-

---

Reprinted with permission of D. Van Nostrand Company, Inc., from Dun J. Li (ed.), *The Essence of Chinese Civilization* (Princeton, N.J., 1967).

ing, she read extensively the great works of the past. Being versed in the classics, she understood large issues better than most people do.

Shortly after she joined our family, my younger sister was to be married. My late mother was worried about her inability to provide enough furniture for the forthcoming wedding because of the lack of funds. Believing that my mother should not burden herself with this worry on account of her advanced age, my wife voluntarily contributed all of her own furniture for this purpose. My mother was pleased and began to eat heartily for the first time in a long period.

The year after my sister was married, I lost my teaching position and had to eat at home. Shortly afterwards my mother left us and went to Heaven. I tried to borrow money from every source I could find, but I did not succeed. Having sensed my helplessness, my wife sold all of her jewels to meet the funeral expenses. . . .

When in the winter I again obtained a teaching position, I took with me the only quilt that we had in our house. My wife was left with a worn-out blanket made of cotton which she held tightly to keep herself warm while sleeping on a bare plank which was our bed. Each evening after the children had gone to sleep, she lit the lamp and began to work. By midnight the little fire in the jug had disappeared, and she was shivering from cold. She walked around the room to keep herself warm, and when she felt warm enough, she started to work again. . . .

T'ANG SHUN-CHIH

A Eulogy for Wang, My Sister-in-Law

She was intelligent, alert, energetic, and generous. She understood the proper way of dealing with people and handling affairs without ever learning about them, and she got along well with all members of our household, high or low. Her father-in-law praised her highly and once said: "My second daughter-in-law knows exactly what I want when she prepares tea or cooks food." Whenever there were guests for tea or dinner, it was Wang who took the primary responsibility for preparing it, while other women in the household only helped. Hearing about her good work in our household, her mother Hsü once said: "'Knowing how she once served me, I have no doubt that she will serve her father-in-law equally well." My wife, Chuang, also praised her, saying that it was Wang who understood her best. Whenever she had misgivings which she could not very well discuss with her husband, she sought advice from Wang. Hearing this, Wang's sisters remarked: "She was the same way with us when she was at home. We knew even then that she would get along well with her future sisters-in-law."

Among her mother's five daughters, Wang was the favorite. Previously, when her father died, her mother, observing the wish of the dead man, gave Wang two hundred taels of silver. She refused to accept the gift on the ground that her mother, being so young as she was, needed the money herself. Later, when her mother distributed her jewels as a farewell gift before she died, Wang received twice as many as any of her sisters. Hoping not to offend her sisters, she refused to take even her own share. . . .

Not only did my brother and his wife love each other dearly; they also admonished each other so as to refine each other's character. At one time only we two brothers stayed at the old house when our father was away as a government official. Whenever my brother became over-active, Wang would show her displeasure and say to him: "If you are not concerned with your own health, how can you face your elder brother who is concerned with yours?" Whenever my brother did something wrong, she would conceal it, being fearful that it might offend me and thus sow the seeds of dissension between us brothers. Whenever my brother did something well, she would be greatly pleased and say: "Do not believe for a moment that you did well because of your own ability. The credit should go to your elder brother who has had such a good influence upon you." Remarks like these moved my brother deeply who, consequently, wished to move even closer to me in brotherhood. The credit should go to this woman Wang who not only encouraged my brother along the road of goodness but also helped the good relationship between us brothers.

It seems that with her ability and virtue she should have enjoyed a long life and been rewarded with many sons. Yet she died young without a child and, more ironically, died in childbirth.

CHOU CHI

On Widowhood

Under present circumstances, a young woman has only two alternatives open to her after the death of her husband. She could either follow her husband by committing suicide or enter a long period of widowhood with all hardships and privations implied in that term. If she chooses the latter course, she would have to serve her parents-in-law loyally and faithfully as well as raising her own children. People say that she should be honored as an example to follow if she chooses widowhood instead of committing suicide, on the laudable ground that life is valuable. Many loyal ministers commit suicide during the period of dynastic change, and philosophers and kings of later ages honor them so as to cultivate good customs, even though their self-inflicted death does not help the dynasty which they have hoped to preserve. Is it not contradictory that we glorify the ministers and scholars who die for their dynasties while condemning severely a helpless woman who simply wishes to follow her dead husband? I believe that a widow who commits suicide during or shortly after the mourning period should be exemplified as an inspiration to others.

RENÉ GROUSSET:

The Lady Wu

Wu Tse-t'ien was a former favourite of the emperor T'ai-tsung. She entered the imperial harem in 637, at the age of fourteen, and was outstanding for her wit and beauty. When the future Kao-tsung was still crown prince, he had seen her among his father's flock of wives, and from that day had nursed a silent love for her. On T'ai-tsung's death his wives and concubines had to cut off their hair and enter a convent. As soon as the official period of mourning came to an end, the new Son of Heaven gave orders for the young woman to

Reprinted with permission of University of California Press, from René Grousset, *The Rise and Splendour of the Chinese Empire* (Berkeley, 1964).

be brought out of retirement, and gave her back her position at court. But a secondary role was not enough for this ambitious concubine. . . . She was prepared to commit any crime, however monstrous, in order to attain her ends. With her own hands she strangled the child she had borne to the emperor and caused the legitimate empress to be accused of the heinous crime. After the birth of the child, a girl, the empress came to pay a visit to Wu Tse-t'ien. She caressed the infant, took it in her arms and congratulated the young mother. As soon as she had left, Wu Tse-t'ien suffocated the newborn child and replaced it in its cradle. The arrival of the emperor was announced. Wu Tse-t'ien received him, her face glowing with pleasure, and uncovered the cradle to show him his daughter. A horrid sight met his eyes; in the cradle lay the dead body of his child. Bursting into tears, Wu Tse-t'ien was careful not to bring any direct accusation against the woman whose ruin she was determined to bring about. Finally, when questioned, she contented herself with incriminating her attendants. As was to be expected, the latter, so as to divert suspicion from themselves, described the visit which the empress had made a few minutes earlier. The scene had been so cleverly contrived that Kao-tsung was convinced of the empress' guilt. She was degraded and Wu Tse-t'ien promoted to her place (655). Despite the opposition of his father's old comrades, the emperor fell completely under the control of his new consort. . . .

From 660 onwards it was Wu Tse-t'ien who directed the affairs of state in the name of the weak Kao-tsung. Through a system of informers which she had established, she was able with impunity to terrorize the court, giving full rein to her jealousy and vindictiveness, and to annihilate her enemies even when they happened to be members of the T'ang imperial family. After bringing about the destruction of the mandarins who opposed her, she forced their widows and daughters to become her slaves. The emperor, weak and helpless, realized the innocence of her victims but did not dare to take any action. It is said that remorse affected his health, but it is possible that his enfeeblement was assisted by the ministrations of his wife. The annalists relate that during the latter days of his life, "his head swelled up and he became like a blind man. His doctor offered to tap the swollen part, but Wu Tse-t'ien cried out that to lay hands on the imperial face was a crime which was punishable by death. The doctor held to his opinion and punctured the swelling, whereupon the emperor's eyesight was greatly improved. . . . The empress, pretending that she was delighted, went to fetch a hundred pieces of silk, which she personally gave to the doctor. A month later, however, it was learned that the emperor had suddenly fallen ill and that he had died without witnesses" (December 27, 683). Acting in the name of her son, Wu Tse-t'ien remained absolute mistress of the empire for twenty-two years (683–705).

Despite her unscrupulous behaviour, Wu Tse-t'ien was a woman of superior ability, and more skilled than her unhappy husband in the management of affairs of state. . . .

In internal affairs Wu Tse-t'ien overcame all obstacles. Everyone gave way before the will of this indomitable woman. So great was her audacity that in 684 she went to the length of deposing her own son, the young emperor Chung-tsung, and had herself proclaimed "emperor" in his place (690). The princes of the blood, ashamed of being ruled over by a former concubine and spurred into action by an appeal from the poet Lo Pin-wang, made an abortive attempt at revolt. Their revolt was put down and their severed heads were brought to the empress. . . .

• 15 •

Chinese Fairy Tales

In all cultures fairy tales embody the myths, superstitions, and beliefs of the people. Behind the charm, fantasy, and apparent innocence of these tales, lie the most cherished values of a civilization. Fairy tales become popular because they teach a lesson.

Here are two traditional Chinese fairy tales. What do you think these stories are about? What kind of religion do you think these people believe in? What lessons do you think these tales are meant to convey? What do these fairy tales tell us about the Chinese?

THE TEN FARMERS

Once upon a time there were ten farmers who were crossing a field together. They were surprised by a heavy thunderstorm, and all took refuge in a half-ruined temple. But the thunder drew ever nearer, and so great was the tumult that the air trembled about them, while the lightning flew around and around the temple in a continuous circle.

The farmers were greatly frightened, and thought that there must be a sinner among them, whom the lightning was trying to strike. To find out which one of them it might be, they agreed to hang up their straw hats outside the door, and he whose hat was blown away was to yield himself up to his fate.

But one of the ten farmers protested. "Surely not one among us is without some sin," said he. "And should any of us be without sin, surely he need have no fear of death." But the others would not listen to him.

No sooner were all the hats outside, than one of them was blown away. Sure enough, it was the hat of the one farmer who had protested. Then all the others laughed, and thrust the unlucky owner out of doors without pity. But as soon as he had left, the lightning ceased circling, and struck the temple with a crash.

For the one whom the rest had thrust out had been the only righteous one among them, and for his sake the lightning had spared the temple. So the nine evil farmers had to pay with their lives for their hardheartedness.

Reprinted with permission of The Peter Pauper Press, from "The Ten Farmers," *Chinese Fairy Tales* (Mount Vernon, N.Y., 1946).

THE THREE EVILS

Once upon a time, in the old days, there lived a young man by the name of Dschou Tschu. He was of more than ordinary strength, and he was unruly and wild. Wherever he was, quarrels arose. Yet the village leaders never ventured to punish him seriously.

He wore a high hat upon his head, always adorned with

Reprinted with permission of The Peter Pauper Press, from "The Three Evils," *Chinese Fairy Tales* (Mount Vernon, N.Y., 1946).

two pheasants' wings. His clothes were of fine embroidered silk, and at his left side hung a tremendous sword. He liked to gamble and to drink, and his hand sometimes took that which belonged to others. Whoever argued with him soon had a fight on his hands, and he always started arguments by mixing in other people's disputes. Thus he kept up his trouble-making for years, and proved himself a pest throughout the neighborhood.

Then a new mandarin came to that district. When he had arrived, he first went quietly about the country and listened to the people's complaints. And they told him that there were three great evils in that district.

Then he clothed himself in coarse old garments, and wept before Dschou Tschu's door. Dschou Tschu was just coming from the tavern, where he had been drinking. He walked slapping his sword and singing in a loud voice.

When he reached his house he asked, "Who is weeping here, and why?"

And the mandarin replied softly: "I am weeping, and I weep for the poor people's distress."

Then Dschou Tschu saw him dressed all in old clothes and he broke out into loud laughter.

"But you are mistaken, my friend," said he. "Revolt is seething round about us like boiling water in a kettle. But here, in our little corner of the land, all is quiet and peaceful. The harvest has been abundant, rice is plentiful, and all go happily about their work. When you talk to me about distress I have to think of the man who groans without being sick. And who are you, old man, who instead of grieving for yourself, are grieving for others? And what are you doing before my door?"

"I am the new mandarin," replied the other. "Since I have come here I have been looking about in the neighborhood. I find the people are honest and simple in their way of life, and every one has sufficient to wear and to eat. This is all just as you state. Yet, strange to say, when the elders come together, they always sigh and complain. And if they are asked why, they answer: 'There are three great evils in our district!' I have come to ask you to do away with two of them. As to the third, perhaps, I had better remain silent. And this is the reason I weep before your door."

"Well, what are these evils?" said Dschou Tschu. "Speak freely, and tell me all!"

"The first evil," said the mandarin, "is the evil dragon at the long bridge, who causes the water to rise so that man and beast are drowned in the river. The second evil is the tiger with the white forehead, who dwells in the hills. And the third evil, my friend Dschou Tschu—is yourself!"

Then the blush of shame mounted to Dschou's cheek, and he bowed and said: "You have come here from afar to be the mandarin of this district, and yet you feel such sympathy for the people? I was born in this place and yet I have only made our elders grieve. What sort of creature must I be? I beg that you will return home again. I will see to it that matters improve!"

Then he ran without stopping to the hills, and hunted the tiger out of his cave. The great tiger leaped into the air so that the whole forest was shaken as though by a storm. Then he came rushing up, roaring and stretching out his claws savagely to seize on his enemy. Dschou Tschu stepped back a pace, and the tiger landed on the ground directly in front of him.

Great was the battle between Dschou Tschu and the tiger that then occurred. The strong man seized the great tiger by the neck, and then he thrust him to the ground with his left hand, and beat him without stopping with his right. The tiger roared, Dschou Tschu panted, but still he held on. Then he took his tremendous sword and struck the beast until it lay dead on the earth. Dschou Tschu loaded the great tiger on his back and went home.

Then he went to the long bridge. He undressed, took his sword in his hand, and thus dived into the water. No sooner had he disappeared, than there was a boiling and hissing, and the waves began to foam and billow. It sounded like the mad beating of thousands of hoofs. After a time a stream of blood shot up from the depths, and the water of the river turned red. Then Dschou Tschu, holding the dying dragon in his hand, rose out of the waves.

The next day he dressed in simple cotton garments, with a plain straw hat, and he went to visit the mandarin. He came into the courtyard where the mandarin was admiring his flowers, and he said with a bow: "My lord, I have cut off the dragon's head, and I have also done away with the tiger.

Thus I have happily accomplished your command. And now I shall wander away so that you may be rid of the third evil as well, and the people will have no more trouble. Lord, watch over my country, and tell the elders that they need sorrow no more!"

But the mandarin would not permit him to leave the district, but made him his chief officer. Thereafter the two of them always went about the countryside together, seeking for ways to help the happiness and the welfare of the hard-working people.

• 16 •

Chinese Parables

A parable is a short allegorical story that is intended to convey some truth or moral lesson. Thus like fairy tales, parables offer insight into the attitudes, values, and modes and codes of behavior of a particular culture.

The parable was the mode by which the Chinese philosopher chose to illustrate his point. The narrator often invented conversations in which the great sages took part in order to give authority to his lesson. The following two parables are from works of two third-century-B.C. thinkers, and contain a particular philosophic point of view. See if you can discover how this view is illustrated in the stories. Why was the man who spurned the machine considered the "perfect" man? Why was it profitless to worry about heaven? Are there any differences (or similarities) between the parables and the fairy tales?

CHUANGTSE

The Man Who Spurned the Machine

When Tsekung, the disciple of Confucius, came south to the state of Ch'u on his way to Chin, he passed through Hanyin. There he saw an old man engaged in making a ditch to connect his vegetable garden with a well. He carried a pitcher in his hand, with which he was bringing up water and pouring it into the ditch, with very great labor and little results.

"If you had a machine here," said Tsekung, "in a day you could irrigate a hundred times your present area. The labor required is trifling compared with the work done. Would you not like to have one?"

"What is it?" asked the gardener, looking up at him.

"It is a contrivance made of wood, heavy behind and light in front. It draws water up smoothly in a continuous flow, which bubbles forth like boiling soup. It is called a well-sweep."

Thereupon the gardener flushed up and said with a laugh, "I have heard from my teacher that those who have cunning implements are cunning in their dealings, and those who are cunning in their dealings have cunning in their hearts, and those who have cunning in their hearts cannot be pure and incorrupt, and those who are not pure and incorrupt in their hearts are restless in spirit. Those who are restless in spirit are not fit vehicles for Tao. It is not that I do not know of these things. I should be ashamed to use them."

Tsekung's countenance fell, humiliated, and he felt discomfited and abashed. It was not till they had gone thirty *li* that he recovered his composure.

"Who was that man?" asked his disciples. "Why did your face change color after seeing him and why did you seem lost for a whole day?"

"I thought," replied Tsekung, "there was only one man (Confucius) in this world. But I did not know there was this man. I have heard from the Master that the test of a scheme

---

is its practicability and the goal of effort is success, and that we should achieve the greatest results with the least labor. Not so this manner of man. Coming into life, he lives among the people, not knowing whither he is bound, infinitely complete in himself. Success, utility and the knowledge of skills would certainly make man lose the human heart. But this man goes nowhere against his will and does nothing contrary to his heart, master of himself, above the praise and blame of the world. He is a perfect man."

LIEHTSE

The Man Who Worried About Heaven

There was a man of the country of Ch'i who was worrying that the sky might one day fall down, and he would not know where to hide himself. This so much troubled him that he could not eat or sleep. There was another who was worried about this man's worry, and he went to explain it to him, saying, "The sky is only formed of accumulated air. There is no place where there is no air. Whenever you move or breathe, you are living right in this sky. Why do you need ever to worry that the sky will fall down?" The other man said, "If the sky were really nothing but air, would not the sun and moon and the stars fall down?" And the man who was explaining said, "But the sun, the moon and the stars are also nothing but accumulated air (gases)* which has become bright. Even if they should fall down, they would not hurt anybody." "But what if the earth should be destroyed?" And the other replied, "The earth is also only formed of accumulated solids, which fill all space. There is no place where there are no solids. As you walk and stamp on the ground, you are moving the whole day on this earth. Why do you ever need to worry that it may be destroyed?" Then that man seemed to understand and was greatly pleased, and the one

* *Ch'i* in Chinese means ether, air, breath, gas and any invisible spiritual force. "Gas" would make better reading here, but the Taoist conception is that all the universe is formed of a certain spiritual force. It is an extremely useful word, bridging the difficulty between material and immaterial concepts, such as we find in the theories of light.

who was explaining it to him also felt he understood and was greatly pleased.

When Ch'anglutse heard about it, he laughed and said, "The rainbow, the clouds and mists, the winds and rains and the four seasons—are all these not formed of accumulated air in the sky? The mountains and high peaks, the rivers and seas, metal and stone, water and fire—are these not formed of accumulated solids on the earth? Since we know they are formed of accumulated air and accumulated solids, how can we say then that they are indestructible? The infinitely great and the infinitesimally small cannot be exhaustively known or explored, or conjectured about—that is a matter taken for granted. Those who worry about the destruction of the universe are of course thinking too far ahead, but those who say they cannot be destroyed are also mistaken. Since the heaven and earth must be destroyed, they will end finally in destruction. And when they are destroyed, why shouldn't one worry about it?"

Liehtse heard about what Ch'anglutse had said, and laughed and said, "Those who say that heaven and earth are destructible are wrong, and those who say they are indestructible are also wrong. Destruction and indestructibility are not things we know anything about. However, they are both the same. Therefore one lives and does not know about death; one dies and does not know about life; one comes and does not know about going away; and one goes away and does not know about coming. Why should the question of destruction or non-destruction ever bother our minds?"

• 17 •

Chinese Proverbs

While parables were intended by the philosophers to teach a great truth, proverbs are the popular sayings (usually of unknown origin) of the people that express commonsense truth. Here is a group of popular Chinese proverbs on a variety of topics. What do these proverbs tell us about the values and ideals of the Chinese people? Are the truths of proverbs the same as those of the parables and fairy tales? Can you discover which proverbs reflect Confucian values, Taoist values, and Buddhist values?

As is the Son of Heaven, so will be his court.

When the prince wants a minister to die, he dies.

When a king makes a mistake, all the people suffer.

The friendship of officials is as thin as paper.

If the family lives in harmony, all affairs will prosper.

Good parents, happy marriages; good children, fine funerals.

It is easy to govern a kingdom but difficult to rule one's family.

Before fathers and mothers, uncles and aunts, itch as you may, you dare not scratch.

To spoil a child is to kill it.

The bamboo stick makes a good child.

Brothers are like hands and feet.

A wife is sought for her virtue, a concubine for her beauty.

Diseases enter by the mouth; misfortunes issue from it.

When there is much soliciting to buy and to sell, trade is not very lively.

Every sect has its truth and every truth its sect.

When times are easy we do not burn incense, but when trouble comes we embrace the feet of the Buddha.

To open a book brings profit.

Hunger is cured by food, ignorance by study.

The more stupid the happier.

Learning is like rowing upstream; not to advance is to drop back.

Even if we study to old age we shall not finish learning.

A load of books does not equal one good teacher.

Wine does not intoxicate a man; he intoxicates himself.

Men are not enticed by vice; they entice themselves.

A lean dog shames his master.

Rivers and mountains may easily change, but human nature is changed with difficulty.

If you do not ask their help, all men are good-natured.

He who rides in the chair is a man; he who carries the chair is also a man.

An army of a thousand is easy to find; but, ah, how difficult to find a general.

Those who have free seats at the play hiss first.

Sorrow is born of excessive joy.

While the boy is small, you can see the man.

If you wish to succeed, consult three old people.

Don't laugh at him who is old; the same will assuredly happen to us.

To see a man do a good deed is to forget all his faults.

Propriety governs the superior man; law, the inferior man.

Rich men have short memories.

If you believe in gambling, in the end you will sell your house.

Ten thousand rivers flow into the sea, but the sea is never full.

When troubles are few, dreams are few.

Preserve the old, but know the new.

A wise man makes his own decisions; an ignorant man follows public opinion.

• 18 •

Chinese Poetry

The T'ang era was China's golden age of poetry. "Whoever was a man was a poet," remarked one historian, illuminating the importance of this literary art. Emperors, statesmen, painters, soldiers, and priests all wrote poems that rank among the finest poetry. The poems give us a view of this era that is difficult to find elsewhere. Here is a small sampling from the works of three of the greatest T'ang poets. What do these poems tell us about China? Can you detect here any Confucian, Taoist, or Buddhist influences? Which of the poems do you like? Why?

LI PO (699-762)

In the Quiet Night

So bright a gleam on the foot of my bed—
Could there have been a frost already?
Lifting myself to look, I found that it was moonlight.
Sinking back again, I thought suddenly of home.

Drinking Alone with the Moon

From a pot of wine among the flowers
I drank alone. There was no one with me—
Till, raising my cup, I asked the bright moon
To bring me my shadow and make us three.
Alas, the moon was unable to drink
And my shadow tagged me vacantly;
But still for a while I had these friends
To cheer me through the end of spring. . . .
I sang. The moon encouraged me.
I danced. My shadow tumbled after.
As long as I knew, we were boon companions.
And then I was drunk, and we lost one another.
. . . . Shall goodwill ever be secure?
I watch the long road of the River of Stars.

TU FU (712-770)

A Spring View

Though a country be sundered, hills and rivers endure;
And spring comes green again to trees and grasses
Where petals have been shed like tears
And lonely birds have sung their grief.
. . . After the war-fires of three months,
One message from home is worth a ton of gold.
. . . I stroke my white hair. It has grown too thin
To hold the hairpins any more.

To Li Po at the Sky's End

A cold wind blows from the far sky. . . .
What are you thinking of, old friend?
The wildgeese never answer me.
Rivers and lakes are flooded with rain.
. . . A poet should beware of prosperity,
Yet demons can haunt a wanderer.
Ask an unhappy ghost, throw poems to him
Where he drowned himself in the Mi-lo River.

PO-CHU YI (772-846)

A Suggestion to My Friend Liu

There's a gleam of green in an old bottle,
There's a stir of red in the quiet stove,
There's a feeling of snow in the dusk outside—
What about a cup of wine inside?

A Song of the Palace

Her tears are spent, but no dreams come.
She can hear the others singing through the night.
She has lost his love. Alone with her beauty,
She leans till dawn on her incense-pillow.

• 19 •

Chinese Short Stories

It was as a result of the influence of the Buddhists and Taoists that the Chinese began to use the short story as a literary form. The stories soon began to be written in the vernacular which had its roots in the oral tradition of storytelling.

The first story is the earliest record in writing of *Cinderella* —recorded in the ninth century. The earliest European version in print is from the sixteenth century. What do the differences between the two versions tell us about life in China as compared with life in the West?

The second story, from the eighth century, combines the popular themes of love and ghosts.

TUANG CH'ENG SHIH

Cinderella

Once, before the time of Chin (222-206 B.C.) and Han (206 B.C.-A.D. 220) there was a chief of a mountain cave whom the natives called Cave Chief Wu. He married two women, one of whom died leaving him a baby girl named Yeh Hsien. She was very intelligent and clever at working on gold and her father loved her dearly, but when he died she was maltreated by her stepmother who often forced her to cut wood and sent her to dangerous places to draw water from deep wells.

One day, Yeh Hsien caught a fish more than two inches long with red fins and golden eyes and she brought it home and placed it in a basin of water. Every day it grew bigger and bigger until the bowl could not hold it any longer, and she placed it in a pond back of her home. Yeh Hsien used to feed it with what she had saved from her own food. When she came to the pond, the fish would rise to the surface and pillow its head on the bank, but if anyone else came to the water's edge it would not appear.

This curious behavior was noticed by the stepmother who often waited for the fish, but it would never come up. One day she resorted to a ruse and said to the girl, "Are you not tired from work? I will give you a new jacket." Then she made Yeh Hsien take off her old clothing and sent her off to a distance of several hundred *li* to draw water from another well. The mother then put on Yeh Hsien's dress, and hiding a sharp knife in her sleeve, went to the pond and called to the fish. When the fish put its head out of the water, she killed it. The fish was by that time over ten feet long, and when it was cooked, it tasted many times better than any other fish. And the mother buried its bones in a dunghill.

Next day, Yeh Hsien came back, and when she arrived at

---

the pond, she saw that the fish was gone. Thereupon she wept until a man with disheveled hair, dressed in a ragged garment, descended from the sky and comforted her, saying, "Do not cry. Your mother has killed the fish, and its bones are buried under a dunghill. Go home and carry the bones to your room and hide them. Whatever you shall want, pray to them and your wish will be granted." Yeh Hsien followed his advice, and it was not long before she had gold and jewelry and finery of such costly texture that they would have delighted the heart of any young maiden.

The night of the Cave Festival Yeh Hsien was told to stay at home and watch the fruit orchard. When the lonely girl saw that her mother had gone a long distance, she arrayed herself in a green silk jacket and went to the festival. Her sister who had recognized her said to the mother, "Is that girl not strangely like my elder sister?" The mother also seemed to recognize her. When Yeh Hsien became aware of their glances she ran away, but in such haste that she dropped one of her slippers, which fell into the hands of the cave people.

When the mother came back home, she found her daughter sleeping with her arms around a tree. She put aside many suspicions she may have had about the identity of the finely dressed girl.

Now near the caves there was an island kingdom called T'o Huan. Through its strong army, it ruled over twenty-four islands, and its territorial waters covered several thousand *li*. The cave people therefore sold the slipper to the T'o Huan Kingdom, where it found its way to the king. The king made the women of his household try it on, but the slipper was an inch too short even for those who had the smallest feet. Then he had all of the women of the kingdom try it, but the slipper would fit none of them.

The king suspected the cave man of getting the slipper from dubious sources and imprisoned and tortured him. The unfortunate man could not tell where the shoe came from. Finally it was placed by the roadside and couriers were sent from house to house to arrest anyone who had the other slipper. The king was greatly puzzled.

All houses were searched and Yeh Hsien was found. She was made to put the slippers on, and they fitted her perfectly. She then appeared in her slippers and her green silk dress, looking like a goddess. Then a report was made to the king, and the king brought Yeh Hsien to his island home, together with her fishbones.

After Yeh Hsien had left the cave, the mother and sister were killed by flying stones. The cave people pitied them and buried them in a pit, erecting a tomb which they called "The Tomb of Regretful Women." The cave people worshiped them as the goddesses of matrimony, and whoever asked them a favor regarding marriage was sure to have her prayer granted.

The king returned to his island and made Yeh Hsien his first wife. During the first year of their marriage, he asked the fishbones for so many jades and precious things that they refused any longer to grant his wishes. He then took the bones and buried them close by the sea, with a hundred bushels of pearls, lined with a border of gold. When his soldiers rebelled against him, he went to the spot, but the tide had washed them away and they have never been found to this day.

This story was told me by an old servant of the family, Li Shih-yuan. He comes from the cave people (aboriginal tribesmen) of Yungchow, and remembers many strange stories of the South.

CHEN HSUANYU

Chienniang

Wang Chou, a young boy of seventeen, had lost his father and was now alone. Steady and more mature than his age indicates, he was old enough to shift for himself. His father had told him on his deathbed that he should go to live with his aunt, who was living in the south at Hengchow, and had reminded him that he was betrothed to his cousin. This was a promise between his father and the father's sister when the babies were being expected; they had said that in case one was a boy and the other a girl, they would be betrothed to each other. Wang Chou disposed of the house and set out to the south accordingly. The young boy's mind was enlivened by the hope of seeing a girl cousin whom he had not seen since the age of six when his father received an appointment in the north. He wondered how she had grown and whether she was still the fragile, affectionate child who used to cling to him as a play companion and wonder at all his doings. He had better hurry, Wang Chou thought, for a girl of seventeen might be betrothed to someone else if he did not show up. But the voyage was slow, and it took him a full month to come down the Hsiang River and then the Tungting Lake and finally reach the mountain city of Hengchow.

His uncle, Chang Yi, ran a shop dealing in herbs and medicinal products. He was a broad-jowled, heavy-voiced man. Every day for the past twenty-five years, he had gone to the shop as regularly as a clock, and he had never traveled or taken a holiday. Cautious, thrifty, and conservative, he had slowly built up his business until he was now quite well-to-do. He had expanded his shop to do wholesale business, added to his property, and built a new house. When Wang Chou saw him at the shop, the uncle growled, "What do you come here for?"

Wang Chou told him. He knew his uncle was a simple and timid man at heart, who wanted only to pay his taxes and have the good opinion of his neighbors. Sober and unimaginative, he had never relaxed from his stern appearance as an elder, having enough trouble keeping himself in the straight and narrow path.

Wang Chou was taken to the uncle's new house, and announced himself as a relative from Taiyuan. The aunt was away at the moment.

Soon he saw a young girl in a blue dress come into the parlor. Chienniang had grown up into a beautiful girl with a very slender figure; she wore a braid of black hair over her shoulder. Her silken smooth face flushed at the sight of her cousin. After a moment's hesitation, she let out a small scream and cried, "You are brother Chou!"

"You are sister Chien!"

The girl was so excited that her eyes filled with tears. "How you have grown!" cried the young girl, eyeing her handsome cousin.

"And so have you!" exclaimed Wang Chou.

Wang Chou looked at the girl with unconcealed admiration, especially with his father's dying words in mind. Soon they were lost in a busy exchange of news of the families and random recollections of their childhood. She had a younger brother several years her junior, who was greatly surprised to see a total stranger who called himself his cousin. They had been separated so long that the family hardly ever spoke of him.

When the mother came back, she gave a hearty, warm welcome to this son of her deceased brother. She was a woman with clear-cut features, a very delicate complexion, and graying hair. A shy, sensitive woman, her lips constantly quivered when she smiled. He informed her that he had finished the district school, and did not know what he was going to do next, and she informed him in turn that his uncle's business was doing well.

"I can see that. You are living in such a beautiful house," said the nephew.

"Your uncle is a very funny man. It took a long time of persuasion on my part and that of the children to get him to move into the new house after he had built it. He is even now regretting how many dollars he is losing by not renting it out. You stay with us. I will ask your uncle to give you a job at the shop. Do your part and don't be afraid of his big voice."

The uncle never came home until evening, and when he did, he was as gruff and as uncommunicative as he had been that morning. The death of his brother-in-law did not seem to concern him, and Wang Chou felt very much like a poor relative and an orphaned young man to be put to the test of apprenticeship. But the aunt was kind and a gentle creature. She was much better educated than her husband and seemed to look upon her husband's businesslike and authoritative attitude with light amusement, although she always obeyed his wishes. She had seen to it, too, that Chien-niang received a perfect education through private tutoring. There was just nothing to talk about at dinner, because the mother and daughter did not understand business, and the father was not much interested in anything else. With his stern appearance and his naturally big voice, he had established himself as the head of the family.

In time, the nephew settled down as a permanent member of the family. Nothing was said about the promised betrothal which was of course verbal between the aunt and her brother when they were both expecting babies. To Wang Chou, the girl in the blue dress would be his choice even if there had been no such promise. Chienniang found Wang Chou's quiet and reserved disposition very much to her liking, too, and as they were thrown into each other's company, before long she had given her heart completely to him.

The mother saw the new happiness on Chienniang's face. When Chienniang cooked something special for the family, she felt as if she was cooking for Wang Chou alone, and a new happiness and pride welled up in her heart. Step by step, she forgot her youthful bashfulness and took over the mending of his clothing and looking after his laundry; she assumed a sort of prior right to take care of him. There was no definite division of jobs, for the daughter was being trained to look after the general household although they had several maids, but the business of cleaning his room and looking after his comforts fell naturally to her. Chienniang would not even permit her younger brother to upset things in his room.

The mother knew that she loved him. One day she said to her daughter dryly, "Chienniang, I see that our dishes are getting more and more salty these days."

Chienniang blushed, for Wang Chou had several times complained that the dishes were not salty enough.

Wang Chou had never dreamed that life could be so sweet and beautiful. He did not mind putting up with his gruff uncle at the shop; he would do anything for the sake of Chienniang and to be near her. Loving Chienniang, he loved all that was connected with her. He felt toward his aunt as if she were his own mother and played with the little boy as if he were his own brother. The father seldom talked at dinner or indulged in jokes with the family, but he was away all day, and was often invited out to business dinners in the evenings.

The Hengchow climate was changeful, varying to extremes between sudden storms coming over the mountains and a scorching heat when the sun was out. Once Wang Chou fell sick and found it so comfortable to lie in bed all day at home, served by his cousin, that he stayed in bed longer than was necessary.

"Now you must go to the shop, or my father will be angry," Chienniang said to him.

"Must I?" asked Wang Chou reluctantly.

One day Chienniang said to him, "You must put more clothing on. I think it is going to rain. If you get sick again, I will be angry with you."

"I would love to," replied Wang Chou impishly, and she understood what he meant.

"Don't be silly," said Chienniang, pouting her lips, and she made him put on extra clothing.

One day Chienniang's elder aunt, the wife of her father's brother, arrived from Changan for a visit. The brother was an extremely wealthy man. He had helped Chang Yi, the girl's father, found the shop with his money; their property was not yet divided and Chang Yi still retained that devotion to his brother which amounted to fear and servile respect for the head of the family. The aunt was royally treated. Family devotion, and Chang Yi's timid nature and natural respect for wealth, both could account for his attitude toward this elder aunt. The best dinners were served every day, and Chang Yi talked and joked at dinner and tried to make himself pleasant to the elder aunt in a way that he had not talked and joked with his wife.

The elder aunt found nothing more pleasant and agreeable than to arrange a match with a rich family for her niece. One day returning from a party with the wealthiest family of the town, the Tsiangs, she said to the girl's mother, in the girl's hearing, "Chienniang is a sweet girl and she is eighteen. I am arranging a match for her with the second son of the Tsiangs. You know of course who the Tsiangs are, and I mean *the* Tsiangs."

"My dear sister-in-law, I have betrothed Chienniang to my brother's son," replied the mother.

"You mean that nephew staying with you? But your brother is already dead."

"That does not make any difference. They seem wonderfully suited to each other." Chienniang, hearing her mother taking the nephew's side, blushed.

The elder aunt broke into loud laughter. "You are crazy! What has he got? I am talking about a respectable match with a decent family with some social standing like ourselves."

Chienniang rose from her seat, left the room, and slammed the door.

"What an ungrateful girl!" the elder aunt shouted after her. "She does not realize what I am doing for her. You have never seen their garden home. Don't be a weak mother. You will thank me when you see the inside of their house. Why their mistress wears a diamond ring almost as big as mine."

The mother did not reply, and excused herself. But the elder aunt, having thought of this match as her best recreation during her stay, would not give up. An engagement would mean dinners and parties, her holiday would be filled with social activities, and she would be happy to have accomplished something memorable during her short stay. But if the mother resisted her suggestion, the elder aunt found in the father of the girl a ready, appreciative, and delighted listener. Chang Yi could not conceive of anything more gratifying to his social ambition and purpose in life. He had always envied one family in the city and that was the Tsiangs. They were an old family and old Mr. Tsiang had been an official in the capital. He had wanted to move in the circle of the Tsiangs and had not been once invited by them. The result was that Chienniang's betrothal to the second son of the Tsiang family was celebrated over the protest of the mother, while the girl lay in bed on a hunger strike.

"No good will come of this," said the mother to her husband. "It is against the girl's wish. You should have gone in and seen the girl crying her heart out in bed. It is her life we have to consider. You have fallen for the Tsiang money."

In time Chienniang was persuaded to eat and get up from bed. She went about the house like one condemned.

The young lover did not care what happened now. He took leave and disappeared for three weeks, trying to drown his sorrow in the Heng mountains. After three weeks, he could not resist the idea of coming back to see his love. When he came back, he found Chienniang suffering from a curious, unknown disease. The day after his departure, the girl lost her memory and did not know who she was. She lay in bed and refused to get up. She did not recognize her own mother and father or her maid. She mumbled words which they did not understand. They feared she had gone out of her mind. But there was something worse. She had no fever, no pains, but she lay in bed all day without food, without drink. They tried to talk to her but her eyes were blank. It was as if her soul had departed from her body, and the body, without the master, stopped functioning altogether. A white pallor settled over her face and the doctors confessed that they had never seen a case like this, and did not know what it was.

With the mother's permission, Wang Chou rushed in to see her. "Chienniang, Chienniang!" he called. The mother watched anxiously. The girl's blank eyes seemed to focus again, her eyelashes moved, and a tinge of red returned to her cheeks.

"Chienniang, Chienniang!" he called again.

Her lips moved and parted in a glad, sure smile.

"It's you," she said quietly.

Tears filled the mother's eyes. "Chienniang, your spirit has returned. You know your mother, don't you?"

"Of course, Mother. What's the matter? What are you crying about? Why am I lying in bed?"

The girl apparently did not know all that had happened. When her mother told her that she had been lying in bed and had not recognized her own mother she could not believe it.

The girl became strong again in a few days. When she was sick, her father had been really frightened, but seeing that she had recovered, he settled back into his authoritative manner again. When the mother described how color returned to Chienniang's cheeks—which she had seen personally—when the nephew came to the girl's bedside, he said, "A fake! The doctors have never seen such a disease. Not knowing her own parents! I do not believe it."

"My dear husband, you have seen the girl lying in bed without food and drink for days. It is in her heart. You should reconsider the engagement—"

"The ceremony is over. Besides, you don't mean that I should break the engagement with the Tsiang family. They will not believe the story. I don't believe it myself."

The aunt who was still staying with them was heard to make sarcastic remarks, implying that the girl's sickness was feigned. "I have lived for fifty years and have never heard of a person not knowing her father and mother."

The father refused to reopen the question. The lovers were miserable and saw no way out. Wang Chou found the situation intolerable. There was nothing he could do. Chagrined and in despair, he informed his uncle that he was leaving for the capital, to be on his own.

"Maybe that is a good idea," replied the uncle curtly.

The night before his departure, the family gave him a

farewell dinner. But Chienniang was heartbroken. She had been lying in bed for two days and refused to get up.

Wang Chou had the mother's permission to go into the girl's room and say good-by. She had not eaten for two days and she was really ill with a high fever. Touching her gently, he said, "I am leaving and have come to say good-by. There is nothing we can do."

"I will die, brother Chou. I have no desire to live when you are gone. But I only know this—living or dead, my spirit shall always be with you wherever you are."

Wang Chou could find no words to comfort her. They parted in tears, and the young man started on his way with an open wound in his heart, believing he should never come back to the house.

His boat had gone about a mile. It was about supper time, and the boat was anchored for the night. Wang Chou lay in bed, sad and lonely, and shedding futile tears. Toward midnight, he heard footsteps drawing nearer and nearer on the bank.

"Brother Chou," he heard a girl whisper. He thought he was dreaming, for he knew she was ill in bed. He peeped out over the gunwale and saw Chienniang standing on the bank. In utter amazement, he jumped ashore.

"I have run away from home," said the girl weakly and fell into his arms. He carried her into the boat quickly, unable to understand how she could cover that distance in her condition except by a superhuman will power, and then he discovered she had come barefooted. How they cried together for joy!

Lying close to his body, caressed with kisses and restored by the warmth, she soon recovered. "Nothing can stop me from following you," she said to him, when she opened her eyes again. It was as if she had completely recovered, and now that they were together and sure of each other, nothing mattered.

It was a long voyage, and during the whole trip, Chienniang expressed only one regret: she felt very sorry for her mother who would be heartbroken when she found that her daughter had disappeared.

They finally arrived at a town in distant Szechwan, where Wang Chou found a small job with a salary barely large enough to support them. In order to make both ends meet, he rented a room in a farmhouse about a mile from the city, a distance which he had to cover on foot daily to and from his office. But he was unbelievably happy. Chienniang washed and cooked and she was contented and happy with him. He looked at his small room, furnished with rustic chairs, a table, and a simple bed, and said that he had all he wanted in life. The farmer who let him have a room upstairs was a simple man and his wife was kind to them. They offered them vegetables from their garden, which helped them to save money for food, and they in turn offered to help in the garden.

Then winter came and Chienniang gave birth to a baby boy, sweet and plump. When spring came, Wang Chou would return to find his wife holding the fat baby in her arms, breast-feeding him. His cup of happiness was full. He never apologized to his wife for making her live like a poor man's wife, for he knew he did not have to. Nevertheless, he knew that she was used to more comfortable living, and was surprised that she had adapted herself to the circumstances so well.

"I wish I could earn more money and hire a maid for you."

His wife stopped him with a soft pressure on his cheeks. It was a complete answer. "You didn't ask me to come. I ran away to follow you," she said simply.

Then they went through that delightful period when every week revealed something new and amazing in their child. The baby was adorable. Now he could grab what he wanted; now he could point to his nose and grab his ear and twitch it. Then the baby learned to crawl and smack his lips, and to say "mamma" and demonstrate those daily miracles of growing intelligence. He was an endless joy who filled their lives. The farmer couple, who were without children, loved the baby and helped Chienniang take care of him.

There was only one thing which marred their happiness. Chienniang kept thinking of her mother and little brother, though she cared not much for her father. Wang Chou was so much in love with her that he could sense her thoughts.

"You are thinking of your mother, I know. If you wish, I will take you home. We are married now and have a baby, and there's nothing they can do about it. At least, it will make your mother happy to see you again."

Chienniang wept with gratitude for his kindness and solicitude for her happiness.

"Let us do it. My mother must have gone crazy thinking that I am lost. And I have this beautiful grandchild to present to my parents."

They started out on the voyage again. After a month on the boat, they arrived at Hengchow.

"You go up first and prepare my parents to receive me," said Chienniang. Taking a gold hair brooch, she gave it to him and said, "Bring this as a token, in case they are still angry and deny you entrance or refuse to believe your story."

The boat anchored on the sandy bank. With Chienniang waiting in the boat, Wang Chou trudged the short distance to her home.

It was about suppertime and the father was at home. Wang Chou knelt on the ground and implored his forgiveness for running away with his daughter. The mother was there and seemed glad to see him, though she looked older, and her hair had turned completely white. He told them that they had now returned and their daughter was waiting in a boat.

"What are you talking about?" replied the father. "Forgive you for what? My daughter has been ill in bed for this entire year."

"Chienniang has never been able to leave her bed since you were gone," said the mother. "It has been sad this long year. She was so ill that at times she went without food for weeks. I could never forgive myself. I promised her that I would break off the engagement, but she was so weak she didn't seem to hear me, as if her spirit had already departed from her body. I was daily hoping for your return."

"I assure you that Chienniang is well and in the boat at this moment. Look, here is her token."

He presented the gold hair brooch. The mother examined it closely and recognized it. The family was greatly confused.

"I tell you she is in the boat. Send a servant to come along with me and see."

The parents were puzzled, but a servant was sent to go with Wang Chou and a sedan chair was ordered. The servant came to the boat and recognized the girl who looked exactly like Chienniang.

"Are my parents well?" the girl asked.

"They are well," replied the servant.

When the family was thus held in suspense and confusion, waiting for the return of the servant, a maid had taken the hair brooch and gone in to see the sick daughter. When the latter heard that Wang Chou had returned, her eyes opened and she smiled. She saw the hair brooch and said, "Indeed I have lost it," and put the brooch in her hair.

Without the maid's notice, the girl got up from her bed, walked out of the house silently like a somnambulist and went straight toward the bank, with a smiling face. Chienniang was leaving the boat already. Wang Chou was holding the baby, waiting for her to get into the sedan chair. He saw the girl on the bank come steadily nearer, and when the two girls met, they merged into one body and Chienniang's dresses became double.

The family was greatly excited when the maid reported that the sick daughter in bed had disappeared. When they saw Chienniang step out of the sedan chair, healthy and well and holding a plump baby in her arms, they were not more delighted than they were astonished and bewildered. They understood then that the girl's spirit, her real self, had gone to live with Wang Chou. For love had wings which broke prison bars. What they had seen in the sick daughter lying in bed was no more than an empty shadow left behind, a body without a soul, from which the conscious spirit had wandered away.

The incident happened in the year A.D. 692. The family kept the story of this strange happening a secret from their neighbors. In time, Chienniang gave birth to several other children, and Wang Chou and Chienniang lived to a happy old age, loving each other more the older they grew.

• 20 •

Chinese Contributions to Civilization

Professor Derk Bodde describes two of the major Chinese inventions that shaped the course not only of Chinese history, but also that of the West. Among other Chinese gifts that were inherited by the rest of the world were gunpowder, compass, astrolabe, porcelain, lacquer, tea, and silk. All of these inventions were indications of the continual change and great variety in Chinese life and technology.

Yet the Chinese never developed any coherent, logical, scientific theory or body of principles. Professor John K. Fairbank offers an explanation for this nondevelopment of science as "a persisting social institution." What do you think were the implications of this failure? Why were the Chinese not primarily concerned with the conquest of man over nature?

DERK BODDE

PAPER

Of all Chinese contributions to the Western world, none can be more clearly traced in its beginnings in China, and then in its gradual spread across Asia to Europe, than can paper. In early times Chinese books were made of narrow vertical strips of bamboo. Many of these, tied together into a bundle, formed one volume. The bulk and clumsiness of such a writing material is obvious. A Chinese philosopher of the fifth century B.C., Mo Tzu by name, used to take along with him three cartloads of such bamboo books wherever he traveled. For writing small documents the Chinese used strips of silk. These were more convenient, but were too expensive for general use. Clearly a new writing material was needed.

The formal invention of paper can be dated exactly in the year A.D. 105, and was the work of one who should surely be honored among the great contributors to human civilization. He was Ts'ai Lun, a man attached to the Chinese imperial court. . . .

There is good reason to suppose that previous attempts to make paper, using raw silk, had already been going on, possibly as early at the third century B.C. What Ts'ai Lun seems to have done, however, was to develop an easy process for manufacture and, above all, to substitute cheaper materials in the place of the expensive silk. His achievement put paper within the reach of everyone.

Following Ts'ai Lun's invention, paper spread with amazing speed throughout all the lands under Chinese domination. . . .

From Central Asia paper pursued its triumphant way westward into the Arabic world, where its first manufacture can be exactly dated in the year 751. In that year, according to Arabic annals, at Samarkand, in the extreme west of Turkestan, the Arabs defeated a Chinese army and captured some of its soldiers. From some of them, who had formerly been papermakers, the Arabs first learned how to manufacture paper.

From Samarkand papermaking spread throughout the Arabic Empire, reaching Syria, Egypt (where it displaced papyrus), and Morocco. From there it finally entered Europe by way of Spain, where its manufacture is first recorded in 1150. From Spain, paper passed on to southern France, and then gradually to the rest of Europe, displacing parchment as it went.

The influence of paper upon the whole course of later Western civilization can hardly be overestimated. Without this cheap material it is unlikely that printing could ever have come into general use. Gutenberg's *Bible,* for example, which is probably the earliest European book printed from movable type, also happens to be one of the few books some of whose copies were printed on parchment instead of paper. It has been estimated that to produce one copy of the *Bible* on parchment, the skins of no less than 300 sheep were required. Had such conditions continued permanently, books would never have been available for more than the richest few, and printing might never have competed successfully with the older, and in some ways more artistic, process of copying manuscripts by hand. . . .

PRINTING

The noble sequel to paper in China was printing. As in the case of most major advances in human civilization, this invention was not the work of any single individual. It came as a climax to several separate processes, developed over a number of centuries. One of these was the invention and spread of paper itself, the significance of which has just been described. Another was the development of a suitable ink.

A third was the process of making what are called rubbings or squeezes. This is a Chinese technique for obtaining on paper exact copies of inscriptions that have been cut on stone monuments and tablets. A sheet of moistened tissue paper is closely fitted upon the face of the engraved stone. The outer surface of this paper is then rubbed with an ink pad so that all parts of the paper touching the raised portions of the underlying stone are inked black. The parts of the paper that fit into the cutout depressions do not receive ink and are left white. Thus an exact black-and-white paper copy of the original inscription is obtained. The Chinese developed this technique of making rubbings because of their eagerness to obtain exact copies of their classics, which were often inscribed on stone monuments.

Most important of all the forerunners of printing was probably the Chinese use of stamp seals. Such seals first appear in human civilization in Mesopotamia, where seals with pictures on them played an important part in man's first development of a system of writing. In China seals began to be used about the third century B.C. . . .

From about the sixth century A.D. onward, however, the Chinese began to stamp their seals in ink, in order to print short inscriptions on paper, in a way similar to our modern rubber stamps. It is from such inked impressions that the true printing of later times gradually developed.

At about the same time, Buddhist and Taoist priests in China began to use such seals. Their seals were only a few inches square and were used to print magical charms and inscriptions by the hundreds. Here was first developed the idea of rapid duplication, an inherent principle of printing. . . .

It is definitely known that actual books were printed in China during the ninth century, and probably such printing goes back considerably earlier. The world's oldest existing printed book is a Buddhist sacred text, dated in the year 868, and beautifully printed in Chinese characters. It was recovered some forty years ago from a cave in Northwest China, just at the point where the great Silk Road leaves China proper to plunge into the deserts of Central Asia. This book was not folded into pages like our modern books, but was a single roll of paper sixteen feet long. . . .

Less than a century later comes the first example of really large-scale book printing in China. This achievement was the printing of nine of the major Chinese classics in 130 volumes. It was carried out between the years 932 and 953 under the direction of a famous official named Feng Tao. From this time onward the flood of printing became ever greater. One modern writer has even estimated that up to the year 1800, more books were printed in China than in the entire rest of the world put together.

All that has hitherto been described refers only to block printing, that is, to printing in which a single block of wood is engraved for each page of the book printed. The first invention of separate movable type, however, is also Chinese. It is the work of a simple artisan named Pi Sheng. Between the years 1041 and 1049 he made a font of movable type of baked clay. In later centuries types made from wood and from various metals replaced such clay types. The use of metal was particularly developed in Korea in the fifteenth century. . . .

At the same time that these developments in movable type were making their appearance in China and surrounding countries, the earlier Chinese invention of block printing was slowly pushing its way toward the Western world. From Turkestan it passed to Persia, where it was known in 1294, and then to Egypt. In Europe itself, we find that the earliest dated example of block printing is a small picture of St. Christopher, accompanied by two lines of text, which was made in the year 1423. . . .

It is not likely that European block printing came as an independent development. Indeed, the beginnings of block printing in Europe can with good probability be traced to several Chinese influences. Among these may have been playing cards, which had long been printed in China, and which first appear in Europe in 1377. . . .

Most important of all, however, was probably the first European acquaintance with printed paper money. Such money began to be printed for the first time in world history in China during the tenth century. . . . Its use spread as far west as Persia, and it is admiringly described by at least eight pre-Renaissance European writers, including Marco Polo. It is difficult to suppose, therefore, that among thoughtful Europeans of the time, there were not some who did not see the possibilities of this strikingly successful example of mass-scale printing, and did not try in their turn to experiment along similar lines.

In Europe, as in China, block printing was followed by

printing with movable type. The first major example of such European printing by means of movable type was Gutenberg's *Bible*. This appeared about 1456, only thirty-odd years after the earliest dated block printing of 1423. No certain proof has yet been found linking this mighty achievement with the similar Chinese invention of movable type more than four hundred years earlier, though such a link is not impossible. But in any case it seems evident that printing with movable type in Europe had a connection with the earlier development of block printing, which itself stems back to China. . . .

JOHN K. FAIRBANK

. . . The brilliant early developments of paper and printing, gunpowder and the compass, the Chinese mathematical discoveries and their perfection of bronze-casting, porcelain and other handicrafts, were not followed by the growth of an organized technology and the formulation of a body of scientific principles. In short, science failed to develop as a persisting social *institution,* a system of theory and practice socially transmitted, though meanwhile there was no lack of inventiveness. During the first thirteen centuries of the Christian era, according to the historian of Chinese science, Joseph Needham, a continuous series of technological inventions came to Europe from China. In addition to the more famous items mentioned above, the wheelbarrow and sailing-carriage, the crossbow, the kite, deep drilling techniques, cast iron, iron-chain suspension bridges, canal lock-gates, the fore-and-aft rig, watertight compartments, and the sternpost rudder, among other things, all seem to have been known in China much earlier than elsewhere. Why did science not result?

The answer, of course, will be complex. In the realm of thought, Chu Hsi* had taught that sincerity of heart was to be approached by a study of external objects, "the investigation of things," after which one might proceed to the understanding of one's self. This phrase, "the investigation of things," however, was interpreted to mean not scientific observation but rather the study of human affairs. Human

---

* [An influential neo-Confucianist philosopher 1130-1200.—Ed.]

society and personal relationships continued to be the focus of Chinese learning, not the conquest of man over nature.

The lack of scientific development is connected with the Chinese failure to work out a fuller system of logic whereby ideas could be tested by ideas, by confronting one statement systematically with another. Philosophers assumed that their principles were self-evident when stated. They made less distinction than the Greeks between grammar and rhetoric, and therefore between abstract and concrete or general and particular. Chinese writers relied more heavily on general ideas of proportion, the balance of opposites, and the harmony of the natural order. Their famous method of chain-reasoning, which was a clincher for Chinese scholars of twenty centuries, was from the Greek point of view a fancy series of non sequiturs.†

Underlying this weakness in logic was the physical nature of the Chinese written language. The use of an ideographic script for the transmission of the cultural inheritance from one generation to the next gave the characters themselves an independent status. They seemed to be enduring entities, not mere tools for the expression of ideas. . . . The tyranny of terms is greater in Chinese than in an alphabetic language. The Chinese have been less able to escape from it than Western thinkers. To question the Confucian virtues would have been to deny the existence of the written characters which expressed them.

This tyranny of language was reinforced by an educational

---

† Take the following key passage from the *Great Learning:*

"The ancients who wished to be illustriously virtuous throughout the kingdom, first ordered well their own states. Wishing to order well their states, they first regulated their families. Wishing to regulate their families, they first cultivated their persons. Wishing to cultivate their persons, they first rectified their hearts. Wishing to rectify their hearts, they first sought to be sincere in their thoughts. Wishing to be sincere in their thoughts, they first extended to the utmost their knowledge. Such extension of knowledge lay in the investigation of things.

"Things being investigated, knowledge became complete. Their knowledge being complete, their thoughts were sincere. Their thoughts being sincere, their hearts were then rectified. Their hearts being rectified, their persons were cultivated. Their persons being cultivated, their families were regulated. Their families being regulated, their states were rightly governed. Their states being rightly governed, the whole kingdom was made tranquil and happy. From the Son of Heaven down to the mass of the people, all must consider the cultivation of the person the root of everything besides."

method in which the Chinese student traditionally memorized the classics before he understood them. . . . The enormous weight of the classic texts which had to be mastered put a premium upon memory, which already played an inordinate part in the learning of Chinese characters. . . .

Behind these shortcomings in thought and action may be seen economic and social circumstances which acted as a check upon the development of science. The state monopoly over large-scale economic organization and production was inimical to private enterprise whenever it threatened to assume large-scale proportions by the use of inventions and machinery. Again, the abundance of manpower militated against the introduction of laborsaving mechanical devices. The dominant position of the official class and their power to tax without check by law made it difficult for new projects to develop except under their wing. In short, the nondevelopment of science was an aspect of the nondevelopment of an industrial economy. This in turn went back to the essentially agrarian and bureaucratic nature of the Confucian state.

PART THREE

CHINA IN TRANSITION

While China was evolving slowly and gradually, adhering to her traditional institutions, reinforced by Confucian principles, far-sweeping and radical changes were taking place in the Western world. Rapid technological, social, and economic changes were leading the Western nations toward commercial and political expansion. At first they sought out the eastern countries only for the raw materials and products demanded at home. However, the industrialists began to see the East as a potential market for the products of their expanding factories, and as a source for investment of accumulated capital. By the early nineteenth century the balance of trade shifted in favor of the West.

The Chinese held fast to their view of foreigners as barbarians who came to China for the blessings of a superior civilization. Given their radically different conceptions of trade, law, and sovereignty, clash was almost inevitable between traditional China and the technologically superior nations of Europe. This clash occurred at a time of dynastic decline while internal rebellion was brewing. The final result was a century of humiliation for China, a period in which she tested a variety of solutions to wrest herself free from the bonds of European imperialism.

• 1 •

Foreigners Describe China

Though China developed in isolation, contact with the outside world was never totally absent. China conducted an indirect silk trade with Rome across the central Asian route. The merchants of the Arab world conducted a great maritime trade with China, bringing back with them many of the great Chinese inventions and intellectual achievements. When European civilization collided with that of the Muslims, stories about China filtered to the western shores of that continent. Many European merchants and traders—aided by the Chinese contributions to navigation—came to China in search of the riches they had heard about. Along with them came the proselytizers—mainly the Jesuits. Eventually an accumulated body of knowledge about China developed.

Here are three descriptions of China from foreign travelers. The first is by Marco Polo, the Venetian merchant who traveled overland to China in the thirteenth century and actually served as a paid employee of the Great Khan of the Mongol (Yuan) dynasty. It was Polo's book on China, among the first to be printed, that created the popular image of China. The second reading is from the journals of Nicholas Trigault, a Jesuit, who accompanied Matteo Ricci, the priest who served the Ming emperor in the sixteenth century. It was the Jesuits who were the chief interpreters of Chinese ideas in the West. The final selection is from the papers of the Earl of Macartney who led a delegation to China in the late eighteenth century from George III in an attempt to establish diplomatic relations between Great Britain and China.

Why were all of these travelers impressed with China? Can you detect any differences among their descriptions? Do you think these accounts are a good source for information on China? How would you describe the attitudes of the travelers? How do you think these writings influenced the European image of China?

MARCO POLO

CONCERNING THE PALACE OF THE GREAT KAAN.

You must know that for three months of the year, to wit December, January, and February, the Great Kaan resides in the capital city of Cathay, which is called *Cambaluc*, and which is at the north-eastern extremity of the country. In that city stands his great Palace, and now I will tell you what it is like.

It is enclosed all round by a great wall forming a square, each side of which is a mile in length; that is to say, the whole compass thereof is four miles. This you may depend on; it is also very thick, and a good ten paces in height, whitewashed and loop-holed all round. . . .

The great wall has five gates on its southern face, the middle one being the great gate which is never opened on any occasion except when the Great Kaan himself goes forth or enters. . . .

Inside of this wall there is a second, enclosing a space that is somewhat greater in length than in breadth. . . . In the middle of the second enclosure is the Lord's Great Palace, and I will tell you what it is like.

You must know that it is the greatest Palace that ever was. . . . The roof is very lofty, and the walls of the Palace are all covered with gold and silver. They are also adorned with representations of dragons [sculptured and gilt], beasts and birds, knights and idols, and sundry other subjects. And on the ceiling too you see nothing but gold and silver and painting. [On each of the four sides there is a great marble staircase leading to the top of the marble wall, and forming the approach to the Palace.]

The Hall of the Palace is so large that it could easily dine 6000 people; and it is quite a marvel to see how many rooms there are besides. The building is altogether so vast, so rich, and so beautiful, that no man on earth could design anything superior to it. The outside of the roof also is all coloured with vermilion and yellow and green and blue and other hues, which are fixed with a varnish so fine and exquisite

---

From Henry Yule (ed.), *The Book of Ser Marco Polo* (London: John Murray, 1871), Vol. I.

that they shine like crystal, and lend a resplendent lustre to the Palace as seen for a great way round. This roof is made too with such strength and solidity that it is fit to last for ever. . . .

Moreover on the north side of the Palace, about a bow-shot off, there is a hill which has been made by art [from the earth dug out of the Lake]; it is a good hundred paces in height and a mile in compass. This hill is entirely covered with trees that never lose their leaves, but remain ever green. And I assure you that wherever a beautiful tree may exist, and the Emperor gets news of it, he sends for it and has it transported bodily with all its roots. . . .

CONCERNING THE CITY OF CAMBALUC, AND ITS GREAT TRAFFIC AND POPULATION.

You must know that the city of Cambaluc hath such a multitude of houses, and such a vast population inside the walls and outside, that it seems quite past all possibility. There is a suburb outside each of the gates, which are twelve in number; and these suburbs are so great that they contain more people than the city itself [for the suburb of one gate spreads in width till it meets the suburb of the next, whilst they extend in length some three or four miles]. In those suburbs lodge the foreign merchants and travellers, of whom there are always great numbers who have come to bring presents to the Emperor, or to sell articles at Court, or because the city affords so good a mart to attract traders. . . .

To this city also are brought articles of greater cost and rarity, and in greater abundance of all kinds, than to any other city in the world. For people of every description, and from every region, bring things (including all the costly wares of India, as well as the fine and precious goods of Cathay itself with its provinces), some for the sovereign, some for the court, some for the city which is so great, some for the crowds of Barons and Knights, some for the great hosts of the Emperor which are quartered round about; and thus between court and city the quantity brought in is endless.

As a sample, I tell you, no day in the year passes that there do not enter the city 1,000 cart-loads of silk alone, from which are made quantities of cloth of silk and gold, and of other goods. . . .

HOW THE KAAN'S POSTS AND RUNNERS ARE SPED THROUGH MANY LANDS AND PROVINCES.

Now you must know that from this city of Cambaluc proceed many roads and highways leading to a variety of provinces, one to one province, another to another; and each road receives the name of the province to which it leads; and it is a very sensible thing. And the messengers of the Emperor in travelling from Cambaluc, be the road whichsoever they will, find at every 25 miles of the journey a station which they call *Yamb,* or, as we should say, the "Horse-Post-House." And at each of those stations used by the messengers there is a large and handsome building for them to put up at, in which they find all the rooms furnished with fine beds and all other necessary articles in rich silk, and where they are provided with everything they can want. If even a king were to arrive at one of these, he would find himself well lodged.

At some of these stations, moreover, there shall be posted some 400 horses standing ready for the use of the messengers; at others there shall be 200, according to the requirements, and to what the Emperor has established in each case. At every 25 miles, as I said, or anyhow at every 30 miles, you find one of these stations, on all the principal highways leading to the different provincial governments; and the same is the case throughout all the chief provinces subject to the Great Kaan. . . .

And in sooth this is a thing done on the greatest scale of magnificence that ever was seen. Never had emperor, king, or lord, such wealth as this manifests! For it is a fact that on all these posts taken together there are more than 300,000 horses kept up, specially for the use of the messengers. And the great buildings that I have mentioned are more than 10,000 in number, all richly furnished as I told you. The thing is on a scale so wonderful and costly that it is hard to bring oneself to describe it. . . .

NICHOLAS TRIGAULT

Due to the great extent of this country north and south as

---

well as east and west, it can be safely asserted that nowhere else in the world is found such a variety of plant and animal life within the confines of a single kingdom. The wide range of climatic conditions in China gives rise to a great diversity of vegetable products, some of which are most readily grown in tropical countries, others in arctic, and others again in the temperate zones. . . . Generally speaking, it may be said with truth that all of these writers are correct when they say that everything which the people need for their well-being and sustenance, whether it be for food or clothing or even delicacies and superfluities, is abundantly produced within the borders of the kingdom and not imported from foreign climes. . . .

This country is so thoroughly covered by an intersecting network of rivers and canals that it is possible to travel almost anywhere by water. Hence, an almost incredible number of boats of every variety pass hither and thither. Indeed there are so many of them that one of the writers of our day does not hesitate to affirm that there are as many people living on the water as there are dwellers on land. This may sound like an exaggeration and yet it all but expresses the truth, as it would seem, if one were to travel here only by water. In my opinion it might be said with greater truth and without fear of exaggeration, that there are as many boats in this kingdom as can be counted up in all the rest of the world. . . .

All of the known metals without exception are to be found in China. Besides brass and ordinary copper alloys, the Chinese manufacture another metal which is an imitation silver but which costs no more than yellow brass. From molten iron they fashion many more articles than we do, for example, cauldrons, pots, bells, gongs, mortars, gratings, furnaces, martial weapons, instruments of torture, and a great number of other things, all but equal in workmanship to our own metalcraft. . . .

The extent of their kingdom is so vast, its borders so distant, and their utter lack of knowledge of a transmaritime world is so complete that the Chinese imagine the whole world as included in their kingdom. . . .

Another remarkable fact and quite worthy of note as marking a difference from the West is that the entire kingdom is administered by the Order of the Learned, commonly known as The Philosophers. The responsibility for orderly management of the entire realm is wholly and completely committed to their charge and care. The army, both officers and soldiers, hold them in high respect and show them the promptest obedience and deference, and not infrequently the military are disciplined by them as a schoolboy might be punished by his master. Policies of war are formulated and military questions are decided by the Philosophers only and their advice and counsel has more weight with the king than that of the military leaders. In fact very few of these, and only on rare occasions, are admitted to war consultations. Hence it follows that those who aspire to be cultured frown upon war and would prefer the lowest rank in the philosophical order to the highest in the military, realizing that the Philosophers far excel military leaders in the good will and the respect of the people and in opportunities of acquiring wealth.

EARL OF MACARTNEY

The Chinese are, perhaps of any people, the most eager in their curiosity about foreigners coming amongst them; it being a sight so rare, except at Canton. But about the countries of such foreigners they are more indifferent. They have been always in the habit of confining their ideas to their own country, emphatically styled the middle kingdom. . . . Regions out of Asia are scarcely mentioned in their books, or noticed in their distorted maps. . . .

No small portion of the people seemed to be in a state approaching indigence; but none were driven to the necessity, or inured in the habit of craving assistance from a stranger. The present time was not, however, one of those times of calamity which destroys or diminishes the resources of the peasant. . . . In such times, however, the Emperor of China always comes forward; he orders the granaries to be opened; he remits the taxes to those who are visited by misfortunes; he affords assistance to enable them to retrieve their affairs:

From Sir George Staunton, *An Authentic Account of an Embassy from the King of Great Britain to the Emperor of China Taken Chiefly from the Papers of His Excellency the Earl of Macartney* (London: W. Bulmer and Co., 1797), Vol. II.

he appears to his subjects, as standing almost in the place of providence, in their favour: he is perfectly aware by how much a stronger chain he thus maintains his absolute dominion, than the dread of punishments would afford. He has shown himself so jealous of retaining the exclusive privilege of benevolence to his subjects, that he not only rejected, but was offended at, the proposal once made to him, by some considerable merchants, to contribute towards the relief of a suffering province. . . .

The houses of the peasants were scattered about, instead of being united into villages. The cottages seemed to be clean and comfortable: they were without fences, gates, or other apparent precaution against wild beasts or thieves. Robbery is said to happen seldom. . . . The wives of the peasantry are of material assistance to their families, in addition to the rearing of their children, and the care of their domestic concerns; for they carry on most of the trades which can be exercised within doors. . . . The women are almost the sole weavers throughout the empire. . . .

The old persons of a family live generally with the young. The former serve to moderate any occasional impetuosity, violence, or passion of the latter. The influence of age over youth is supported by the sentiments of nature, by the habit of obedience, by the precepts of morality ingrafted in the law of the land, and by the unremitted policy and honest arts of parents to that effect. They who are past labour, deal out the rules which they had learned, and the wisdom which experience taught them, to those who are rising to manhood, or to those lately arrived at it. Plain sentences of morals are written up in the common hall, where the male branches of the family assemble. Some one, at least, is capable of reading them to the rest. In almost every house is hung up a tablet of the ancestors of the persons then residing in it. References are often made, in conversation, to their actions. Their example, as far as it was good, serves as an incitement to travel in the same path. The descendants from a common stock visit the tombs of their forefathers together, at stated times. This joint care, and indeed other occasions, collect and unite the most remote relations. They cannot lose sight of each other; and seldom become indifferent to their respective concerns. The child is bound to labour and to provide for his parents' maintenance and comfort, and the brother for the brother and sister that are in extreme want; the failure of which duty would be followed by such detestation, that it is not necessary to enforce it by positive law. Even the most distant kinsman, reduced to misery by accident or ill health, has a claim on his kindred for relief. . . .

The city [Pekin] walls were about forty feet in height. The thickness of the walls was at the base about twenty feet. . . . The walls were flanked on the outside by square towers, at about sixty yards distance from each other, and projecting from the curtain between them forty or fifty feet. Several horsemen were able to ride abreast upon the ramparts, ascending to them upon slopes of earth raised on the inside.

Pekin exhibited, on the entrance into it, an appearance contrary to that of European cities, in which the streets are often so narrow, and the houses so lofty, that from one extremity of a street the houses appear at the other to be leaning towards, and closing upon, each other. Here few of the houses were higher than one story; none more than two; while the width of the street which divided them was considerably above one hundred feet. It was airy, gay, and lightsome.

The street was unpaved, and water sprinkled on it to keep down the dust. . . .

There are properly but three classes of men in China. Men of letters, from whom the mandarines are taken; cultivators of the ground; and mechanics, including merchants. In Pekin alone is conferred the highest degree of literature upon those who, in public examinations, are found most able in the sciences of morality and government, as taught in the ancient Chinese writers; with which studies, the history of their country is intimately blended. Among such graduates all the civil offices in the state are distributed by the Emperor; and they compose all the great tribunals of the empire. The candidates for those degrees are such as have succeeded in similar examinations in the principal city of each province. Those who have been chosen in the cities of the second order, or chief town of every district in the province, are the candidates in the provincial capital. They who fail in the first and second classes have still a claim on subordinate offices, proportioned to the class in which they had succeeded. Those examinations are carried on with great solemnity, and apparent fairness. Military rank is likewise given to those who are found, upon competition, to excel in the military art, and in warlike exercises.

• 2 •

China Rejects the West

The European nations, especially the British, wished to establish diplomatic relations with the Chinese mainly for the purpose of extending their trading interests. China completely rejected these overtures. Here, recorded in an official document of the Court of Peking, was the Chinese answer to the British request. What is the Chinese attitude toward the British? On what basis did the emperor justify his position? How do you think the British reacted to this mandate?

EMPEROR'S MANDATE OF 1790

You, O King, from afar have yearned after the blessings of our civilization, and in your eagerness to come into touch with our converting influence have sent an Embassy across the sea bearing a memorial. . . .

Hitherto, all European nations, including your own country's barbarian merchants, have carried on their trade with our Celestial Empire at Canton. Such has been the procedure for many years, although our Celestial Empire possesses all things in prolific abundance and lacks no product within its own borders. There was therefore no need to import the manufactures of outside barbarians in exchange for our own produce. But as the tea, silk and porcelain which the Celestial Empire produces, are absolute necessities to European nations and to yourselves, we have permitted, as a signal mark of favour, that foreign *hongs* should be established at Canton,

From E. Backhouse and J.O.P. Bland, *Annals and Memoirs of the Court of Peking* (Boston: Houghton Mifflin Company, 1914).

so that your wants might be supplied and your country thus participate in our beneficence. But your Ambassador has now put forward new requests which completely fail to recognise the Throne's principle to "treat strangers from afar with indulgence," and to exercise a pacifying control over barbarian tribes, the world over. Moreover, our dynasty, swaying the myriad races of the globe, extends the same benevolence towards all. Your England is not the only nation trading at Canton. If other nations, following your bad example, wrongfully importune my ear with further impossible requests, how will it be possible for me to treat them with easy indulgence? Nevertheless, I do not forget the lonely remoteness of your island, cut off from the world by intervening wastes of sea, nor do I overlook your excusable ignorance of the usages of our Celestial Empire. . . .

Your Ambassador requests facilities for ships of your nation to call at Ningpo, Chusan, Tientsin and other places for purposes of trade. . . . For the future, as in the past, I decree that your request is refused.

The request that your merchants may establish a repository in the capital of my Empire for the storing and sale of your produce. . . . This request is also refused.

Your request for a small island near Chusan, where your merchants may reside and goods be warehoused, arises from your desire to develop trade. . . . England is not the only barbarian land which wishes to establish relations with our civilisation and trade with our Empire: supposing that other nations were all to imitate your evil example and beseech me to present them each and all with a site for trading purposes, how could I possibly comply? This also is a flagrant infringement of the usage of my Empire and cannot possibly be entertained.

If these restrictions were withdrawn, friction would inevitably occur between the Chinese and your barbarian subjects, and the results would militate against the benevolent regard that I feel towards you. From every point of view, therefore, it is best that the regulations now in force should continue unchanged. . . .

I have even gone out of my way to grant any requests which were in any way consistent with Chinese usage. Above all, upon you, who live in a remote and inaccessible region, far across the spaces of ocean, but who have shown your submissive loyalty by sending this tribute mission, I have heaped benefits far in excess of those accorded to other nations. But the demands presented by your Embassy are not only a contravention of dynastic tradition, but would be utterly unproductive of good result to yourself, besides being quite impracticable. . . . If, after the receipt of this explicit decree, you lightly give ear to the representations of your subordinates and allow your barbarian merchants to proceed to Chêkiang and Tientsin, with the object of landing and trading there, the ordinances of my Celestial Empire are strict in the extreme, and the local officials, both civil and military, are bound reverently to obey the law of the land. Should your vessels touch the shore, your merchants will assuredly never be permitted to land or to reside there, but will be subject to instant expulsion. In that event your barbarian merchants will have had a long journey for nothing. Do not say that you were not warned in due time! Tremblingly obey and show no negligence! A special mandate!

• 3 •

The Humiliation of Opium

Traditionally in China, trade was conducted according to the tribute system, a system which embodied the Chinese view of their position in the world. Outsiders, or "barbarians," were irresistibly attracted to the Middle Kingdom and came bearing "gifts." The Emperor revealed his benevolence to all men by bestowing, through his subordinates, "gifts" on the foreigners. Thus, the exchange of products took place between superior and inferior, firmly based upon the Confucian principle of reciprocity. The kowtow—the humbling of the inferior before the Son of Heaven—became the ritual expression of this relationship.

While the states of East Asia submitted to this gesture, it could hardly be expected that the Europeans, with their notions of national sovereignty and free trade, would become "tributaries" of China.

The city of Canton was the major port through which tribute was paid. At first the European mercantile companies reached a working compromise with the Chinese at Canton, but as these trading companies dissolved—by the beginning of the nineteenth century—private traders began to demand an end to all restrictions on commerce, and an opening of more ports for their products. It was these traders, primarily British but also of other national origins, including Americans, who introduced opium into China. (They had the support of many Chinese merchants and officials who also got rich from the opium.)

This conflict finally erupted into war between China and Britain which resulted in the total humiliation of the Chinese, and the forced opening of their ports to Western trade.

In the first reading, Lin Tse-hsü, commissioner of Customs at Canton, urges Queen Victoria to bring a halt to the opium trade, indicating that to the Chinese opium was not merely a matter of economics. What did the Chinese expect from the British? The next two selections—official pronouncements by Commissioner Lin and a Chinese Censor—outline the methods by which the Chinese hoped to curtail the opium trade themselves. What attitudes are revealed in these memorials? Why do you think these methods proved to be unsuccessful? The fourth selection, Lord Palmerston's instructions to the British envoy in China, reveals the official attitude of the British government. How would you describe it? The final two readings present two of the early treaties concluded after the Opium War—the first between Britain and China, the second between the United States and China. How does the American treaty differ from the British treaty? Why are these treaties referred to as the "unequal treaties?" Why did the Chinese consider the terms to be humiliating? How do you think the opium trade and these treaties influenced Chinese views of and attitudes toward the West?

LIN TSE-HSÜ (March, 1839)

We find that your country is sixty or seventy thousand *li* [three *li* make one mile, ordinarily] from China. Yet there are barbarian ships that strive to come here for trade for the purpose of making a great profit. . . . Even though the barbarians may not necessarily intend to do us harm, yet in coveting profit to an extreme, they have no regard for injuring others. Let us ask, where is your conscience? I have heard that the smoking of opium is very strictly forbidden by your country; that is because the harm caused by opium is clearly understood. Since it is not permitted to do harm to your own country, then even less should you let it be passed on to the harm of other countries—how much less to China! . . .

The goods from China carried away by your country not only supply your own consumption and use, but also can be divided up and sold to other countries, producing a triple profit. Even if you do not sell opium, you still have this threefold profit. How can you bear to go further, selling products injurious to others in order to fulfill your insatiable desire? . . .

. . . Only in several places of India under your control such as Bengal, Madras, Bombay, Patna, Benares, and Malwa has opium been planted from hill to hill, and ponds have been opened for its manufacture. For months and years work is continued in order to accumulate the poison. The obnoxious odor ascends, irritating heaven and frightening the spirits. Indeed you, O King, can eradicate the opium plant in these places, hoe over the fields entirely, and sow in its stead the five grains [i.e., millet, barley, wheat, etc.] Anyone who dares again attempt to plant and manufacture opium should be severely punished. . . .

Now we have set up regulations governing the Chinese people. He who sells opium shall receive the death penalty and he who smokes it also the death penalty. Now consider this: if the barbarians do not bring opium, then how can the Chinese people resell it, and how can they smoke it? The fact is that the wicked barbarians beguile the Chinese people into a death trap. . . . Therefore in the new regulations, in regard to those barbarians who bring opium to China, the penalty is fixed at decapitation or strangulation. This is what is called getting rid of a harmful thing on behalf of mankind.

. . . May you, O King, check your wicked and sift your vicious people before they come to China, in order to guarantee the peace of your nation, to show further the sincerity of your politeness and submissiveness, and to let the two countries enjoy together the blessings of peace. How fortunate, how fortunate indeed! After receiving this dispatch will you immediately give us a prompt reply regarding the details and circumstances of your cutting off the opium traffic. . . .

LIN TSE-HSÜ (August, 1839)

Lin, high imperial commissioner, &c., and Tang, governor of the two Kwang, &c., A proclamation giving clear commands.

Whereas the English foreigners, in their overbearing pride and unpracticability, have withstood the prohibitory enactments; these depraved individuals who deal in opium, have continued to linger at Macao; the empty store-ships which had surrendered their opium have thus long remained anchored in the outer seas; and newly-arrived merchant vessels, neglecting to surrender what opium they have brought, have assembled at Hongkong and the neighborhood, neither entering Whampoa, nor yet sailing back again; whereby occasion was given in a drunken brawl to cause the death of Lin Weihe, one of the people of the empire: and whereas, we, the commissioner and the governor, have reiteratedly issued commands to the superintendent Elliot, justly to investigate and take proceeding therein, he has still withstood us, has not received our commands, and has sheltered and failed to deliver up the murderer (acts of contumacy, and of stiff-necked presumption that cannot be surpassed):—Therefore, we the commissioner and the governor have given strict commands to the local officers, civil and military, at every point, by land and by water, faithfully to intercept and wholly to cut off from the English all supplies, that they may be made to fear and to pay the tribute of fealty. . . .

We make proclamation to all the gentry and elders, the shopkeepers and inhabitants of the outer villages and hamlets, along the coast, for their full information. Pay you all obedience hereto; assemble yourselves together for consultation; purchase arms and weapons; join together the stoutest of your villagers, and thus be prepared to defend yourselves.

From Harley F. MacNair (ed.), *Modern Chinese History: Selected Readings* (Shanghai: Commercial Press, Limited, 1923).

If any of the said foreigners be found going on shore to cause trouble, all and every one of the people are permitted to fire upon them, to withstand and drive them back, or to make prisoners of them. They assuredly will never be able, few in number, to oppose the many. Even when they land to take water from the springs, stop their progress, and let them not have it in their power to drink. But so long as the said foreigners do not go on shore, you must not presume to go in boats near to their vessels, causing in other ways disturbance, which will surely draw on you severe investigations.

A CENSOR'S MEMORIAL (1840)

The English barbarians are an insignificant and detestable race, trusting entirely to their strong ships and large guns; but the immense distance they have traversed will render the arrival of seasonable supplies impossible, and their soldiers, after a single defeat, being deprived of provisions, will become dispirited and lost. Though it is very true that their guns are destructive, still in the attack of our harbors they will be too elevated, and their aim moreover rendered unsteady by the waves; while we in our forts, with larger pieces, can more steadily return the fire. Notwithstanding the riches of their government, the people are poor, and unable to contribute to the expenses of an army at such a distance. Granted that their vessels are their homes, and that in them they defy wind and weather, still they require a great draft of water; and, since our coasts are beset with shoals, they will certainly, without the aid of native pilots, run ashore, without approaching very closely. Though waterproof, their ships are not fireproof, and we may therefore easily burn them. . . . While guarding the approaches to the interior, and removing to the coast the largest guns, to give their ships a terrific reception, we should at the same time keep vessels filled with brushwood, oil, saltpetre, and sulphur, in readiness to let them drive, under the direction of our marine, with wind and tide against their shipping. When once on fire, we may open our batteries upon them, display the celestial terror, and exterminate them without the loss of a single life.

From Harley F. MacNair (ed.), *Modern Chinese History: Selected Readings* (Shanghai: Commercial Press, Limited, 1923).

LORD PALMERSTON (May, 1841)

Experience has shown that it is entirely beyond the power of the Chinese Government to prevent the introduction of opium into China; and many reasons render it impossible that the British Government can give the Chinese Government any effectual aid toward the accomplishment of that purpose. But while the opium trade is forbidden by law it must inevitably be carried on by fraud and violence; and hence must arise frequent conflicts and collisions between the Chinese preventive service and the parties who are engaged in carrying on the opium trade. These parties are generally British subjects; and it is impossible to suppose that this private war can be carried on between British opium smugglers and the Chinese authorities, without events happening which must tend to put in jeopardy the good understanding between the Chinese and British Governments.

H. M. Government makes no demand in this matter; for they have no right to do so. The Chinese Government is fully entitled to prohibit the importation of opium, if it pleases; and British subjects who engage in a contraband trade must take the consequences of doing so. But it is desirable that you should avail yourself of every favorable opportunity to strongly impress upon the Chinese Plenipotentiary, and through him upon the Chinese Government how much it would be for the interest of the Chinese Government itself to alter the law of China on this matter, and to legalize, by a regular duty, a trade which they cannot prevent.

From Harley F. MacNair (ed.), *Modern Chinese History: Selected Readings* (Shanghai: Commercial Press, Limited, 1923).

TREATY OF NANKING, 1842

Victoria, by the Grace of God, Queen of the United Kingdom of Great Britain and Ireland, Defender of the Faith, etc., etc., etc. To All and Singular to whom these Presents shall come, Greeting! Whereas a Treaty between Us and Our Good

From *Treaties, Conventions, Etc., between China and Foreign States* (Shanghai: Statistical Department of the Inspectorate General of Customs, 1908), Vol. I.

Brother The Emperor of China, was concluded and signed, in the English and Chinese Languages, on board Our Ship the *Cornwallis,* at Nanking, on the Twenty-ninth day of August, in the Year of Our Lord One Thousand Eight Hundred and Forty-two, by the Plenipotentiaries of Us and of Our said Good Brother, duly and respectively authorized for that purpose; which Treaty is hereunto annexed in Original:—

ARTICLE I.

There shall henceforward be Peace and Friendship between Her Majesty the Queen of the United Kingdom of Great Britain and Ireland, and His Majesty the Emperor of China, and between their respective Subjects, who shall enjoy full security and protection for their persons and property within the Dominions of the other.

ARTICLE II.

His Majesty the Emperor of China agrees, that British Subjects, with their families and establishments, shall be allowed to reside, for the purpose of carrying on their Mercantile pursuits, without molestation or restraint at the Cities and Towns of Canton, Amoy, Foochow-fu, Ningpo, and Shanghai. . . .

ARTICLE III.

It being obviously necessary and desirable, that British Subjects should have some Port whereat they may careen and refit their Ships, when required, and keep Stores for that purpose, His Majesty the Emperor of China cedes to Her Majesty the Queen of Great Britain, etc., the Island of Hongkong. . . .

ARTICLE IV.

The Emperor of China agrees to pay the sum of Six Millions of Dollars as the value of Opium which was delivered up at Canton in the month of March 1839, as a Ransom for the lives of Her Britannic Majesty's Superintendent and Subjects, who had been imprisoned and threatened with death by the Chinese High Officers.

ARTICLE VI.

The Government of Her Britannic Majesty having been obliged to send out an Expedition to demand and obtain redress for the violent and unjust Proceedings of the Chinese High Authorities towards Her Britannic Majesty's Officer and Subjects, the Emperor of China agrees to pay the sum of Twelve Millions of Dollars on account of the Expenses incurred. . . .

ARTICLE XII.

On the assent of the Emperor of China to this Treaty being received and the discharge of the first instalment of money, Her Britannic Majesty's Forces will retire from Nanking and the Grand Canal, and will no longer molest or stop the Trade of China. The Military Post at Chinhai will also be withdrawn, but the Islands of Koolangsoo and that of Chusan will continue to be held by Her Majesty's Forces until the money payments, and the arrangements for opening the Ports to British Merchants be completed.

TREATY OF WANG-HEA, 1844

ARTICLE I.

There shall be a perfect, permanent, and universal peace and a sincere and cordial amity between the United States of America on the one part, and the Ta-Tsing Empire on the other part, and between their people respectively, without exception of persons or places.

ARTICLE II.

Citizens of the United States resorting to China for the purpose of commerce will pay the duties of import and export prescribed by the Tariff which is fixed by and made a part of this Treaty. They shall in no case be subject to other or higher duties than are or shall be required of the people of any other nation whatever. . . . If the Chinese Government desire to modify in any respect the said Tariff, such modifications shall be made only in consultation with Consuls or

From *Treaties, Conventions, Etc., between China and Foreign States* (Shanghai: Statistical Department of the Inspectorate General of Customs, 1908), Vol. I.

other functionaries thereto duly authorised in behalf of the United States, and with consent thereof. And if additional advantages or privileges of whatever description be conceded hereafter by China to any other nation, the United States and the citizens thereof shall be entitled thereupon to a complete, equal, and impartial participation in the same.

ARTICLE III.

The citizens of the United States are permitted to frequent the five ports of Quangchow, Amoy, Fuchow, Ningpo, and Shanghai, and to reside with their families and trade there, and to proceed at pleasure with their vessels and merchandise to or from any Foreign port and either of the said five ports, and from either of said five ports to any other of them; but said vessels shall not unlawfully enter the other ports of China, nor carry on a clandestine and fraudulent trade along the coasts thereof; and any vessel belonging to a citizen of the United States which violates this provision shall, with her cargo, be subject to confiscation to the Chinese Government.

ARTICLE XIX.

All citizens of the United States in China peaceably attending to their affairs, being placed on a common footing of amity and goodwill with subjects of China, shall receive and enjoy, for themselves and everything appertaining to them, the special protection of the local authorities of Government, who shall defend them from all insult or injury of any sort on the part of the Chinese.

If their dwellings or their property be threatened or attacked by mobs, incendiaries, or other violent or lawless persons, the local officers, on requisition of the Consul, will immediately despatch a military force to disperse the rioters, and will apprehend the guilty individuals and punish them with the utmost rigour of the law.

ARTICLE XXI.

Subjects of China who may be guilty of any criminal act towards citizens of the United States shall be arrested and punished by the Chinese authorities according to the laws of China, and citizens of the United States who may commit any crime in China shall be subject to be tried and punished only by the Consul or other public functionary of the United

States thereto authorised according to the laws of the United States; and in order to the prevention of all controversy and disaffection, justice shall be equitably and impartially administered on both sides.

• 4 •

Dynastic Decline: The Taiping Rebellion

Although the Manchu dynasty (1644–1912) had incorporated the traditional Chinese institutions and had received the support of the bureaucracy, it had tried to maintain (though not very successfully) its separate cultural identity. It was never popular with the Chinese who regarded them as aliens. Two hundred years of relative internal peace had led to dynastic decay and inefficiency. A great increase in population—the result of internal security and the introduction of new food crops—intensified pressure on the land and brought the creaky machinery of government to a virtual halt. Flood, famine, disease—the traditional signs of dynastic decline—seemed imminent. The disgrace brought on by China's failures in the Opium Wars further decreased the little moral authority the Manchus continued to possess.

The Taiping Rebellion (1851–1864), begun in the southern provinces nearest to Canton (hence most closely in contact with the Western intrusion), was a major uprising that tested the authority of the imperial regime. Similar in many ways to earlier rebellions, the Taiping also bore more than a hint of the Western influence. In this selection, from the Taiping economic program, perhaps you can detect these influences. Which are Chinese? Which are Western? A major reason for the failure of the Taiping Rebellion was that the scholars, as well as the Western powers, threw their support to the government.

ANONYMOUS TAIPING REBELLION PUBLICATION

All officials who have rendered meritorious service are to receive hereditary stipends from the court. For the later adherents to the Taiping cause, every family in each military district *(chün)* is to provide one man to serve as a militia man. During an emergency they are to fight under the command of their officers to destroy the enemy and to suppress bandits. In peacetime they are to engage in agriculture under the direction of their officers, tilling the land and providing support for their superiors. . . .

The distribution of all land is to be based on the number of persons in each family, regardless of sex. A large family is entitled to more land, a small one to less. The land distributed should not be all of one grade, but mixed. Thus for a family of six, for instance, three are to have fertile land and three barren land—half and half of each.

All the land in the country is to be cultivated by the whole population together. If there is an insufficiency [of land] in this place, move some of the people to another place. If there is an insufficiency in another place, move them to this one. All lands in the country are also to be mutually supporting with respect to abundance and scarcity. If this place has a drought, then draw upon the abundant harvest elsewhere in order to relieve the distress here. If there is a drought there, draw upon the abundant harvest here in order to relieve the distress there. Thus all the people of the country may enjoy the great blessings of the Heavenly Father, Supreme Ruler, and Lord God-on-High. The land is for all to till, the food for all to eat, the clothes for all to wear, and money for all to spend. Inequality shall exist nowhere; none shall suffer from hunger or cold.

Every person sixteen or over, whether male or female, is entitled to a share of land; those fifteen or under should receive half the share of an adult. . . .

Mulberry trees are to be planted along the walls [of villages] throughout the country. All women are required to grow silk-

---

worms, to do weaving, and to make clothes. Every family of the country is required to raise five hens and two hogs, in keeping with the proper breeding seasons.

During the harvest season, the Group Officer should direct [the grain collection by] the sergeants. Deducting the amount needed to feed the twenty-five families until next harvest season, he should collect the rest of the produce for storage in state granaries. The same method of collection is applicable to other kinds of products, such as barley, beans, ramie fiber, cotton clothes, silk, domestic animals, silver and copper cash, etc., for all people under Heaven are of one family belonging to the Heavenly Father, the Supreme Ruler, the Lord God-on-High. Nobody should keep private property. . . .

• 5 •

China Seeks Ways to Combat the West

With the collapse of the Taiping Rebellion, the Manchu dynasty was given a respite and an opportunity to determine its future course with the West. Chinese leaders were forced to reevaluate China's position *vis-à-vis* the West, and to seek methods to free itself from the imposed subjugation.

In this group of readings, a provincial official, Li Hung-chang, the scholar Feng Kuei-fan, and a reformer, Liang Ch'i-ch'ao, outline their ideas for meeting the challenge of the West. How would you evaluate these ideas?

LI HUNG-CHANG (1872)

A Call for More Military Strength

The Westerners particularly rely upon the excellence and efficacy of their guns, cannon, and steamships, and so they can

---

Reprinted with permission of Harvard University Press, from Ssu-yü Teng and John K. Fairbank, *China's Response to the West.* Copyright 1954 by the President and Fellows of Harvard College.

overrun China. The bow and spear, small guns, and native-made cannon which have hitherto been used by China cannot resist their rifles, which have their bullets fed from the rear opening. The sailing boats, rowboats, and the gunboats which have been hitherto employed cannot oppose their steam-engined warships. Therefore, we are controlled by the Westerners.

To live today and still say "reject the barbarians" and "drive them out of our territory" is certainly superficial and absurd talk. Even though we wish to preserve the peace and to protect our territory, we cannot preserve and protect them unless we have the right weapons. They are daily producing their weapons to strive with us for supremacy and victory, pitting their superior techniques against our inadequacies, to wrangle with and to affront us. Then how can we get along for one day without weapons and techniques?

The method of self-strengthening lies in learning what they can do, and in taking over what they rely upon. Moreover, their possession of guns, cannon, and steamships began only within the last hundred years or so, and their progress has been so fast that their influence has spread into China. If we can really and thoroughly understand their methods—and the more we learn, the more improve—and promote them further and further, can we not expect that after a century or so we can reject the barbarians and stand on our own feet? . . .

Your minister humbly thinks that all other expenditures of our nation can be economized, but the expenses for supporting the army, establishing defense measures, drilling in guns and cannon, and building warships should by all means never be economized. If we try to save funds, then we shall be obliged to neglect all these defense measures, the nation will never have anything to stand upon, and we shall never be strong. . . . The amount which has already been spent will, in turn, become a sheer waste. Not only will we be a laughing stock to foreigners, but we will also strengthen their aggressive ambitions. . . .

FENG KUEI-FAN (ca. 1860)

ON THE ADOPTION OF WESTERN KNOWLEDGE

The world today is not to be compared with that of the Three Dynasties (of ancient China). . . .

If today we wish to select and use Western knowledge, we should establish official translation offices at Canton and Shanghai. Brilliant students up to fifteen years of age should be selected from those areas to live and study in these schools on double rations. Westerners should be invited to teach them the spoken and written languages of the various nations, and famous Chinese teachers should also be engaged to teach them classics, history, and other subjects. At the same time they should learn mathematics. (Note: All Western knowledge is derived from mathematics. Every Westerner of ten years of age or more studies mathematics. If we now wish to adopt Western knowledge, naturally we cannot but learn mathematics. . . .)

If we let Chinese ethics and famous [Confucian] teachings serve as an original foundation and let them be supplemented by the methods used by the various nations for the attainment of prosperity and strength, would it not be the best of all procedures? . . .

. . . Our officers from generals down, in regard to foreign countries are completely uninformed. . . . The Chinese officials have to rely upon the stupid and silly "linguists" as their eyes and ears. The mildness or severity, leisureliness or urgency of their way of stating things may obscure the officials' original intent after repeated interpretations. Thus frequently a small grudge may develop into a grave hostility. At the present time the most important administrative problem of the empire is to control the barbarians, yet the pivotal function is entrusted to these people. No wonder that we understand neither the foreigners nor ourselves, and cannot distinguish fact from unreality. . . .

If my proposal is carried out, there will necessarily be many Chinese who learn their written and spoken languages; and

---

when there are many such people, there will certainly emerge from among them some upright and honest gentlemen who thoroughly understand the fundamentals of administration, and who would then get hold of the essential guiding principles for the control of foreigners. . . .

ON THE MANUFACTURE OF FOREIGN WEAPONS

What we then have to learn from the barbarians is only the one thing, solid ships and effective guns. . . .

Funds should be assigned to establish a shipyard and arsenal in each trading port. Several barbarians should be invited and Chinese who are good in using their minds should be summoned to receive their instructions so that they may in turn teach many artisans. When a piece of work is finished and is indistinguishable from that made by the barbarians, the makers should be given a *chü-jen* degree as a reward, and be permitted to participate in the metropolitan examination on an equal footing with other scholars. Those whose products are superior to the barbarian manufacture should be granted a *chin-shih* degree as a reward, and be permitted to participate in the palace examinations on the same basis as others. The workers should be double-paid so as to prevent them from quitting.

Our nation has emphasized the civil service examinations, which have preoccupied people's minds for a long time. Wise and intelligent scholars have exhausted their time and energy in such useless things as the eight-legged essays [highly stylized essays for the civil service examination, divided into eight paragraphs], examination papers, and formal calligraphy. . . . Now let us order one-half of them to apply themselves to the pursuit of manufacturing weapons and instruments and imitating foreign crafts. . . .

Some suggest purchasing ships and hiring foreign people, but the answer is that this is quite impossible. If we can manufacture, can repair, and can use them, then they are our weapons. If we cannot manufacture, nor repair, nor use them, then they are still the weapons of others. When these weapons are in the hands of others and are used for grain transportation, then one day they can make us starve; and if they are used for salt transportation, one day they can deprive us of salt. . . . Eventually we must consider manufacturing, repairing, and using weapons by ourselves. . . . Only thus will we be able to pacify the empire; only thus can we play a leading role on the globe; and only thus shall we restore our original strength, and redeem ourselves from former humiliations.

LIANG CH'I-CH'AO (ca. 1900)

Praise of Country of China

The greatest country in the greatest of the five continents of the world,—which is it? My country, the Middle State, the Flowery Land! The people who number one-third of the human race,—who are they? My countrymen of the Middle State, the Flowery Land! Annals which extend back without a break for over four thousand years,—of what country are these? Of my country, the Middle State, the Flowery Land! My country contains four hundred million inhabitants, who all speak what is fundamentally the same language, and use the same script: of no other country can this be said. Her ancient books hand down events which have occurred during more than thirty centuries past: of no other country can this be said.

Of old, there were five States: China, India, Persia, Egypt, and Mexico. Of four of these the territory remains, but as States all four have disappeared. Wandering over the deserted sites, you see only traces of the ruins left by the ironclad horsemen, followers of Mahomet, or the arenas where once warlike Caucasian tribes gloried in the song and dance. But my country, the Middle State, the Flowery Land, stands proudly alone, having survived, in one unbroken line, ever increasing in size and brilliancy, down to the present day. And in the future it will spread into a myriad branches, to be fused together in one furnace. Ah, beautiful is my country! Ah, great are my countrymen! . . .

China is a huge country with a learning of its own, which has been handed down for several thousand years and which is so well fortified by defences that foreign ideas do not easily find their way in. Even if they do get in, for many—perhaps a hundred—years their influence will not succeed in rumpling

From Liang Ch'i-ch'ao, "My Country," in Herbert A. Giles (ed.), *Gems of Chinese Literature* (Shanghai: Kelly & Walsh, Limited, 1922).

the hair of one's head. It is like throwing ink into water. If the water is in a foot-wide bowl or in a ten-foot pool, the ink will very rapidly discolour it all; but if the same ink is thrown into a mighty rushing river or into the wide and deep ocean, can these be easily stained in the same way? Again, although China is not receptive of foreign learning, from what she does receive she makes a point of extracting all the excellences and adapting these to her own advantage. She transmutes the substance and etherializes its use, thus producing a new factor of civilization which is altogether her own. Her blue is thus bluer than the original indigo-blue of foreigners; her ice is colder than their water. . . .

• 6 •

Westerners Observe the Chinese

Following the Opium Wars, and the privileges exacted in the unequal treaties, Westerners came in large numbers to China—merchants, traders, industrialists, government representatives, missionaries, teachers, scholars. Many wrote down their observations, and their published works became a major source of information about China for the general public in the West. These works also give a glimpse into the attitudes that permeated Western thought about China.

First we have some notes written by Thomas Meadows, a British interpreter. The second selection is an excerpt from a geography text prepared by William Swinton and designed for American children. In the third selection an Englishman, Goldsworthy L. Dickinson, tries to step inside Chinese shoes, in the guise of "John Chinaman," in order to see things from a Chinese view. Then we have a missionary, Henry Dore, describing Chinese religious practices. Finally, there is an attempt by an American, Rodney Gilbert, to sum up the Chinese mind and character. What do you think would be the cumulative effect of these views on the Western mind? How would you describe the attitudes expressed in these works?

THOMAS MEADOWS (1847)

Notes on the Government and People of China

"It is in the great size and wealth and the numerous population of our country; still more in its excellent institutions, which may contain some imperfections, but which after all are immeasurably superior to the odd confused rules by which these barbarians are governed; but, above all, in its glorious literature which contains every noble, elegant, and in particular, every profound idea; everything, in short, from which true civilization can spring, that we found our claim to national superiority." So thinks even the educated Chinese; and so the whole nation will continue to think until we have proved to them—no easy nor short task—our mental as well as our physical superiority. . . .

At present they take the tone of superiors quite unaffectedly, simply because they really believe themselves to be superior. . . . For instance, when a mandarin who has never spoken to a barbarian, and never seen one of their books, who, perhaps, has hitherto always doubted that they had anything deserving of the name, is first shown one, he admires the decided superiority of the paper at once; but when he finds that instead of commencing at the left hand, as it (according to his belief) *of course* ought, its beginning is at the (Chinese) end; when he sees that all the lines, instead of running perpendicularly down the page, in the (to a Chinese) natural way, go sidling across it; when he further asks the meaning of the words in a sentence, and finds, as may easily happen, that the first comes last, and the last first, "Ah!" says he, without however the slightest intention of giving offence, "it's all confused, I see; you put the words anywhere, just as it suits your fancy. But how do you manage to read it?" When you, however, explain to him at length, that there is no *natural* way for the lines to run, and no absolutely proper place for books to begin; that there can scarcely be said to be any natural order for the succession of words in sentences, but that it is fixed by custom, and differs in every language, and that the uneducated Englishman would consider the Chi-

From Thomas Meadows, *Desultory Notes on the Government and People of China* (London: W.H. Allen and Co., 1847).

nese method as quite absurd; when you explain this to him, and he begins to comprehend your reasoning, there is no obstinate *affectation* of contempt. He cannot, of course, have much respect for the shallow productions of barbarian minds, but he handles the book gravely, no longer regarding it as an absurdity.

All Chinese who have seen them are perfectly ready to allow that our ships, our guns, watches, cloths, etc., are much superior to their own articles of the like sort; and most of them would frankly admit us to be superior to them in all respects, if they thought so. But as above said, they do not. They are quite unable to draw conclusions as to the state of foreign countries, from an inspection of the articles produced or manufactured in them. They cannot see that a country where such an enormous, yet beautiful fabric as a large English ship is constructed—an operation requiring at once the united efforts of numbers and a high degree of skill—*must* be inhabited by a people not only energetic but rich and free to enjoy the fruits of its own labor; that such a country *must*, in short, have a powerful government, good laws, and be altogether in a high state of civilization. All this the Chinaman, having never compared the various states of different nations, is not only quite unable to perceive of himself, but often not even when it is pointed out to him at great length. We have, it is true, the power to do some great and extraordinary things, but so have the elephants and other wild animals he occasionally sees and hears of; in his eyes, therefore, we are all barbarians, possessing perhaps some good qualities, congregated perhaps together in some sort of societies, but without regular government, untutored, coarse, and wild. . . .

WILLIAM SWINTON (1875)

The Chinese Empire

2. The first thing to be noticed about China is the vast number of human beings that live there. The number of people in China is over 400 millions; but this is so great a number

From William Swinton, *Elementary Course in Geography Designed for Primary and Intermediate Grades* (New York: Ivison, Blakeman and Company, 1875).

PUNCH, OR THE LONDON CHARIVARI.—December 22, 1860.

WHAT WE OUGHT TO DO IN CHINA.

that no person can realize it, for it would take one very many years to count 400 millions. Perhaps, then, we may get a better idea of the population of China by remembering that it is more than ten times the population of the whole United States, or that one in three of all the inhabitants of the globe is a subject of that Emperor who is styled the "Brother of the Sun and Moon." . . .

4. China is one of the oldest of civilized nations. By this is meant that several thousand years ago, when the people of Europe were still savages, the Chinese had a regular government, and a written language, and a knowledge of many of the mechanical arts. They had invented the mariner's compass, gunpowder, and the art of printing, many centuries before these became known in Europe. But we cannot say that the Chinese are a civilized people according to our standard, for they are not progressive: their way of doing things and thinking about things is today just as we find it described in their books to have been 2,500 years ago. . . .

IV. THE PEOPLE

11. There are very many things that might be said about the ways of the Chinese, but there is room to speak of only a few here. The men tie up their hair into a long tail which hangs down over the back. The girls of the wealthier families are kept with their feet bandaged from infancy, so that when they grow up their feet are mere stumps, on which they can barely hobble along. The Chinese eat with chopsticks, in place of knives and forks. There are schools for boys in all the villages, and almost every Chinaman can read and write, but the girls are not thought to be worth educating. The Chinese are exceedingly industrious, thrifty, and imitative; but they are often treacherous, knavish, and immoral. They are great opium-smokers. . . .

1. *Of what does the Chinese Empire consist?*

The Chinese Empire consists of China Proper, together with various provinces, all united under one government, the head of which is the Emperor of China.

2. *What can you say of China?*

China is the oldest and most populous country on the globe. It contains 400 millions of inhabitants, or one third of all the people in the world.

3. *What of its civilization?*

The Chinese are not a progressive people, having made little advancement in the arts and sciences for 3,000 years.

GOLDSWORTHY L. DICKINSON ("JOHN CHINAMAN") (1901)

Chinese and Western Civilization Compared by a Westerner

Our civilization is the oldest in the world. It does not follow that it is the best; but neither, I submit, does it follow that it is the worst. On the contrary, such antiquity is, at any rate, a proof that our institutions have guaranteed to us a stability for which we search in vain among the nations of Europe. But not only is our civilization stable, it also embodies, as we think, a moral order; while in yours we detect only an economic chaos. Whether your religion be better than ours, I do not at present dispute; but it is certain that it has less influence on your society. You profess Christianity, but your civilization has never been Christian; whereas ours is Confucian through and through. But to say that it is Confucian, is to say that it is moral; . . . Whereas, with you (so it seems to us) economic relations come first, and upon these you endeavor, afterward, to graft as much morality as they will admit.

This point I may illustrate by a comparison between your view of the family and ours. To you, so far as a foreigner can perceive, the family is merely a means for nourishing and protecting the child until he is of age to look after himself. . . . As soon as they are of age, you send them out, as you say, to "make their fortune"; and from that moment, often enough, as they cease to be dependent on their parents, so they cease to recognize obligations toward them. They may go where they will, do what they will, earn and spend as they choose; and it is at their own option whether or not they maintain their family ties. With you the individual is the unit, and all the units are free. No one is tied, but also no one is rooted. Your society, to use your own word, is "progressive";

From Goldsworthy L. Dickinson, *Letters from A Chinese Official: Being an Eastern View of Western Civilization* (New York: McClure, Phillips, 1907). Published in 1901 (London: R.B. Johnson), as *Letters from John Chinaman.*

you are always "moving on." Everyone feels it a duty (and in most cases it is a necessity) to strike out a new line for himself. To remain in the position in which you were born you consider a disgrace; a man, to be a man, must venture, struggle, compete, and win. To this characteristic of your society is to be attributed, no doubt, its immense activity, and its success in all material arts. But to this, also, is due the feature that most strikes a Chinaman—its unrest, its confusion, its lack (as we think) of morality. Among you no one is contented, no one has leisure to live, so intent are all on increasing the means of living.

Now, to us of the East all this is the mark of a barbarous society. We measure the degree of civilization not by accumulation of the means of living, but by the character and value of the life lived. Where there are no humane and stable relations, no reverence for the past, no respect even for the present, but only a cupidinous ravishment of the future, there, we think, there is no true society.

HENRY DORE (1914)

What [the author] tells us therein, he has witnessed with his own eyes, or heard from the lips of the people with whom he came into daily contact. Real China exists little in the Open Ports. Civilisation has there done its work, and raised the Chinaman to a higher level than his fellow countrymen. Whosoever, therefore, would study him in real life, must needs see him in the remote regions, the quaint old towns, and the secluded villages of some distant province. . . .

The work will, doubtless, fulfil a useful and scientific purpose both in the Far East and at home. The principal intention of the Author in publishing it has been to help his fellow Missionaries in the field, chiefly those recently arrived from home, and yet unacquainted with the life and religious conditions of the Chinese people. These men shall one day be brought into contact with the superstitions of the country. They must, therefore, have some knowledge of what the people think, believe and worship. Thus equipped, they will

From Henry Dore, *Researches into Chinese Superstitions*, preface by M. Kennelly, S.J. (tr.) (Shanghai: T'uswei Printing Press, 1914).

offend less native prejudice and promote better the great work of implanting Christian truth in the land. . . .

The notion of *the true God* has almost disappeared, or at least is but dimly known. For the greater part of the people, their God is the *"Pearly Emperor," Yuh-hwang* 玉 皇, of Taoist origin; *Buddha* or *Fuh* 佛, *Amitabha* 阿 彌 陀 佛 (O-mih-t'o-fuh), the Ruler of the Western Paradise; *Kwan-yin* 觀 音, the Goddess of Mercy; some local or tutelary divinity to whom they give the title of *"Venerable Sire or Lord," Lao-yeh* 老 爺; the God of Riches, the God of the Hearth, the God of Fire. Carpenters have their Patron God, also play-actors, wrestlers, fencers, musicians, and even gamblers. It would seem that every need of man has its corresponding divinity, the Gods being thus, as with the Romans, largely names for these various needs. . . . The modernists among them are utter atheists and materialists. For them, God is but an abstract principle, identified with *Reason* or *Law,* that is, he is nothing else but the moral sense of man, exalted thus to be his own Lord and Lawgiver. Practically, they are as superstitious as the masses, and will burn mock-money, though this is a Buddhist practice, at the tombs of their ancestors.

China's popular religion is, therefore *a medley of superstitions,* varying according to places, but essentially the same in their fundamental features. Hence the popular adage: *"the three religions are one", San-kiao wei-yih* 三 教 爲 一. Each person in fact selects or adopts what suits best his fancy, or meets his present requirements. The Powers of Nature, Spirits, the Hosts of Heaven, Genii and deified Heroes, Ancestors are also worshipped; even animals, especially the Dragon and the Tortoise, not omitting the mineral world. The whole affords a pitiful spectacle which excites compassion, and has held the people in bondage throughout the past, as well as it degrades them at the present day. . . .

The present-day Chinese, especially the higher and intelligent classes, are thoroughly dissatisfied with their crude and primitive ideas, and look around for a religion which will enlighten the individual and the nation of God, the soul, and the spiritual world . . . and this they will find in the Catholic Church.

RODNEY GILBERT (1926)

The Chinese have all the native charm of children and all their weaknesses. They are kind, as children are kind; and cruel, as children are cruel. Children either love a pet to death or subject it to tortures that would shame the lowest savage just to see it squirm and squeal—so do the Chinese indulge themselves. . . . The Chinese are as trustful and loyal as children, and yet suspicious, secretive and circuitous in their methods as only children can be. They are suspicious and sensitive, but affectionate and trusting—as only children are. Like children they are wilful, proud, independent, recalcitrant and resentful of correction, but under sustained and reasonable discipline are the most docile, tractable and responsive people on earth—like nothing so much in fact as good schoolboys. We all know how graspingly mean and selfish a child can be at one moment and how foolishly and lavishly generous he can be the next, acting under impulses which we cannot grasp; the Chinese are the same. They are timid, but bold; peace loving, but warlike; painstaking and indefatigable workers, and at the same time careless, slipshod and shirking, just as they happen to be used and inspired, as children are. . . .

Superficially China has a great many serious problems to face and the world has much to do to arrange for lasting placid relations between the East and West. But it is the purpose of these essays to demonstrate what will here be stated as a fundamental hypothesis: that most of China's ills have grown out of her own and our failure to appreciate that the Chinese mind is a child's mind—the mind of a precocious child at its best and worst. If China's ills are to be laid at our door, as her propagandists say, it is because we have failed to realize that we are dealing with children, because we have treated the individual Chinese as an adult and the nation as a grown-up. . . .

To any intelligent person living in the East, it is evident

Reprinted with permission of John Murray (Publishers), Ltd., from Rodney Gilbert, *What's Wrong with China* (London, 1926).

enough that China's present state is primarily due to the complete breakdown of discipline and of respect for authority, upon which the maintenance of order has depended since the beginning of things Chinese, and without which the Chinese masses are no more a nation than a masterless horde of young hoodlums at large is a school.

It is also apparent to students of Oriental history that, for peculiar reasons of their own, the Chinese are utterly incapable of restoring order dependent upon respect for native authority, chiefly because no native authority worthy of respect exists or is likely to exist, and because weaklings and hypocrites can no more restore order in a nation of schoolboy minds than they can govern and reshape a demoralized school.

It is further obvious to all of us in the East that foreign influence and imported ideas had, of necessity, much to do with the collapse of that imperial authority which sufficed for China's good order before we meddled with her, but having done the damage, it would be a feeble sense of responsibility indeed that would prompt us to say "hands off" now, just because the demoralized Chinese shouted for it, when a firm hold upon the situation would right matters.

• 7 •

The Boxer Rebellion

The second half of the nineteenth century were years in which the Western powers staked out their claims in China. Armed with the provisions of the unequal treaties, they carved China into spheres of influence and were granted economic concessions. The Sino-Japanese War (1895) was a further humiliation for the Chinese, as Japan—China's former tributary—vigorously entered the race for concessions. It seemed possible that China would cease to exist as a sovereign state. The Open Door policy of the United States (1899) did little to appease Chinese fears.

The Boxer Rebellion (1900) was a peasant rebellion supported by many Chinese officials and was aimed at expelling the foreigners from China. It was specifically anti-Christian and anti-imperialist, but the Boxers were also opposed to those Chinese who had come under the tutelage of Western influence and recognized that China's salvation lay in the direction of modernization. (A brief, but abortive period of reform—the Hundred Days of 1898—had failed and only intensified the efforts of the Boxers.) From the beginning the rebellion was doomed, and its failure represented perhaps the last gasp of a dying empire, and reaped further disgrace and humiliation for China.

First, Jung Lu, a devoted confidant of the Empress, explains his reasons for opposing the Boxers. In the second selection, the dowager empress describes her role in the uprising and gives her reactions to its failure as reported by the Princess Der Ling, First Lady in Waiting. Then there is the protocol stating the conditions laid down by the allied powers for peace, which the Chinese were "behooved to accept in their entirety." In the last reading, "John Chinaman" (in reality the Britisher, Goldsworthy L. Dickinson) tries to picture the Chinese reaction to the failure and disgrace of the rebellion. What do these readings tell us about the state of mind in China at the turn of the century, and of the effects of the Boxer Rebellion upon that state of mind?

JUNG LU

Opposition to Boxers

[June 22, 1900] at the Hour of the Dog (7–9 P.M.).—I learn that Jung Lu has just sent off a courier with a telegram, which Yüan Shih-K'ai is to send on to the Viceroys of Canton, Nanking and Wuch'ang. Prince Li has sent me a copy, which I am to keep secret; it reads as follows:—

"With all respect I have received your telegrams. Where one weak people dares to oppose ten or more powerful nations, the inevitable result can only be complete ruin. . . . Shall the fate of the Dynasty be staked on a single throw? It requires no peculiar sagacity to see that these Boxers' hopes

---

From J.O.P. Bland and E. Backhouse, *China Under the Empress Dowager* (London: William Heinemann, Ltd., 1910).

of success are nothing but the shadow of a dream. It is true and undeniable that, from Their Majesties on the Throne down to the very lowest of our people, all have suffered from the constant aggression of foreigners and their unceasing insults. For this reason these patriotic train-bands have been organized, claiming a divine mission of retaliation; but the present crisis is all-serious, and although I have used every effort to explain its dangers, I have laboured in vain. . . .

"All the Princes and Ministers of State who surround the Throne now cry out against me with one voice, as your Excellencies can readily believe. I dare not quote in this place the words of Her Majesty, but I may say that the whole of the Imperial family have joined the Boxers, and at least two-thirds of our troops, both Manchu and Chinese, are with them. They swarm in the streets of our capital like a plague of locusts, and it will be extremely difficult to disperse them.

"Even the divine wisdom of Her Majesty is not sufficient to stand against the will of the majority. If Heaven is not on our side how can I oppose its will? For several days past I have been pondering night and day on some way out of our difficulties, some forlorn hope of escape. Therefore yesterday morning (June 20th) I arranged for a meeting with the foreign Ministers at the Tsung-li Yamen, with a view to providing a safe-conduct for the entire foreign community, with my own troops, to Tientsin. This course appeared to me to hold out some reasonable chances of success, but Prince Tuan's soldiery slew the German Minister, and since then the situation continues to develop from hour to hour with such extraordinary rapidity that words fail me to describe it . . . The situation here is well-nigh lost, but it remains for your Excellencies to take all possible steps for the protection of your respective provinces. Let each do his utmost, and let proper secrecy be maintained." Signed "Jung Lu, with tears in his eyes."

DOWAGER EMPRESS TZ'Ū HSI

Do you know I have often thought that I am the most clever woman that ever lived and others cannot compare with

---

From Princess Der Ling, *Two Years in the Forbidden City*, from Harley F. MacNair (ed.), *Modern Chinese History: Selected Readings* (Shanghai: Commercial Press, Limited, 1923).

REPRODUCED WITH PERMISSION, FROM PUNCH.

me. . . . I have 400,000,000 people, all dependent on my judgment. Although I have the Grand Council to consult with, they only look after the different appointments, but anything of an important nature I must decide myself. What does the Emperor know? I have been very successful so far, but I never dreamt that the Boxer movement would end with such serious results for China. That is the only mistake I have made in my life. I should have issued an Edict at once to stop the Boxers practising their belief, but both Prince Tuan and Duke Lan told me that they firmly believed that the Boxers were sent by Heaven to enable China to get rid of all the undesirable and hated foreigners. Of course they meant mostly missionaries, and you know how I hate them and how very religious I always am, so I thought I would not say anything then but would wait and see what would happen. . . .

Prince Tuan then came to my private Palace and told me that the Boxer leader was at the Palace Gate. . . . I immediately became very angry and told him that he had no right to bring any Boxers to the Palace without my permission; but he said that this leader was so powerful that he was able to kill all the foreigners and was not afraid of the foreign guns, as all the gods were protecting him. Prince Tuan told me that he had witnessed this himself. A Boxer shot another with a revolver and the bullet hit him, but did not harm him in the least. . . .

Yung Lu looked grieved when he learned what had taken place at the Palace, and said that these Boxers were nothing but revolutionaries and agitators. They were trying to get the people to help them to kill the foreigners, but he was very much afraid that the result would be against the Government. I told him that probably he was right, and asked him what should be done. He told me that he would talk to Prince Tuan, but the next day Prince Tuan told me that he had had a fight with Yung Lu about the Boxer question, and said that all of Peking had become Boxers, and if we tried to turn them, they would do all they could to kill everyone in Peking, including the Court; that they (the Boxer party) had the day selected to kill all the foreign representatives; that Tung Fou Hsiang, a very conservative General and one of the Boxers, had promised to bring his troops out to help the Boxers to fire on the Legations. When I heard this I was very much worried and anticipated serious trouble, so I sent for Yung Lu at once and kept Prince Tuan with me. Yung Lu came, looking very much worried, and he was more so after I had told him what the Boxers were going to do. He immediately suggested that I should issue an Edict saying that these Boxers were a secret society and that no one should believe their teaching, and to instruct the Generals of the nine gates to drive all the Boxers out of the city at once. When Prince Tuan heard this he was very angry and told Yung Lu that if such an Edict was issued, the Boxers would come to the Court and kill everybody. When Prince Tuan told me this, I thought I had better leave everything to him. After he left the Palace, Yung Lu said that Prince Tuan was absolutely crazy and that he was sure that these Boxers would be the cause of a great deal of trouble. Yung Lu also said that Prince Tuan must be insane to be helping the Boxers to destroy the Legations; that these Boxers were a very common lot, without education, and they imagined the few foreigners in China were the only ones on the earth and if they were killed it would be the end of them. They forgot how very strong these foreign countries are, and that if the foreigners in China were all killed, thousands would come to avenge their death. . . . One day Prince Tuan and Duke Lan came and asked me to issue an Edict ordering the Boxers to kill all the Legation people first and then all remaining foreigners. I was very angry and refused to issue the Edict. . . . He issued these Edicts unknown to me and was responsible for a great many deaths. . . . You need not feel sorry for me for what I have gone through; but you must feel sorry that my fair name is ruined. That is the only mistake I have made in my whole life and it was done in a moment of weakness. Before, I was just like a piece of pure jade; every one admired me for what I have done for my country, but the jade has a flaw in it since this Boxer Movement and it will remain there to the end of my life. I have regretted many, many times that I had such confidence in, and believed that wicked Prince Tuan; he was responsible for everything.

PROTOCOL FOR ENDING THE BOXER REBELLION

During the months of May, June, July, and August of the present year serious disturbances broke out in the northern provinces of China and crimes unprecedented in human history—crimes against the law of nations, against the laws of humanity, and against civilization—were committed under peculiarly odious circumstances. The principal of these crimes were the following:

1. On the 20th of June His Excellency Baron von Ketteler, German Minister, proceeding to the Tsung-li Yamen, was murdered while in the exercise of his official duties by soldiers of the regular army, acting under orders of their chiefs.

2. The same day the foreign legations were attacked and besieged. These attacks continued without intermission until the 14th of August, on which date the arrival of foreign troops put an end to them. These attacks were made by regular troops, who joined the Boxers, and who obeyed orders of the Court, emanating from the Imperial Palace. . . .

3. The 11th of June Mr. Sugiyama, Chancellor of the Legation of Japan, in the discharge of an official mission, was killed by regulars at the gates of the city. At Peking and in several provinces foreigners were murdered, tortured, or attacked by Boxers and regular troops, and only owed their safety to their determined resistance. Their establishments were pillaged and destroyed.

4. Foreign cemeteries, at Peking, especially, were desecrated, the graves opened, the remains scattered abroad. These events led the foreign Powers to send their troops to China in order to protect the lives of their Representatives and their nationals, and to restore order. During their march to Peking the Allied Forces met with the resistance of the Chinese armies and had to overcome it by force. China having recognized her responsibility, expressed her regrets, and manifested the desire to see an end put to the situation created by the disturbances referred to, the Powers have decided to accede to her request on the irrevocable conditions enumer-

---

From William W. Rockhill (ed.), *Treaties and Conventions with or concerning China and Korea, 1894-1904* (Washington, D.C.: Government Printing Office, 1904).

ated below, which they deem indispensable to expiate the crimes committed and to prevent their recurrence:

1. *(a)* Dispatch to Berlin of an extraordinary mission, headed by an Imperial Prince, to express the regrets of His Majesty the Emperor of China, and of the Chinese Government, for the murder of His Excellency the late Baron von Ketteler, German Minister.

(b) Erection on the place where the murder was committed of a commemorative monument suitable to the rank of the deceased, bearing an inscription in the Latin, German, and Chinese languages, expressing the regrets of the Emperor of China for the murder.

2. The severest punishment in proportion to their crimes for the persons designated in the Imperial decree of September 25, 1900, and for those whom the Representatives of the Powers shall subsequently designate. . . .

3. Honorable reparation shall be made by the Chinese Government to the Japanese Government for the murder of Mr. Sugiyama, Chancellor of the Japanese Legation.

4. An expiatory monument shall be erected by the Imperial Chinese Government in each of the foreign or international cemeteries which have been desecrated and in which the graves have been destroyed.

5. Maintenance, under conditions to be settled between the Powers, of the prohibition of the importation of arms as well as of material used exclusively for the manufacturing of arms and ammunition.

6. Equitable indemnities for governments, societies, companies, and private individuals, as well as for Chinese who have suffered during the late events in person or in property in consequence of their being in the service of foreigners. China shall adopt financial measures acceptable to the Powers for the purpose of guaranteeing the payment of said indemnities and the interest and amortization of the loans.

7. Right for each Power to maintain a permanent guard for its legation and to put the legation quarter in a defensible condition. Chinese shall not have the right to reside in this quarter.

8. The Taku and other forts, which might impede free communication between Peking and the sea, shall be razed.

9. Right of military occupation of certain points, to be determined by an understanding between the Powers, for

keeping open communication between the capital and the sea.

10. *(a)* The Chinese Government shall cause to be published during two years in all subprefectures an Imperial decree embodying:

Perpetual prohibition, under pain of death, of membership in any antiforeign society; . . .

(b) An Imperial decree shall be issued and published everywhere in the Empire declaring that all Governors-General, Governors, and Provincial or local officials shall be responsible for order in their respective jurisdictions, and that whenever fresh antiforeign disturbances or any other treaty infractions occur, which are not forthwith suppressed and the guilty persons punished, they, the said officials, shall be immediately removed and forever prohibited from holding any office or honors.

11. The Chinese Government will undertake to negotiate the amendments to the treaties of commerce and navigation considered useful by the Powers, and upon other subjects connected with commercial relations, with the object of facilitating them.

12. The Chinese Government shall undertake to reform the Office of Foreign Affairs and to modify the court ceremonial relative to the reception of foreign Representatives in the manner which the Powers shall indicate.

Until the Chinese Government has complied with the above to the satisfaction of the Powers, the Undersigned can hold out no expectation that the occupation of Peking and the Province of Chihli by the general forces can be brought to a conclusion.

Peking, December 22, 1900.

For Germany,	A. MUMM.
For Austria-Hungary,	M. CZIKANN.
For Belgium,	JOOSTENS.
For Spain,	B. J. DE COLOGAN.
For United States of America,	E. H. CONGER.
For France,	S. PICHON.
For Great Britain,	ERNEST SATOW.
For Italy,	SALVAGO RAGGI.
For Japan,	T. NISSI.
For Netherlands,	F. M. KNOBEL.
For Russia,	MICHEL DE GIERS.

GOLDSWORTHY L. DICKINSON ("JOHN CHINAMAN")

Chinese Response to the Boxer Treaty As Imagined by a Westerner

Consider for a moment the conditions you have imposed on a proud and ancient empire, an empire which for centuries has believed itself to be at the head of civilization. You have compelled us, against our will, to open our ports to your trade; you have forced us to permit the introduction of a drug which we believe is ruining our people; you have exempted your subjects residing among us from the operation of our laws; you have appropriated our coasting traffic; you claim the traffic of our inland waters. Every attempt on our part to resist your demands has been followed by new claims and new aggressions. And yet all this time you have posed as civilized peoples dealing with barbarians. You have compelled us to receive your missionaries, and when they by their ignorant zeal have provoked our people to rise in mass against them, that again you have made an excuse for new depredations, till we, not unnaturally, have come to believe that the cross is the pioneer of the sword, and that the only use you have for your religion is to use it as a weapon of war. Conceive for a moment the feelings of an Englishman subjected to similar treatment; conceive that we had permanently occupied Liverpool, Bristol, Plymouth; that we had planted on your territory thousands of men whom we had exempted from your laws; that along your coasts and navigable rivers our vessels were driving out yours; that we had insisted on your admitting spirits duty free to the manifest ruin of your population; and that we had planted in all your principal towns agents to counteract the teachings of your Church and undermine the whole fabric of habitual belief on which the stability of your society depends. Imagine that you had to submit to all this. Would you be so greatly surprised, would you really even be indignant, if you found one day the Chinese Legation surrounded by a howling mob and Confucian missionaries everywhere hunted to death? What right then have you to be

---

From Goldsworthy L. Dickinson, *Letters from a Chinese Official: Being an Eastern View of Western Civilization* (New York: McClure, Phillips, 1907). Published in 1901 (London: R.B. Johnson) as *Letters from John Chinaman.*

surprised, what right have you to be indignant at even the worst that has taken place in China? What is there so strange or monstrous in our conduct? A Legation, you say, is sacrosanct by the law of nations. Yes; but remember that it was at the point of the sword that you forced us to receive Embassies whose presence we have always regarded as a sign of national humiliation. But our mobs were barbarous and cruel. Alas! Yes. And your troops? And your troops, nations of Christendom? Ask the once fertile land from Peking to the coast; ask the corpses of murdered men and outraged women and children; ask the innocent mingled indiscriminately with the guilty; ask the Christ, the lover of men, whom you profess to serve, to judge between us who rose in mad despair to save our country and you who, avenging crime with crime, did not pause to reflect that the crime you avenged was the fruit of your own iniquity!

Well, it is over—over, at least, for the moment. I do not wish to dwell upon the past.

• 8 •

Sun Yat-sen Plans a New China

Dr. Sun Yat-sen was a member of that first generation which came to maturity under the influence and impact of Western ideas. He was expelled from China for engaging in revolutionary activities, and joined a group of anti-Manchu Chinese in Japan where he witnessed China's humiliation in the Sino-Japanese War, Boxer Rebellion, and Russo-Japanese War. It was the dynasty's role in the Boxer Rebellion that convinced this group that Chinese political institutions were not then capable of taking the necessary steps toward modernization. Revolution—not reform—was the answer.

When the dynasty was overthrown in 1912, the revolutionaries called Dr. Sun back from abroad where he was trying to raise money from overseas Chinese for the revolution. He became the head of China's first republic, and maintained a position of leadership intermittently until his death in 1925. He founded his party, the Kuomintang (Nationalist), along the lines of Western parliamentary political parties. During his tenure in office, he was faced with the overwhelming problem of unity, but he began to design plans that would make China the equal of Western nations, and that would enable China to prosper.

In the interview reprinted here, Dr. Sun talks about how he hopes to put his plans into effect. In the second selection, Dr. Sun outlines the Three Principles of the Kuomintang—his hope for the salvation of China. Can you detect the influence of Western ideas in Dr. Sun's thinking? Can you find any traces of traditional Chinese thought? Why do you think this plan had appeal? Were the Three Principles a valid answer to China's problems? Why is Dr. Sun considered a hero today by all Chinese?

SUN YAT-SEN

(An Interview)

At last the doctor entered and shook hands with me. Grave and pensive, he gave one the impression of a frock-coated, Protestant pastor; of medium height and with a high forehead, he seemed a little older than his portraits had led one to expect, but no more than his real age, forty-six. . . .

We chatted for some time, and I will set down only those remarks that applied to his economic plans, at that time the subject of popular curiosity.

"You are blamed," I remarked, "for planning things on too grand a scale; six hundred and forty million pounds to be spent on railways seems a stupendous undertaking, and you are no doubt aware that it has been severely criticized!"

"No doubt," he replied, "but you must remember that the realization of my plan will take time. In announcing it, I could only sketch an ideal programme. I have been blamed," he continued, smiling, "for not having given any details. Every Chinese enterprise gives rise to so much competition that it is impossible to satisfy everybody, and there cannot fail to be critics!"

Reprinted with permission of Gerald Duckworth and Co. Ltd., from Fernand Farjenal, *Through the Chinese Revolution*, Margaret Vivian (tr.) (London, 1915).

"You propose, do you not, to seek the co-operation of foreigners, and it is in this connection that difficulties arise?"

"Certainly," he replied; "all the republican leaders who understand such matters are fully convinced that the best way to hasten the advent of our prosperity, and the exploitation of our native wealth, is to seek the help of foreign capitalists. We are ready to concede to them a maximum of advantages, but on the sole condition that none of the concessions granted by us shall be employed for political ends."

The conspirator in Sun Yat-sen here made his appearance. "It is a fact," he exclaimed, "that every time we have sought to make terms with foreigners they have used us as coinage to pay the expenses of diplomatic ventures. We have fought against the dynasty, because it was dragging us, little by little, into a state of complete servitude. This was the real cause of the revolution, and it is patriotic sentiments that have enabled us to triumph. The movement actually began on account of a dispute regarding a railway. Today, however, we are in hopes that the world at large will understand our attitude, and that those who provide us with funds will be satisfied with reasonable profits, which we shall discuss beforehand."

These remarks seemed to me most reasonable, but I wondered to myself whether the famous Chinese patriot was not assuming too much.

(The Three Principles of the People)

The Principles of the Kuomintang are no other than the Three Principles of the people. . . .

(1) *The Principle of Nationalism.*

There are two aspects to this principle—namely, self-emancipation of the Chinese nation and equality of all races within Chinese territory.

(a) The principle of nationalism seeks to make China a free and independent nation. . . .

(b) . . . The *Kuomintang* solemnly declares . . . that after the completion of the National Revolution a free and united

---

Reprinted with permission of The Sylvan Press, from "Manifesto of the First National Congress, January 30th, 1924," quoted in N. Gangulee (ed.), *The Teachings of Sun Yat-sen* (London, 1945).

Republic of China, based on the voluntary union of all races, will be established.

(2) *The Principle of Popular Sovereignty.*

This principle envisages a system of direct popular authority in addition to that of indirect popular authority; that is to say, the people will enjoy the rights of election, initiative, referendum and recall. . . . The so-called modern system of popular government is often a monopoly of the property class, to be used as an instrument of oppression, whereas the principle of popular sovereignty is for the masses and not for the few. . . .

(3) *The Principle of the People's Livelihood.*

This principle contains two fundamental aspects—equalization of land and regulation of capital. Since the right of owning land is controlled by a few, the State should enact a land law, a law for the utilization of land, a land expropriation law, a land taxation law. Private landowners shall declare the value of their land to the government. It shall be taxed according to the value so declared and the government may buy it at that price in case of necessity. Private industries, whether belonging to Chinese or foreign nationals, which are either monopolistic in character or beyond the capacity of private individuals to develop—such as banking, railways, and navigation—shall be undertaken by the State, so that private-owned capital shall not control the economic life of the people.

China is an agricultural country, and the peasants are the class that have suffered most. The *Kuomintang* stands for the policy that those peasants owning no land should be given land by the State for cultivation. . . . The livelihood of Chinese labourers being unprotected by any sort of guarantee, the State should find remedies for the unemployment and enact labour laws to improve their livelihood. Other auxiliary measures such as those relating to the support of the aged, care of the young, relief of the sick and disabled, the dissemination of knowledge, shall be prosecuted until they are carried into effect.

In China today . . . poor peasants and overworked labourers are to be found everywhere. Because of the sufferings which they have undergone and their aspirations for liberation, there is in both of them a powerful will to revolt against imperialism. Therefore the success of the National Revolution depends upon the participation of the peasants and the labourers of the whole country. . . .

• 9 •

Chinese Nationalism: The May Fourth Movement

The May Fourth Movement began as a student demonstration in Peking against the treaty drawn up at the Paris Peace Conference in 1919. Once more the Chinese felt they had been cheated, disgraced, and humiliated as Germany's spheres of influence in China were handed over to Japan, and Western imperialism attempted to renew its hold on China. Warlordism had factionalized the new Republic, and the weakened regime in Peking had meekly accepted the terms of the treaty. What was at first a public expression of indignation, motivated by youthful patriotism, soon became a ground swell of nationalist feeling, affecting all classes of people and all areas of Chinese life. It was this movement that marked an abrupt shift from attitudes of the past, and paved the way for the revolutionary movements that were determined to place China squarely in the modern world as an equal, sovereign state. One Chinese student manifesto described this feeling:

> ". . . We now approach a crisis in which our country is threatened with subjugation and her territory is going to be ceded. If her people still cannot unite in indignation in a twelfth-hour effort to save her, they are indeed the worthless race of the twentieth century. They should not be regarded as human beings. Are there not some of our brethren who cannot bear the torture of being slaves and beasts of burden and steadfastly desire to save their country? Then the urgent things we should do right now are to hold citizens' meetings, to make public speeches, and to send telegrams to the government in support of our stand. As for those who willingly and traitorously

sell out our country to the enemy, as a last resort we shall have to rely on pistols and bombs to deal with them. Our country is in imminent peril—its fate hangs on a thread! We appeal to you to join our struggle."*

Hu Shih, a key figure in the movement, discusses its significance from an intellectual and cultural point of view.

HU SHIH

The Renaissance was the name given by a group of Peking University students to a new monthly magazine which they published in 1918. They were mature students well trained in the old cultural tradition of the country, and they readily recognized in the new movement then led by some of their professors a striking similarity to the Renaissance in Europe. Three prominent features in the movement reminded them of the European Renaissance. First, it was a conscious movement to promote a new literature in the living language of the people to take the place of the classical literature of old. Second, it was a movement of conscious protest against many of the ideas and institutions in the traditional culture, and of conscious emancipation of the individual man and woman from the bondage of the forces of tradition. It was a movement of reason versus tradition, freedom versus authority, and glorification of life and human values versus their suppression. And lastly, strangely enough, this new movement was led by men who knew their cultural heritage and tried to study it with the new methodology of modern historical criticism and research. In that sense it was also a humanist movement. In all these directions the new movement which began in 1917 and which was sometimes called the "New Culture Movement," the "New Thought" movement, or "The New Tide," was capturing the imagination and sympathy of the youth of the nation as something which promised and pointed to the new birth of an old people and an old civilization. . . .

Reprinted with permission of Paragon Book Reprint Corp., from Hu Shih, *The Chinese Renaissance* (New York, 1963).

* Chow Tse-tung, *The May Fourth Movement* (Cambridge, Mass.: Harvard University Press, 1960), pp. 107-108.

The Renaissance movement of the last two decades differs from all the early movements in being a fully conscious and studied movement. Its leaders know what they want, and they know what they must destroy in order to achieve what they want. They want a new language, a new literature, a new outlook on life and society, and a new scholarship. They want a new language, not only as an effective instrument for popular education, but also as the effective medium for the development of the literature of a new China. They want a literature that shall be written in the living tongue of a living people and shall be capable of expressing the real feelings, thoughts, inspirations, and aspirations of a growing nation. They want to instill into the people a new outlook on life which shall free them from the shackles of tradition and make them feel at home in the new world and its new civilization. They want a new scholarship which shall not only enable us to understand intelligently the cultural heritage of the past, but also prepare us for active participation in the work of research in the modern sciences. This, as I understand it, is the mission of the Chinese Renaissance.

The conscious element in this movement is the result of long contact with the people and civilization of the West. It is only through contact and comparison that the relative value or worthlessness of the various cultural elements can be clearly and critically seen and understood. . . .

. . . I began to study the history of our literature with a new interest and with a new methodology. I tried to study it from the evolutionary standpoint and, to my great surprise and unlimited joy, the historical development of Chinese literature presented to me a continuous though entirely unconscious movement of struggle against the despotic limitations of the classical tradition, a continuous tendency to produce a literature in the living language of the people. I found that the history of Chinese literature consisted of two parallel movements: there was the classical literature of the scholars, the men of letters, the poets of the imperial courts, and of the élite; but there was in every age an undercurrent of literary development among the common people which produced the folk songs of love and heroism, the songs of the dancer, the epic stories of the street reciter, the drama of the village theater, and, most important of all, the novels. I found that every new form, every innovation in literature, had come never from the imitative classical writers of the upper classes, but always from the unlettered class of the countryside, the village inn, and the marketplace. I found that it was always these new forms and patterns of the common people that, from time to time, furnished the new blood and fresh vigor to the literature of the literati, and rescued it from the perpetual danger of fossilization. . . .

Then an unexpected event occurred which suddenly carried the literary movement to a rapid success. The Peace Conference in Paris had just decided to sacrifice China's claims and give to Japan the freedom to dispose of the former German possessions in the province of Shantung. When the news reached China, the students in Peking, under the leadership of the students of the Peking University, held a mass meeting of protest and, in their demonstration parade, broke into the house of a pro-Japanese minister, set fire to the house, and beat the Chinese minister to Tokyo almost to death. The government arrested a number of the students, but public sentiment ran so high that the whole nation seemed on the side of the university students and against the notoriously pro-Japanese Government. The merchants in Shanghai and other cities closed their shops as a protest against the peace negotiations and against the government. The Chinese Delegation at the Paris Conference was warned by public bodies not to sign the treaty; and they obeyed. The government was forced by this strong demonstration of national sentiment to release the students and to dismiss from office three well-known pro-Japanese ministers. The struggle began on May 4, and lasted till the final surrender of the government in the first part of June. It has been called the "May Fourth Movement." . . .

. . . All of a sudden, the revolution in literature had spread throughout the country, and the youths of the nation were finding in the new literary medium an effective means of expression. Everybody seemed to be rushing to express himself in this language which he could understand and in which he could make himself understood. In the course of a few years, the literary revolution had succeeded in giving to the people a national language, and had brought about a new age of literary expression.

WHEN A FELLER NEEDS A FRIEND

1922

REPRINTED WITH PERMISSION, FROM SAN FRANCISCO CHRONICLE.

Do you think this cartoon accurately illustrates the problems the Chinese had to face during the years following World War I?

• 10 •

The Aims and Tactics of Revolution

Marxism and communism entered the Chinese scene as a result of the influx of Western ideas which were part of the literary renaissance, and as a result of Sun Yat-sen's efforts to receive the aid of foreign governments in assisting China's reformation. Communist Russia seemed to be the only nation bent on condemning the imperialists and in fact rescinded its concessions in China, temporarily. The mere fact of the Russian Revolution and its professed aims had tremendous effect not only on the Chinese, but on most other areas under the control of the West. The Chinese Communist Party was formed in 1921, and early became a pawn in the power struggle going on in the Comintern between Stalin and Trotsky. The party formed a temporary alliance with the Kuomintang, itself reorganized along Leninist lines. In 1927, Chiang Kai-shek, Sun's successor, purged the Kuomintang of Communists. This debacle for the Communists was mainly the result of horrendous political advice from their Russian advisers.

After Chiang's "white terror," the Communists were forced to flee from urban areas into the countryside and mountains. It was here that new methods had to be devised, and that a new leader emerged. Here also, during the course of their experiments in the countryside, the Communists first achieved success, and laid the foundation for their continuing struggle with Chiang and the Kuomintang.

In these selections from his works, Mao discusses two major strains in the Communist movement: anti-imperialism, and the importance of the peasants. Do you think his account of China's recent history is accurate? Were there any similarities or differences between his tactics and those employed in the Russian Revolution? What do you think was the appeal of Maoism to the peasants?

MAO TSE-TUNG

Condemnation of the West—1927

The imperialist powers started many wars of aggression against China as, for example, the Opium War launched by Britain in 1840 . . . the Eight-Power Allied Army in 1900. Having defeated China in war, they not only occupied many states bordering on China that were under her protection, but seized or "leased" part of her territory. For example, Japan occupied Taiwan and the Pescadores and "leased" Port Arthur, Britain seized Hongkong, and France "leased" Kwangchow Wan. Apart from these territorial annexations they exacted from China huge sums of indemnities.

They forced China to conclude numerous unequal treaties by which they acquired the right to station their land and sea forces in China and to enjoy consular jurisdiction, and China has even been divided up into spheres of influence among a number of imperialist powers.

The imperialists have gained control of all the important trading ports in China by unequal treaties and have marked off parts of many of these ports as concessions under their direct administration. . . .

The imperialist powers are also running many light and heavy industries in China in order to make immediate use of China's raw materials and cheap labour, thereby directly exerting economic pressure on China's own industries and hampering the development of her productive forces. . . .

The imperialist powers supply the reactionary government in China with large quantities of arms and ammunition and a host of military advisers in order to foment the mixed fight among the warlords and oppress the Chinese people.

Besides, the imperialist powers have never slackened their efforts to poison the minds of the Chinese people, that is, to carry out a policy of cultural aggression. Carrying on missionary activities, establishing hospitals and schools, publishing newspapers and enticing Chinese students to study abroad, are the ways this policy is implemented. Their aim is

From Mao Tse-tung, "Report of An Investigation into the Peasant Movement in Hunan (1927)," *Selected Works of Mao Tse-tung* (New York: International Publishers, 1954), Vol. I.

to train intellectuals to serve their interests and to fool the great masses of the Chinese people.

The Question of "Going too Far"—1927

There is another section of people who say, "Although the peasant association ought to be formed, it has gone rather too far in its present actions." This is the opinion of the middle-of-the-roaders. But how do matters stand in reality? True, the peasants do in some ways "act unreasonably" in the countryside. The peasant association, supreme in authority, does not allow the landlords to have their say and makes a clean sweep of all their prestige. This is tantamount to trampling the landlords underfoot after knocking them down. The peasants threaten: "Put you in the special register"; they impose fines on the local bullies and bad gentry and demand contributions; they smash their sedan-chairs. Crowds of people swarm into the homes of the local bullies and bad gentry who oppose the peasant association, slaughtering their pigs and consuming their grain. They may even loll for a minute or two on the ivory beds of the young mesdames and mademoiselles in the families of the bullies and gentry. At the slightest provocation they make arrests, crown the arrested with tall paper-hats, and parade them through the villages: "You bad gentry, now you know who we are!" Doing whatever they like and turning everything upside down, they have even created a kind of terror in the countryside. This is what some people call "going too far," or "going beyond the proper limit to right a wrong," or "really too outrageous."

The opinion of this group, reasonable on the surface, is erroneous at bottom.

First, the things described above have all been the inevitable results of the doings of the local bullies and bad gentry and lawless landlords themselves. For ages these people, with power in their hands, tyrannised over the peasants and trampled them underfoot; that is why the peasants have now risen in such a great revolt. The most formidable revolts and the most serious troubles invariably occur at places where the local bullies and bad gentry and the lawless landlords were

From Mao Tse-tung, "Report of An Investigation into The Peasant Movement in Hunan (1927)," *Selected Works of Mao Tse-tung* (New York: International Publishers, 1954), Vol. I.

the most ruthless in their evil deeds. The peasants' eyes are perfectly discerning. As to who is bad and who is not, who is the most ruthless and who is less so, and who is to be severely punished and who is to be dealt with lightly, the peasants keep perfectly clear accounts and very seldom has there been any discrepancy between the punishment and the crime.

Secondly, a revolution is not the same as inviting people to dinner, or writing an essay, or painting a picture, or doing fancy needlework; it cannot be anything so refined, so calm and gentle, or so mild, kind, courteous, restrained and magnanimous. A revolution is an uprising, an act of violence whereby one class overthrows another. A rural revolution is a revolution by which the peasantry overthrows the authority of the feudal landlord class. If the peasants do not use the maximum of their strength, they can never overthrow the authority of the landlords which has been deeply rooted for thousands of years. In the rural areas, there must be a great, fervent revolutionary upsurge, which alone can arouse hundreds and thousands of the people to form a great force. All the actions mentioned above, labelled as "going too far," are caused by the power of the peasants, generated by a great, fervent, revolutionary upsurge in the countryside. Such actions were quite necessary in the second period of the peasant movement (the period of revolutionary action). In this period, it was necessary to establish the absolute authority of the peasants. It was necessary to stop malicious criticisms against the peasant association. It was necessary to overthrow all the authority of the gentry, to knock them down and even trample them underfoot. All actions labelled as "going too far" had a revolutionary significance in the second period. To put it bluntly, it was necessary to bring about a brief reign of terror in every rural area; otherwise one could never suppress the activities of the counter-revolutionaries in the countryside or overthrow the authority of the gentry. To right a wrong it is necessary to exceed the proper limits, and the wrong cannot be righted without the proper limits being exceeded.

• 11 •

The Decades of Turmoil

The first half of the twentieth century were years of chaos for the Chinese. Rebellion, revolution, warlordism, civil war, foreign aggression, renewed civil war—these were the events that marked these decades. China meanwhile continued to be exploited by the imperialists, in spite of certain concessions made. While China's leaders were trying to forge a new social order, apparently against insurmountable odds, the Chinese people continued to suffer.

Each of the following group of readings surveys some aspect of the Chinese scene during these years. The first selection, by the noted British author, William Somerset Maugham, describes that pathetic figure, the Chinese coolie. Anne Morrow Lindbergh next describes the flood-ravaged areas she and her husband witnessed from the skies in 1931. A Chinese village on the verge of famine is observed by Nikos Kazantzakis, the Greek author who traveled in China in 1935. Finally, two American correspondents, Theodore H. White and Annalee Jacoby, describe peasant life during the war years. What do you find to be the cumulative effect of these essays? Do these authors find anything changing in China? Anything of durable value?

W. SOMERSET MAUGHAM (1922)

The Beast of Burden

At first when you see the coolie on the road, bearing his load, it is as a pleasing object that he strikes the eye. In his blue rags, a blue of all colours from indigo to turquoise and

---

then to the paleness of a milky sky, he fits the landscape. He seems exactly right as he trudges along the narrow causeway between the rice fields or climbs a green hill. His clothing consists of no more than a short coat and a pair of trousers; and if he had a suit which was at the beginning all of a piece, he never thinks when it comes to patching to choose a bit of stuff of the same colour. He takes anything that comes handy. From sun and rain he protects his head with a straw hat shaped like an extinguisher with a preposterously wide, flat brim.

You see a string of coolies come along, one after the other, each with a pole on his shoulders from the ends of which hang two great bales, and they make an agreeable pattern. It is amusing to watch their hurrying reflections in the paddy water. You watch their faces as they pass you. They are good-natured faces and frank, you would have said, if it had not been drilled into you that the oriental is inscrutable; and when you see them lying down with their loads under a banyan tree by a wayside shrine, smoking and chatting gaily, if you have tried to lift the bales they carry for thirty miles or more a day, it seems natural to feel admiration for their endurance and their spirit. But you will be thought somewhat absurd if you mention your admiration to the old residents of China. You will be told with a tolerant shrug of the shoulders that the coolies are animals and for two thousand years from father to son have carried burdens, so it is no wonder if they do it cheerfully. And indeed you can see for yourself that they begin early, for you will encounter little children with a yoke on their shoulders staggering under the weight of vegetable baskets.

The day wears on and it grows warmer. The coolies take off their coats and walk stripped to the waist. Then sometimes in a man resting for an instant, his load on the ground but the pole still on his shoulders so that he has to rest slightly crouched, you see the poor tired heart beating against the ribs: you see it as plainly as in some cases of heart disease in the out-patients' room of a hospital. It is strangely distressing to watch. Then also you see the coolies' backs. The pressure of the pole for long years, day after day, has made hard red scars, and sometimes even there are open sores, great sores without bandages or dressing that rub against the wood; but the strangest thing of all is that sometimes, as though nature sought to adapt man for these cruel uses to which he is put, an odd malformation seems to have arisen so that there is a sort of hump, like a camel's, against which the pole rests. But beating heart or angry sore, bitter rain or burning sun notwithstanding, they go on eternally, from dawn till dusk, year in year out, from childhood to the extreme of age. You see old men without an ounce of fat on their bodies, their skin loose on their bones, wizened, their little faces wrinkled and apelike, with hair thin and grey; and they totter under their burdens to the edge of the grave in which at last they shall have rest. And still the coolies go, not exactly running, but not walking either, sidling quickly, with their eyes on the ground to choose the spot to place their feet, and on their faces a strained, anxious expression. You can make no longer a pattern of them as they wend their way. Their effort oppresses you. You are filled with a useless compassion.

In China it is man that is the beast of burden.

"To be harassed by the wear and tear of life, and to pass rapidly through it without the possibility of arresting one's course,—is not this pitiful indeed? To labour without ceasing, and then, without living to enjoy the fruit, worn out, to depart, suddenly, one knows not whither,—is not that a just cause for grief?"

So wrote the Chinese mystic.

ANNE MORROW LINDBERGH (1931)

The Floods

Looking down on it from the air on our flight to Nanking, we saw that there was nothing to stop a flood. Flat fields for miles and miles—and the great massive river. . . . The Yangtze valley, despite the immense expanse of land, still seems crowded. Every inch of ground is cultivated, not in big tracts, like our farms, but in narrow strips of rice fields, slivering off at right angles to the river. No wild land, no forests; just thin back-yard strips of field with occasionally a crowded village of mud huts, representing thousands of people.

One did not have to be told that this was a land in which there could be no waste; that people here lived literally from day to day; that there was no "extra" stored away; that even the shucks of the crop and the dry grass were saved for fuel, because the trees had gone long ago.

This was the type of country into which the floods came, destroying crops, homes, and people. . . .

Flying lower we could see suggestions of what the land was like under the flood: fields under water; hundreds of small villages standing in water, many of them up to their roofs; towns whose dykes and walls had given way, whose streets were canals; in some places, nothing but the tops of a few trees, with here and there a smear of brown on the surface, where a dyke or a road or a mud village had once been. In this last territory one dared not think how many lives had been lost. There was no trace left. In less badly flooded country the people had built up temporary mud dykes around their villages and pulled inside their first crop. But it was a hopeless fight. For these hastily slapped-up walls, guarding a group of huts and a rescued grain stack, were rapidly crumbling before the constant lapping of little waves, whipped up by the wind.

There was no dry land for miles around. Most of the people who were near enough to the border to escape had crowded into the outlying cities. Thousands of refugees had put up temporary grass shelters along the dykes lining the Grand Canal and on an uncompleted road just south of the flooded area. But there were thousands more who would never get out, who, their homes completely destroyed, were living in flat-bottomed sampans, with a grass roof rigged up in one end for shelter. Moored in the old streets or floating about the flooded fields, these refugees were apparently living only on the few straws of grain they had saved and what fish they might catch.

The small sampan driven by oar or pole seemed to be the only possible means of transportation in this vast area. Looking down on them, myriads of gnats on the surface of the water, we began to realize the hopelessness of the situation. How could relief ever reach these people? The water was not deep enough for large boats. There were no roads and probably never had been. There were almost no large centers from which food could be distributed, just thousands of small isolated villages—or what remained of them—stretched out over an area larger than Massachusetts.

Some things could be and were being done by the Relief Commission. Food could be taken to the refugee camps in or near the few larger centers, and, what was even more needed, medical supplies and assistance to stop the epidemics which inevitably follow a flood. We could not help to carry food, as the weight would be prohibitive in a plane; but we could perhaps carry medical supplies and a doctor.

My husband was trying to do this the day he set out for Hinghwa. We had seen the walled city from the air on our first day's flight. It was marooned in the center of a large flooded area; the nearest dry ground was more than twenty-five miles to the south. Medical aid, the Commission felt, was probably as badly needed there as anywhere, and it would be a good center for distribution. So one morning my husband took off from Nanking, carrying with him in the plane a Chinese doctor, an American doctor, and several packages of medical supplies. I had given up my place to one doctor. The baggage compartment had been cleared of much emergency equipment to lighten the load and make room for the second.

In less than an hour they completed a trip which would have taken days by canal. The plane landed on flooded fields outside the city walls. A few stray sampans were the only signs of life on the calm waters. The Chinese doctor, who was to land with supplies, waved at them and finally persuaded one boat to pull up alongside. Others straggled behind curiously. Slowly the doctor climbed down out of the cockpit and stepped from the pontoon into the sampan. Carefully a package of medicines was handed down after him. An old woman took it in her arms, put it down on the floor of the sampan, and sat on it firmly.

There was a stir of curiosity in the surrounding boats. By now there were ten or twenty of them poling about. Men, women, and children, sullen and hungry, looked at the package and began to murmur among themselves. "Food," they were saying, "there must be food in the box." They pushed forward and soon surrounded the doctor's boat as it poled out. Others pressed nearer the plane.

My husband stood up in the cockpit and motioned them back. (One of the heavy prows could easily knock a hole in our pontoons.) But they paid no attention to him. And there were more sampans coming every minute, attracted by the strange craft. They sprang up from nowhere like flies on a summer day. The American doctor began to shout to them in Chinese, telling them to keep back. But the starving people were thinking only of one thing. They made cups out of their hands and pretended to be eating with chopsticks. "The foreigners must understand now; we want food." The word spread like fire leaping across a field in a high wind. It reached the outer circle of boats, and people began jumping from one boat to another toward the plane. For they could no longer pole any nearer. There were literally hundreds of sampans now, boat jammed against boat on all sides. The nearest were right under the wings and tail surfaces. A sampan under the left wing had a small fire dangerously near its grass hood. Shouting, either in English or Chinese, had no effect and—worse still—there were even more coming. In the distance one could see a solid stream of boats rounding the city wall.

"Have you a gun?" the American doctor shouted.

"Yes—" said my husband, "a thirty-eight revolver—but someone in that crowd"—looking out at thousands of sullen and desperate faces—"may have a rifle—probably several—fatal to show a gun in a crowd like that."

Nevertheless he hid it under his parachute, planning not to use it unless they started to board the plane. People were hanging on to wings, pontoons, and tail surfaces but no one had yet actually tried to climb on.

Suddenly a man stood up and put his foot on the left pontoon. As though at a signal the rest surged forward. Now a man was on the other pontoon. They had begun to board.

My husband grabbed his revolver and covered the nearest man. He stopped but did not move back. My husband turned to the right side. Those faced with the gun hesitated, but the men on the other side moved up. He whipped the gun from the right side to the left quickly, shooting straight up in the air as he turned. Each side thought someone had been shot on the other. He moved it back and forth quickly, covering always the nearest person. Slowly they edged back. . . .

The American doctor in the meantime was hauling up the anchor as fast as he could. There was no time to stow it in the pontoon anchor-hatch, where it usually fitted in the neat coils of rope. He stuffed it, rope and all, in the baggage compartment, and started to climb in on top. They were clear, ready to go.

No—there was a single sampan just in front of the plane, an old man and an old woman poling it. My husband raised himself up in the cockpit and covered them with his gun. The American doctor jumped out on the wing and shouted, "Get out of the way! We'll kill you!"

They made no move. The old woman looked up sullenly, "What does it matter?" she said slowly. "We have nothing."

The plane swung slightly in the wind, pointing clear of the of the sampan. My husband pressed the starter. The engine caught—an answering roar. They took off dead ahead, over flooded fields, between fences, collapsed roofs, and grave-mounds, regardless of wind direction—anything to get off, to shake that trailing wake of hundreds of sampans, those arms paddling as fast as they could in a vain attempt to follow. . . .

Looking down on the spot they had just left, the men in the plane were acutely conscious of the miracle of their escape. A moment before they had been down in that crowd of starving people, some of whom might live until spring; many would die before the waters receded. . . . The fliers had crossed over from one world to another as easily, as swiftly, as one crosses from the world of nightmare to the world of reality in the flash of waking.

NIKOS KAZANTZAKIS (1935)

A Chinese Village

One day I went to a small Chinese village in order to try my psychic and physical endurance. Low houses built of mud and straw crowded in the middle of an endless mud-colored plain and through them passed the river, moving slowly. Half-naked men and women dipped in the river up to their waists and brought water in pails to water their rice fields. Pigs and children happily wallowed in mud. A corpse of a dog at the end of the water rotted, full of worms and crabs. And next to the corpse in the flaming sun, the Chinese slept with their mouths open, and between their sparse yellow teeth flies went in and out. . . .

Life is really hard, I think, as I walk in this ghastly village where you can't see even a single person laughing, not even a flower in a pot nor a bird anywhere. Outside of every door there are two pails full of human excrement. Sometimes at the door yellow figures appear, anxious to see that the pails are still there and have not been stolen by the neighbors. When they are filled, they hang them at the ends of a thick cane; they take them across their shoulders and empty them on their rice fields.

Naked children, like erect piglets, covered with mud, make a circle around me; others deride me and touch me; others hold stones in their hands. Their glance is full of poison; if looks could kill, I would be lost. Red papers with thick black letters on the walls. The urchins point them out to me and look at me hard. I wonder what these letters say. I secretly unglue one and put it in my pocket. When I went to Nanking I showed it to a Chinese whom I knew. "What does this paper say?" I asked. "Death to foreigners!" . . .

The sun sets, the ragged beggars crawl on the streets, dig the garbage, look secretly from the doors, seek to find something to eat or to steal. Others, naked, covered with straw below the waist; others heavily loaded with all their rags. Whatever they own they carry; whatever they find they pass through their belt—old shoes, cucumbers, penknives, cans, bells. Old men and women, tall and husky young men, girls seven and eight years old, naked. Lame lepers with missing hands. The blind go one after the other, they make up gangs and pass through the villages; they clear the streets; many fall dead of starvation on the way. Stench and hunger—these are the two greatest deities of China; Confucius, Lao-tze and Buddha do not have so many followers.

THEODORE H. WHITE and ANNALEE JACOBY

A Peasant Village

The village is a cluster of adobe huts and shelters. If it is a large village, there is a wall of mud and rubble round it; a small village consists of ten or twelve houses clustered close to each other for protection. In a prosperous village the walls of the adobe huts are whitewashed, and green trees shade the larger houses; a poor village—and most of them are poor—is a mass of crumbling weathered yellows and browns. The homes have no ceilings but the raftered roofs; they have no floors but the beaten earth. Their windows are made of greased paper, admitting so little light that the inner recesses are always dim. In his house the peasant stores his grain; in it he keeps his animals at night; in it is the ancestral shrine that he venerates. By day the street is empty of men—pigs wallow in it, chickens cackle in the alleyways. . . . At dusk the men return from the fields, and all over China at the same hour the villages are covered with a blue haze of smoke that curls from each homestead as the evening meal is cooked. At the same moment in every village, timed only to the setting of the sun, the same spiraling wisps of smoke go up from the houses to the sky. In the larger villages yellow light may gleam for a few hours from the doorways of the more comfortable, who can afford oil for illumination; but in the smaller villages the smoke fades away into the dark, and when night is come, the village sleeps, with no point of light to break its shadows.

Men and women come together in the village to produce children, till the land, and raise crops. The unity of man, village, and field is total and rigid. All the work is done by hand, from the sowing of the rice grains in early spring, through the laborious transplanting of the tufts in water-filled paddies in late spring, to the final harvesting by sickle in the fall. The Chinese farmer does not farm; he gardens. He, his wife, and his children pluck out the weeds one by one. He hoards his family's night soil through all the months of the year; in the spring he ladles out of mortar pits huge stinking buckets of dark green liquid offal, and carefully, without wasting a drop, he spreads the life-giving nitrogen among his vegetables and plants. When harvest time comes, the whole family goes out to the field to bring in the grain. The family helps him thresh his grain, either by monotonously beating it with a flail or by guiding animals that draw huge stone rollers round and round in a circle over the threshing floor. All life is attached to the soil; the peasant works at it, eats of it, returns to it all that his body excretes, and is finally himself returned to the soil.

Certain basic differences exist between the Chinese farmer and the farmer of America. The Chinese peasant's acres are pocket-handkerchief plots. The average Chinese farm, including those of the sparsely populated northwest, is less than 4 acres; in some of the densely settled provinces of the south and west the average is between one and one and a half acres per farm. Even this meager morsel is poorly laid out, for it consists of scattered strips and bits here and there, and the farmer must walk from one of these to another to serve each in turn. The average farmer has few animals. He cannot spare precious grain for feeding pigs or beef cattle or precious meadow land for dairy products. He may have one or two pigs, but these, like his chickens, feed on kitchen scraps. If he is well off, he may have an ox or buffalo to pull his plow, but most farmers with their small holdings cannot afford even that.

The farmer himself is uneducated. He is illiterate, and full of superstitions and habit ways that make it difficult to reach him by print. His horizons are close drawn. Off the main highways transportation is as tedious as it was a thousand years ago; the people he sees and talks to all live within a day's walk of his birthplace and think as he does. His techniques are primitive. He knows little of proper seed selection, and till recently his government has done little to improve seed strains; he knows nothing about combating plant diseases; his sickles, crude plows, flails, and stone rollers are like those his forefathers used. Frugality governs all his actions. He gathers every wisp of grass and twists it together for fuel. He sows beans or vegetables on the narrow ridges that separate one paddy field from another, so that no square foot of growing land is lost. He weaves hats, baskets, and sandals out of rice straw; out of the pig's bladder he makes a toy balloon for the children; every piece of string, every scrap of paper, every rag is saved.

Last and most important, the yield of his back-breaking labor is pitifully small. Although the yield per acre is fair—80 to 90 percent of what the American farmer gets from the same amount of land—the yield is miserably small in terms of man-hours, in terms of mouths and human lives. One American farmer with his machines, draft animals, good seeds, and broad acres will produce 15 pounds of grain each year while the Chinese farmer is producing one. This means that the Chinese farmer is constantly at war with starvation; he and his family live in the shadow of hunger. . . .

Peasants in the Twentieth Century

The ancient trinity of landlord, loan shark, and merchant is a symbol hated throughout Chinese history. It represents a system that has shackled China's development for five centuries. During the last century, however, the system has tightened about the Chinese peasant as never before because of the impact of the West, by commerce and violence, on its timeworn apparatus. Concentration of landholding had usually been stimulated in olden times by famine, flood, or disaster, when the peasant was forced to sell or mortgage his lands to meet his emergency needs. But the impact of Western commerce created new forms of liquid wealth in China and concentrated it in the hands of the relatively minute number of go-betweens of Western industry and the Chinese market. This new commercial wealth lacked the know-how, the courage, or the proper conditions to invest in industrial enterprises, as commercial wealth historically did everywhere else; it found in land its safest and most profitable form of investment. Particularly in the vicinity of such cities as Shanghai and Canton, where the new wealth was created, it poured into the countryside; land values shot upward, and the peasant was crushed by a process he could not understand. . . . Absentee landlords living in urban comfort far from the landlord's legal title gave him what was called "bottom" rights, but the tenant possessed "surface" rights, the right to farm the soil, and no landlord could sell the surface rights out from under the peasant or dispossess him of his means of livelihood. Such quaint customs, however, dissolved as the acid of modern speculation ate away into the ancient system of landholding. . . .

Another grim factor for a generation past has been civil commotion. The warlords who tore the interior to pieces were most of them shrewd, brutal men who wished to crystal-

---

lize permanently both their gains and their social position; this could be done best by acquiring land. Peasants were beaten off their fields, or their ownership was taxed away. In one county near Chengtu, in western China, 70 percent of the land is held by a single person, a former warlord. These warlords, even though their military fangs are now drawn, are still potent economic forces.

Crushed by speculation, warlords, and Western commerce, straitjacketed by their ancient feudal relationships, the peasants of China have been gradually forced to the wall. Despite all the new railways and factories and the humane paper legislation of the Central Government, some scholars think that China is perhaps the only country in the world where the people eat less, live more bitterly, and are clothed worse than they were five hundred years ago.

Many Western and Chinese students have looked at China through the eyes of her classics. Seeing it through such a medium, they have regarded China as "quaint" and found a timeless patina of age hanging over the villages and people. The biblical rhythm of the fields makes Chinese life seem an idyl, swinging from season to season, from sowing to harvest, from birth to death, in divinely appointed cadences. Chinese intellectuals, writing of their country and their people for foreign consumption, have stressed this piquant charm along with the limpid purity of the ancient philosophy. This composite picture of China is both false and vicious. Beneath the superficial routine of the crops and the village there is working a terrible ferment of change, which now, with ever-increasing frequency, is bursting into the main stream of Chinese politics. Those who see in the peasant's life an imaginary loveliness are the first to stand terrified at the barbarities his revolts bring about in the countryside when he is aroused. There is no brutality more ferocious than that of a mass of people who have the chance to work primitive justice on men who have oppressed them. The spectacle of loot and massacre, of temples in flames, of muddy sandals trampling over silken brocades, is awesome; but there is scant mercy or discrimination in any revolution, large or small.

• 12 •

The Triumph of Communism

One of the great controversies of modern times has surrounded the question as to how and why Mao Tse-tung and the Communists were able to defeat Chiang Kai-shek and the Nationalists in the years following World War II. All kinds of charges have been leveled on all sides, and at times the atmosphere of the debate has approached hysteria. Professors John K. Fairbank, Edwin O. Reischauer, and Albert M. Craig present a sober analysis of the Communist victory that places the question within the context of Chinese events.

JOHN K. FAIRBANK, EDWIN O. REISCHAUER, and ALBERT M. CRAIG

Communist Victory Over Chiang Kai-shek

The eight-year Japanese invasion was followed by four years of civil war, 1946-49, one of the big wars of modern times. The Nationalist forces totaled at the beginning about three million men, the Communists about one million. The cost of United States aid to China between August 1945 and early 1948 was estimated at over two billion dollars—this in addition to the billion and a half committed during World War II. By sheer weight of arms the Nationalist forces spread out to major cities and provincial capitals, and, when eventually permitted by Russia, into Manchuria. Innumerable factors undid them: the Nationalist forces, going against American advice, became overextended; the military under Chiang were out of civilian economic control and never established a sound economic base; a postwar American-style military reorganization produced confusion; the Whampoa clique dis-

---

Reprinted with permission of Houghton Mifflin Company, from John K. Fairbank, Edwin O. Reischauer and Albert M. Craig, *East Asia: The Modern Transformation* (Boston, 1965).

criminated against provincial commanders and armies, particularly those of Kwangsi. The strategy of the Nationalists was to hold strong positions defensively; their instinct was to hoard supplies and wait for others to move first; their field tactics were sometimes masterminded by the Generalissimo from a great distance. Corruption, demoralization, and desertion steadily depleted their armies.

The Communists pursued opposite tactics, maneuvering in the countryside, recruiting among the populace, destroying railroads, avoiding unfavorable terms of battle. They grew in numbers and armament, both from the big Japanese Manchurian stocks made available by Russia and from Nationalist defections and surrenders. By June 1948 the CCP roughly equaled the Nationalists in numbers of men, rifles, and cannon. Having cut off the government's Manchurian garrisons, in October 1948 they forced their surrender—a third of a million men.

The Nationalist cause had meanwhile been gutted in its city bases by an economic collapse. During World War II Chungking had steadily increased its expenditures, with income lagging far behind outlay. In 1941, when revenues provided only 15 percent of expenditures, the government took over the land tax in kind and kept its bureaucracy alive on rice stipends. But the situation deteriorated. Prices doubled at first every few months, then by the week. In September 1945 the volume of note issue was 465 times that of July 1937. The end of World War II gave a brief respite as the Nationalist currency spread back over all China, but large government expenditures continued. Hyperinflation was resumed. Prices doubled 67 times between January 1946 and August 1948 and then rose 85,000 times in six months, destroying the last remnant of urban enthusiasm for the Nationalist cause.

Intellectuals meanwhile had been increasingly alienated from the government. When many professors joined in widespread agitation for domestic peace and against civil war, the CCP catered to this feeling, but KMT rightists tried to suppress it by force, even by assassination—such as the shooting in Kunming in mid-1946 of the Tsing Hua professor Wen I-to, a poet and patriot educated in the United States. More and more students crossed the lines to join the CCP cause, which now seemed to possess the "Mandate of Heaven."

The showdown in the civil war came in a great two-month

battle fought in the old Nien area of the Huai River basin. Chiang (against the advice of his staff) committed 50 divisions, out of 200 remaining, to form a strong point on the plains around Hsuchow. The Communists, however, not only controlled the villages but, by reactivating railways as they advanced, were able to deploy large forces and to surround and immobilize the well-armed Nationalists. By mid-November four Nationalist army groups, about 340,000 men, had been cut off and encircled on the plain. By late December the 130,000 surviving Nationalists, out of 66 divisions now committed, were squeezed into six square miles, surrounded by 300,000 of the People's Liberation Army. They surrendered on January 10, 1949. Of 550,000 Nationalists lost, the Communists claimed 327,000 surrendered. Jealous noncooperation among the Whampoa commanders, failure to use the Nationalist monoply of the air, inability to bring their American weapons to bear on the enemy, every aspect of this great defeat underlines the old adage that armament alone cannot bring victory. Tientsin and Peking, long since cut off, surrendered in January 1949. In April the Communists stormed across the Yangtze, in May they entered Shanghai, in October Canton, in November Chungking. Chiang Kai-shek and most of the National Government leaders established themselves on Taiwan.

PART FOUR

CONTEMPORARY CHINA

What China will be tomorrow will be determined by what is happening in China today. For some this is the tragedy of recent Chinese history. For others this will be the result of one of the most noble social experiments ever undertaken. In any event, the China of today and tomorrow will continue to be shaped, in spite of the most radical changes, by the China of yesterday. This is the nature of the historical experience.

The People's Republic of China was proclaimed in 1949 as the Communist troops consolidated their control of the mainland, and as the party leaders began to restore some semblance of political unity. The decades that followed have been years of growth, experimentation, setback, consolidation, and most recently, disruption and disorder. China has emerged as a power to be reckoned with, and has frequently asserted her independence, if not her strength, in international politics. Change, both domestic and on the world scene, has been the key theme in these decades. The China of today is vastly different, but not unrecognizable from the China of the past.

• 1 •

Life in Contemporary China: Blue Ants or Proud Men?

What is life like in China? What have been the achievements? The failures? Are the people content? Are conditions better than they used to be? Would conditions be even better if not for Communist rule? The answers given to these questions are controversial, often misleading, and frequently confusing. Here are a group of eye-witness reports describing various aspects of contemporary Chinese life. All of these visitors came to China in the 1960s—a period in which the Chinese were beginning to recover from several years of hardship. These readings are excerpts from the works of two Germans, A.E. Johann and Hugo Portisch, a Belgian, Jørgen Bisch, and an Australian, Myra Roper. The answers they provide to the above questions differ considerably and are, at best, tentative. The reader will have to reach his own conclusions.

A.E. JOHANN (1963)

The years of terrible famine had ended when I reached China last winter, yet nourishment even compared with that of the poorest classes in southern Italy remains terribly meager. The rice allotment this past winter ranged between twenty-eight to forty pounds of rice per month, depending on how strenuous a job the worker had. And rice is the basic foodstuff of the Chinese. There was also a monthly ration of one to two pounds of vegetable oil at thirty cents per pound; two pounds of meat, mostly pork, for seventy cents; and along the coast, fish. Tickets must be used in the factory canteens. However, in contrast to the years of famine, the free market

---

Reprinted with permission, from A.E. Johann, "In the Land of the Blue Ants," *Atlas* Magazine (September 1963). Translated from *Christ Und Welt*, Stuttgart.

offered vegetables and fruit. But everything that does not belong in the category of basic foodstuffs comes high. Chicken is ninety cents a pound. And hardly anybody can afford that. Even today the Chinese diet hovers precariously close to a bare subsistence level.

Anyone who does not want to wear the clothing issued by the state must also pay relatively high prices. Shirts cost between $1.75 and $3. Printed cotton material costs between $1.75 and $2.75 a yard.

Amusements are very cheap. Movies cost five or ten cents; theater tickets are about twice that, and tickets for guest appearances of famous artists from the capital cost only twenty or twenty-five cents—or slightly more than a pack of the best cigarettes. . . .

This does not sound very attractive to us. But for China and the Chinese—and that is what counts—it represents such progress as nobody dared dream of fifteen years ago. Although I could scarcely believe it myself, China has attained in one leap the world of modern civilization that originated in Europe. She has reached only the bottom step of the stairway, but she has started along the irreversible path that the Western Europeans, the North Americans, the Japanese and the Russians have already taken.

There is no doubt that if China's leaders do not indulge in dangerous domestic political experiments or embark on foreign political adventures they will raise their country to Japan's level in a matter of decades. This is made doubly certain because the masses of China have always displayed patience, discipline, obedience, the capacity to suffer and the ability to endure the deprivation of personal freedom.

The standard of living of the masses has risen noticeably. If the purpose of modern government is to develop an economic policy that will advance the welfare of the common man, then the present government has achieved greater success than any Chinese government since the revolution of 1911. The fact that the methods used are distasteful to us and go against our grain is beside the point. Our objections mean nothing to the Chinese. . . .

HUGO PORTISCH (1965)

Red China Today

The train stopped in each of the larger stations for about ten to twenty minutes. During these stops, the train attendants would jump off, armed with mops, pails, and rags, to wash down the coaches from roof to rails with honest zeal. Most of the passengers also got off, to the accompaniment of rhythmic music issuing from the loudspeakers inside the train and others mounted on the platform. With the music came vocal instructions for gymnastics. Many of the passengers lined up along the platform and did the setting-up exercises as directed. Like every other place where the new Chinese state can reach a large number of people, the railroad has become a large drill ground.

On the long stretch of track between Canton and Peking, I observed another ritual conscientiously carried out by the railroad in its role of "socialistic training institution." Whenever the train entered a station, martial music blared over the platform. Dozens of railroad personnel stood at the edge of the platform at parade rest. Each was positioned precisely at a coach entrance, and they all waved red and green flags in salute. The same thing occurred when the train was about to pull out. There was the order to go aboard, to shut the doors, then the martial music and the salute by the personnel. A "train of socialism" got into motion. From then until the next stop, socialism was on the move over the loudspeakers in the coaches.

The platforms were painstakingly clean; whole columns of broom-wielding women worked to keep them so. Small vendors' carts were wheeled along for the passengers to buy ice cream, Chinese bread (a sort of puff pastry containing meat), chocolate bars, bonbons, cigarettes, wines, and spirits.

Apparently foreigners were not expected to mix with the Chinese, or to make their own purchases. When I approached one of these carts in a station, I found the attendant of my pullman at my elbow, giving me to understand that I should not buy a box of matches there. He guided me out of the crowd on the platform into a small park where, he indicated, I could stroll among the blooming jasmine shrubs and the fountains. Perhaps his sole concern was for my comfort. Two minutes before departure time, my attendant ceremoniously escorted me out of the park to the pullman, handing me a box of matches of markedly superior quality to those I had already bought at the cart—apparently he hadn't noticed my purchase. Later, I found these first-quality match boxes in all the hotels for foreigners in China. . . .

We approached Wuhan, that industrial center on the Yangtze (Chang). The ground here was neither green nor gray but black as coal, and the sky was obscured by low-hanging smoke plumes from countless smokestacks.

This view from the window was the first indication I had that Chinese industry still lacks modern installations. I was to find this impression confirmed repeatedly in many of the industrial areas I visited.

Along the track, an unending procession of coal heaps passed my window. On each of these heaps, dozens, hundreds of people were busy shoveling coal and coal dust into small carrying baskets. Baskets balanced on poles across their shoulders, they raced down the slope, emptied each basket into a cart, and scurried back up the slope. The full carts were pulled by people, mostly women and girls, hitched to them by ropes. The sight of so many toiling, hurrying human beings must have given rise to the appellation "ants," used by former travelers in China to describe the great unresting masses of Chinese workers.

But such an impression of industrial backwardness may be deceiving. . . .

I remembered reading travel accounts, some quite recent, that told how the trains from Canton would reach the terminus at Wuhan on the banks of the Yangtze, how the travelers had to be ferried across by boat to board the train for Peking on the other side. But our train did not stop; its speed merely decreased somewhat as it rolled thunderously onto a bridge, which one could not really identify as such at first. Because the rail line is so high above the waters of the Yangtze, one has the sensation of swooping in flight over the many junks plying between the two banks.

In the 1950s Russian and Chinese engineers succeeded in

throwing this first bridge across the Yangtze. Even in comparison with similar structures in Europe and the United States it is one of the greatest construction feats of its kind, a truly brilliant technical achievement. It stood there in startling contrast to those thousands of coolies, whom just a moment ago I had seen running past my window with sweat-drenched, naked torsos, carrying their loads on poles.

JORGEN BISCH (1964)

Visit to China—1964

I had first visited China in 1958, for only twenty days. While duly impressed by monuments such as the Great Wall and Peking's Forbidden City, I found the people looking poor and working very hard. Swarming through fields and factories, clad in drab blue uniforms, they had elicited the title "blue ants" from critical visitors.

This time food seemed more plentiful, and many trees had been planted in Peking. The drab work clothes had largely given place to more individual and attractive attire. . . .

As in other underdeveloped countries I've visited, China is eager to impress strangers with industries.

I knew my fate. "Yes, sir, thank you very much indeed," I said politely when Cheng invited me to visit Textile Factory No. 3. . . .

The mill has 5,500 workers—average age twenty-six. Its 19,000 spinning units and 3,200 weaving machines, all made in China, produce 123,000 pounds of cotton cloth per day.

As we walked into the factory halls, all the workers applauded and, as is the local custom, we all applauded back. The leaders pointed out that the halls were air-conditioned, with "spring temperatures." In view of this pride, I felt it would be impolite to comment on the white snow of cotton dust falling steadily through the air.

An official explained that 65 percent of the workers were women. The birth of a child brings a working mother a 56-day holiday and a congratulation premium of four yuan—about $1.70—for each of the first two children. . . .

Amid the clatter of the machines, I questioned one elderly

Reprinted with permission, from Jorgen Bisch, "This Is the China I Saw," *National Geographic*, Vol. 126 (November 1964).

man about his earnings. His family, he told me, numbered fourteen—he and his wife, five daughters, one son, two sons-in-law, and four grandchildren. Five of them worked at the factory, earning a total of 366 yuan, about $150 a month. All fourteen shared a four-room furnished apartment, for which they paid 15 yuan per month. Food came to 166 yuan, clothes to 51 yuan, other expenses to 94 yuan. Left over—40 yuan, to be used for small luxuries like the theater or motion pictures.

To a Westerner this income seems very low, but the Chinese point out that no tax is levied on it and that workers receive numerous benefits, such as free medical aid. Further, most commodities cost little: $2 for shoes, $2.50 for a good shirt; a few cents for a six-pound basket of vegetables or a pound of fish. A large bottle of beer—a luxury to most Chinese—costs twelve cents. Prices, I noticed, had dropped considerably since my visit in 1958, while wages had held steady. . . .

Some 1,400 new electric buses—all manufactured in China—glide quietly through the main avenues, carrying workers to and from their jobs for fares of less than a penny. I saw few automobiles, and all seemed to be government-owned cars or taxis. While the number of taxis had more than quadrupled since my earlier visit, they remain far beyond the means of most citizens. . . .

Mao Tse-tung, Chairman of the Chinese Communist Party, has pronounced "body building" good, so one sees Chinese exercising everywhere. I saw factory workers exercising between shifts, and even restaurant customers while waiting for service. Later, in Shanghai, every morning at five o'clock I saw hundreds of citizens performing calisthenics on the wide stone esplanade along the Whangpoo River. In the same place, old masters of sword dancing and other traditional gymnastics taught their art to any eager child free of charge.

"The Americans think only about painting their faces or buying fancy clothes," Cheng told me. "We think about building healthy bodies." . . .

If the part of China I was allowed to visit was a fair sample, the Communists have at least raised the poor from their timeless misery. Nowhere did I see starvation; nowhere did I see a beggar. And, while I saw numerous men and women with fascinating patterns of patches on their blue working trousers, I saw none in rags.

MYRA ROPER (1966)

A Young Wife Describes Life under Communism

She had been born near Hangchow on the east coast, about one hundred and fifty miles from Shanghai, where she had gone to work in a cotton mill on leaving school. When the Peking factory wanted skilled workers in 1956 she had been offered a job, her fare and accommodation in the hostel, and had decided to accept. At some factory function she had met Chung-yi and they had been married in a simple, civil ceremony.

Though she had stayed at school until sixteen, she was not as well educated as her husband; already he had mastered some three thousand characters of the Chinese language and passed examinations in three subjects of his textile engineer's diploma-course, for which he studied three nights a week at the mill classes.

She worked eight hours a day, six days a week, earning about sixty-two yuan a month*; her husband's wages were eighty-five yuan; their flat cost four-and-a-half yuan a month, food and clothing about one hundred yuan, with very little for extras; so they reckoned to save about 40 yuan a month, more if they got good bonuses. They had saved up for the radio, Chung-yi had just achieved a bicycle he had been longing for and next month Mei-lang would have her wristwatch—her eyes sparkled with anticipatory pleasure as she told me this and I found myself clapping my hands quite spontaneously to indicate, wordlessly, my own delight at her achievement. She went on, almost breathless with extra excitement, to explain that this was not all—they had even saved up nearly enough to take them back to Hangchow to visit her parents on their next holiday!

When I asked her about other living costs Mei-lang explained that there weren't many because all medical services were free for her and Chung-yi and only half fees were

---

* About £9 [about $25—Ed.]

charged for Jen-bao and Grandma. When she was expecting Jen-bao she had fifty-five days' maternity leave on full pay.

"What about your spare time; what sort of amusements have you and how much do they cost?" I asked.

They could get into the city, she said, for a few pennies and a half-day in the Peihai Park or the Summer Palace was very cheap; even theatre seats cost very little; but there was so much going on at the mill that they did not often need to seek amusement in the city. There were television sets in the public rooms and films or theatrical performances in the mill theatres three times a week as well as indoor and outdoor sports; table tennis she especially enjoyed. She explained, too, that she wanted time to take part in factory affairs and attend meetings where local and national problems were discussed as well as methods of increasing the mill's production. In addition, each block of flats had a Family Committee working along with the Street Committee, and this met regularly to help all the women with child-care—"and husband-care," she added with a grin.

• 2 •

Man and the State: Individuals or Robots?

In traditional Chinese society, the individual was subordinate to the group, whether the group was the family or the government. Much has been written on how the present Chinese government has carried out this subjugation of the individual to an even greater extent than was practiced in Confucian China—how every institution in Chinese life is designed to mold and to test the loyalty of the citizen to the Party and the state. However, a paradoxical argument exists. Some who admit that institutionalization and regimentation are excessive, argue that the individual Chinese is freer today than ever before because of the social and economic changes that have taken place.

These readings explore several areas of Chinese life and institutions, and offer some clues as to the relationship between the individual and the state. Hugo Portisch describes the complex triangle that exists in the union of male, female, and the state. G. Leslie Wilcox, a Canadian doctor, describes achievements in Chinese medicine—both modern and traditional. His article offers some interesting suggestions concerning the relationship between medicine and the state. In the next reading, Hans Koningsberger describes a movie he saw in China. In all cultures today, perhaps film is the most significant influence on moods and attitudes. Next, Theodore Hsi-en Chen, an American professor of Asian Studies, analyzes the Chinese educational system. Is Chinese education merely a method of brainwashing? In the final selection, Myra Roper discusses what is perhaps the most controversial and least understood of Chinese institutions, the communes. What is the purpose of the commune system? Does this system offer the individual any measure of his humanity, or is he only the pawn of the state? What conclusions can you draw from the cumulative effects of this group of readings?

HUGO PORTISCH (1965)

Guided Love

In the Communist Youth Association, whose members are aged thirteen to twenty-five, I asked about the attitude of the Party toward love and marriage. I was told, "For us, the main question is the young couple's correct concept of love and marriage."

"What is the correct concept?"

"Both parties must have the same political ideology, and their main concern must be production."

The first of these requirements was clear enough from a communist viewpoint, but what was meant by the second?

"Only what is good for production is good for marriage. Work must take precedence over love, and a married couple must show a proper understanding of this."

In other words, a couple must renounce love and even marriage if the government, the Party, the factory, or the commune so decides. They do so decide when they separate

---

young couples by assigning them to different cities or villages. They decide when they require overtime, night shifts, and special assignments. From married couples they may demand total dedication, forcing parents to leave their children in kindergartens or boarding schools. In the opinion of the Communist Youth Association and the Party, only those who are prepared to go to these lengths have the correct attitude toward love and marriage. . . .

In the institutions of higher learning the young people are urged through instruction and ideological training not to form any romantic attachments. Likewise, the plays, films, and operas produced by the youth groups, although mainly intended for adults, serve a twofold purpose. Love occurs everywhere (in one movie I saw, four couples were romantically involved), but marriage is always depicted as far in the future. A young couple love each other, but they never even hold hands, much less kiss. It is really platonic love that is portrayed, in a manner almost painful to Westerners.

For example, in one film a girl discovers her girl friend knitting a pair of men's gloves, obviously intended as a present for a young man. The embarrassed knitter buries her face in her hands, then runs and hides in a corner of the room.

In the next scene the young lovers meet in a park. They have important things to talk about; a difficult problem has arisen at work and has to be discussed. They arrive at a solution which will double production. Both of them are ecstatic. They bid each other farewell. At that point the girl holds out the gloves to her boyfriend and leaves swiftly. The young man stares at the gloves. Then he gets the idea. Dumfounded, he looks for the girl, who has long since disappeared. After another glance at the gloves, he presses them to his chest and then hides them under his sweater. Interestingly enough, the audience got very excited during this scene. There were loud comments, and some of the women giggled.

There was one further reference to love in this movie. The young lady in question, twenty-five years old and an engineer by profession, discovers her friend after midnight in his office. He has fallen asleep over a weighty mathematical computation, the results of which will be required by the factory in the morning. Until dawn, she works out his mathematical formula and leaves before he wakes. This too is a sign of love. . . .

This sort of puritanical morality is widespread in China nowadays. It is noticeable when one strolls through the parks in the evening. I have seen many young couples, but never lovers kissing.

G. LESLIE WILCOX (1966)

MEDICINE AND MEDICAL TRAINING

I visited the Peking Medical College. As on my other official visits to a plant and a commune, there was a brief introduction. The director told me of the great increase in student enrollment, staff, and teaching facilities that had occurred since the time of Liberation. Students have a six-year course which, in essence, is similar to our own, with the addition of courses in politics and traditional Chinese medicine. The director said it was desirable that the students be both "red and expert." By red, he meant politically conscious and loyal to the cause.

Political indoctrination is a part of all Chinese education, from kindergarten through high school, university, and even medical school. . . .

I visited the classrooms and laboratories in the basic science buildings. They were very well equipped, and the training appeared to be very similar to our own. In the Neuroanatomy Department they showed me excellent slides and preparations and told me that Dr. Wilder Penfield of the Montreal Neurological Institute had visited their laboratory about two months before.

In Chinese medicine and in medical training, great emphasis is placed on public health and preventive medicine. Disease was a major problem in China, and they have accomplished a great deal in preventing the large epidemics. The infant mortality rate has dropped until it now is similar to our own. . . .

I visited several of the newer hospitals in Peking. The number of available beds has increased tremendously. The wards were bright and airy and a little austere by our standards as far as the frills and conveniences were concerned. The medical

---

care was excellent. Charting was identical to our own. On the general surgical ward I found the kinds of operations and the preoperative and postoperative care almost the same as in my own practice. The instruments were from many European countries, as well as from Shanghai. The whole routine and environment was such that I felt right at home and thought I could have carried on a surgical practice in any one of their hospitals without changing my pace or taking time out to get accustomed to a different situation. . . .

At the conclusion of any interviews or discussion in China it is customary for the Chinese participant to make a small incantation to the effect that all this is due to the correct leadership of Chairman Mao Tse-tung, the Communist Party of China and the three red banners of the correct party, the Great Leap Forward, and the People's Commune. Most of our hosts were able to say this little speech without difficulty. I was amused to find that my Chinese medical confreres kept forgetting to finish with these remarks, and I had the occasion to prompt one of them in the final sentence. . . .

RESEARCH FACILITIES

The facilities for research in Peking Medical College were excellent. The latest medical equipment was available. In my own hospital the equipment we use to test pulmonary functioning comes from Holland. The makers of the equipment told me that they have sold more of their machines to China than to any other country. . . .

TRADITIONAL CHINESE MEDICINE

I wanted to see the practice of traditional Chinese medicine, and I visited the Research Institute of Acupuncture and Moxibustion at the Academy of Traditional Chinese Medicine in Peking. . . . "Acupuncture" means needle puncture, and "moxibustion" means the burning of a *moxa,* or a dried herb, not unlike the punks we used as children for lighting firecrackers. They are part of the traditional Chinese therapeutic methods which have been handed down for centuries. Stone needles were used some 4,000 years ago. Solid, stainless steel needles are now inserted into points along about eleven pairs of lines, or channels, on the body. These channels, or meridians, are reputed to conduct vital energy. Depending on the diagnosis, needles are inserted at various points corresponding to the organ involved. Harmful excesses of body humors and moribund essences are drawn off. Stagnating vital forces flow freely again, restoring the balance between *yin* and *yang*. . . .

. . . The waiting rooms and hallways were jammed with patients waiting their turn. I saw hypertension treated by needles inserted into the forehead and in the wrists. A lady with a protruded intraverbal disk had needles inserted into her forehead and both ankles. Small portions of moxa, looking like bits of cigarettes, were placed on the ends of the needles and set on fire. . . .

HANS KONINGSBERGER (1966)

At this stage of the Chinese revolution, a film particularly is no private effort but in a way made by the entire government of the People's Republic.

There is as an example *A Life in Flames*, a film based on a fragment from *The Red Crag*, one of those multitudinous, popular novels, which came out a few years ago. The film is a big hit, a Chinese *Gone with the Wind*. . . . *A Life in Flames* is fascinating, even if the nobility of the good guys becomes a bit much at times for the more sophisticated members in the audience. (The Chinese are no mean movie makers; they provide films for all the non-Communist countries in Asia.) It is set in Chungking, the river city on the upper Yangtse, in the last year of the civil war when Chiang Kai-shek was still in power there.

The film opens on scenes of the town during those final months: its glitter, corruption, spies, miseries, and hopes—so much in the classic Western tradition of great adventure movies that a Parisian, who went to see it at my urging, later said: "I expected any minute to see Humphrey Bogart appear." Jeeps dash through the streets, coffee shops are packed, fortune tellers and beggars are thick as flies, convicts and political prisoners unload ships at the river quay. From one of the river boats the hero of the film, a Communist underground leader, steps ashore. He is dressed fashionably in American style to avoid suspicion, and he cuts through the

---

crowds, the tramps, and the policemen with all the impressive disdain of the rich Chinese to whom such people were simply invisible.

But this image of Chungking during the last days of Chiang is not a propaganda caricature. It shows life as it must have been, downs and ups, including a big neon advertisement for Coca-Cola and a hawker with old copies of *Life* Magazine for sale. Such subtle humor is indeed a rare item in Asia, and it is startling that the makers of the film had so much feeling not only for the sordidness of that time but also for its color and bustle and excitement—gone from their own more antiseptic days. One cannot help but wonder which Communist official wrote what memorandum to whom in order to get a Coca-Cola neon sign manufactured.

The only American in the movie is an officer, a political adviser; he looks convincing which is no surprise since he is played by an American actor, an ex-Korea P.O.W. The movie American is by no means a caricature either, and the advice he gives the Chiang officers sounds straight out of a State Department White Paper. The movie hero is captured during a café rendezvous with a traitor, and he is taken to Chungking prison which had a fame of its own in those days. Eventually, as he refuses to collaborate, he is executed just before the Communist Army enters Chungking. The music plays *The Internationale,* and some people in the audience cry.

Chinese movies usually draw their material from that ample source, the "national myth" of the new republic. The Chinese myth is different from that of most other countries in being so recent; it is one part Japanese war, one part civil war. (Its American equivalent would be Valley Forge, Gettysburg, the Wild West, and both World Wars rolled into one.) This was the great experience of the older generation, and the government considers it a prime source of inspiration for the younger ones who, not having known the bad old times, might flag in their enthusiasm and self-discipline if not repeatedly confronted with these. The same subject matter makes up the new "revolutionary opera" which has pushed aside the classic opera. The triumph of the good guys (the Communists) over the bad guys (Kuomintang, Americans, and Japanese) is treated at length but not quite ad nauseam: these films and operas have more entertainment value than the dreary label, propaganda, might lead one to expect.

Good versus Bad is of course the basic theme of most drama, and to the audience it does not make too much difference who is who. The types remain the same; the blustering major may now be an officer of Chiang rather than of Emperor Chiung-chen, the peasant rebel may clutch a tommy gun instead of a sword, and the virtuous old lady with smooth grey hair may be shot rather than strangled; the characters are all there; the crooks and the dubious people are usually much more real than the pink-cheeked goodies; the overwhelming sense of continuity the Chinese have about themselves is not broken.

THEODORE HSI-EN CHEN (1966)

The Nature of Communist Education

One of the most noteworthy features of Chinese Communist education is the systematic schooling given to adults in their after-work hours without interference with their employment. This instruction does not take place in the regular schools: classes are held aboard ship for crews, as well as on farms and in factories.

"Spare-time" education is a major form of education for workers and peasants and the most important means of combatting illiteracy. . . .

In addition to spare-time schools, there are part-time schools in which young students spend some time in productive labor. Full-time schools, therefore, constitute only a fraction of the educational facilities available to the population. Taking into consideration spare-time schools, part-time schools, and full-time schools, as well as numerous short-term institutes, correspondence courses, and indoctrination classes, one can see some justification for the Communist claim that one out of every four persons in China is receiving some kind of schooling. At any rate, there exists a vast network of educational and indoctrinational agencies which aim to produce an impact on the minds of the people. . . .

WHAT TO EDUCATE FOR

In a country where schooling and scholarship have traditionally commanded social esteem and prestige, the new opportunities for education are welcomed and eagerly sought by young people. Yet young people seem to have been besieged by doubts in regard to the purpose of education. Such doubts have been expressed in the correspondence section of publications like *China Youth.* Young people ask many questions. Do they go to school for academic learning, for productive labor, or for political training? If one is judged by his labor and political record, is it necessary to put effort into academic learning, or to be in school at all? . . .

Young people in China also ask whether there is any other purpose of education than service to the Party-state. They wish that their personal interests and preferences could be given more consideration. For a young couple to be separated by assignment to jobs in different cities may be accepted as temporarily necessary, but prolonged separation inevitably raises questions and doubts, if not resentment. . . .

The Communists believe that the human mind and heart are as subject to conditioning as human behavior, and that thought, attitudes, desires, and ambitions can be "remolded" as easily as overt action. . . .

The Communists launch campaigns and call them off to suit their purpose. Today, the nation is "mobilized" to take Taiwan by force; tomorrow the propaganda line is changed and the aroused emotions are supposed to subside. Yesterday, "learning from the Soviet Union" was the guide for the entire nation, and schools followed the Soviet "model" in curriculum and methods and taught Russian instead of English; today, the Russians are revisionists and traitors to the revolution, and the schools are teaching English once more. Yesterday, the "old intellectuals" were to be replaced by new "proletarian intelligentsia" and "red experts"; today, young people are asked to respect the "old teachers" and learn from the "old experts." The Communists seem to believe that the mind of the people can be wiped clean at any moment—clean not only of bourgeois ideas, but also of discarded Party lines—to make room for any new thoughts and ideas the manipulators of "public opinion" may choose to implant.

But the human mind has a way of breaking through the

walls that confine it. A person exposed to education—although no more than indoctrination and propaganda—is likely to think beyond what he is asked to think. An illiterate person, hitherto taking no interest in affairs outside his home and village, who learns to read and write and participate in political affairs, may become interested in things other than those prescribed by the rulers. . . .

MYRA ROPER (1966)

The Communes

Among all Chinese myths and legends reaching the West the communes hold pride of place. They have been presented as quasiconcentration camps. We read of peasants herded into military-style barracks, separated from their families, always hungry after "staggering food-production failures." . . .

Having visited some eight communes, and spent several days in one of them, I could not find any foundation for all this. To begin with, far from being fenced in, a commune has no obvious boundaries. I had at first vaguely expected at least to pass through a gate and be aware that I was well and truly in such and such a commune; in fact, I was no more aware of moving from one to another than I am of crossing from Yorkshire into Lancashire or Victoria into New South Wales. Only the locals know which village is in which commune, for the term "commune" is really an administrative and social one, referring to roughly the age-old division of the Chinese countryside into *hsiangs* or townships, each containing a number of villages. I noticed that, as for centuries, the village today counts its inhabitants by households rather than individuals; the family is still the important unit.

It struck me, too, that the commune as an administrative unit bore some resemblance to the English County Council, though its role is more inclusive and its control far wider. Not only is the commune responsible for agricultural production and organization, but also for primary and some secondary education, for shops, canteens, light industries, hospitals, clinics and sporting and entertainment facilities. . . .

The size of communes varies greatly, both in area and

---

population, not only according to the productivity of the land, but also to the traditional habits and occupations of the region, for, in communes, as elsewhere, the Communist Party does not use force or direction when discussion, persuasion, reeducation will serve its purpose better. From the question of ancestor-worship and funeral customs down to the planting of the odd acres of land, the government is usually prepared to wait for local decisions to be thrashed out. Of course, every village has long had its Communist cadres, its Peking-trained young men and women who have acted as a stimulus to modernization and Marxist-Leninist thinking, but after some initial mistakes they have worked as far as possible within the local traditions and with some of the local people. . . .

Wages are lower than in the cities and the general standard of living may, generally speaking, fall below its urban counterpart. But, even so, conditions are more than satisfactory compared with the miseries of the old days, when flood, drought and the depredations of war were endemic. And wages have increased tenfold since 1949. . . . In addition, today, most peasants have a house, or part of a house, of their own; they are allocated supplies of basic foods from the commune's stock and can augment these from the vegetable or animal produce of their own private plots which they cultivate assiduously. Education is very nearly free, medical services free or very cheap, and sporting and entertainment facilities are increasing. . . . Because of the close-knit character of the whole life, few can be lonely and the old and the sick are cared for. Families temporarily without the breadwinner for any reason are supplied by the commune welfare fund. There will be no privacy on a commune, but no loneliness or neglect, either.

Village amenities are steadily improving and it is estimated that the majority of villages now have electric light. Certainly, I found it in all the dozen or so that I visited. Furniture, once very scanty indeed, is now becoming commonplace, radios are almost taken for granted, and most peasants have, or are saving up for, a bicycle and a wristlet watch. It is government policy to do everything to ensure that the standard of living in the country shall approximate to that in the cities as far as possible.

This is not to say that the peasants have a particularly comfortable existence. In most of China modern production techniques as we know them are wholly inadequate. The shortage of chemical fertilizers is lamentable, and even the increased output of the new fertilizer factories, which have diverted labour and materials from certain heavy industrial plants, is still far from adequate. Even in the more prosperous communes I saw, as late as 1965, innumerable handcarts doing the job of a couple of trucks, and innumerable muscles straining to give the pushing, pulling or lifting power of one tractor, crane or bulldozer. . . .

In the communes there are still tensions and strains, resulting both from habits of mind retained by some former wealthy peasants and landlords, who resent communization and the equality of all commune members, and from mishandling by Communist cadres or by impractical "experts." These are problems of which no casual visitor to however many communes can be more than dimly aware. But they are not wholly concealed by the government. . . . But all this does not invalidate the concept of the commune as a viable rural unit for China; it indicates weaknesses but not failure; it mainly indicates that people living in communes are human.

Small-scale, nonmechanized farming is as outmoded for China as for Australia, the United States or the United Kingdom; and far from being a curb on China's agricultural development, the communes have been its spur. . . .

• 3 •

In Defense of the New China

Probably no other position in Chinese life has so radically changed as has the role of Chinese women. It should be noted that this change, like many other economic and social changes, has been accelerated, rather than begun, in the last twenty years. The great upheaval in the first half of the twentieth century witnessed, under the aegis of Western influence, the beginning of the breakdown of many of China's traditional social institutions. Myra Roper has transcribed an interview with

Wu Y-feng, a woman of the new China. Why does Madame Wu prefer the new China? Do you find her definition of freedom valid? Would you agree with her impressions of the United States?

WU Y-FENG (1966)

A Woman of New China Defends Communist China

It was immediately apparent that one of the main reasons for her support of the regime was its release of woman from positions of subordination as "the second sex." Wu Y-feng explained this to me in detail:

Woman has stood up in the New China; she can say to any man, "I am a human being like you." Before Liberation only a few could honestly feel that. Look at my struggle, even in a Christian family, to get the same education as my brother. There is a story about this. A woman was left alone in her house for almost the first time in her life. When someone knocked at the door she was too shy to answer at first, so the visitor knocked again and asked, "Is anyone at home?" "Nobody is at home," came the whispered reply. She just didn't count herself as anybody!

So, as a woman, I had to support a government that gave us real equality and a chance to fill any position in the land. And also as an educationist. Under the KMT* and in the civil war, there were appalling shortages of everything—labs, equipment, books, desks and teachers. Now everyone can go to a school of some kind, for education is a main concern of the government. Nanking, as you will have heard, is a large educational centre, with many schools and colleges and especially good medical and technical institutions.

And, also, as a patriot, I must do all I can for a regime which has ended corruption, inflation and starvation and already brought us, for the first time in a century, a generation of peace. Only those as old as I, who remember the suffering of preliberation times, can know what all this means. Just to have food enough to keep alive is still a marvel to the poor

---

* [Kuomintang—Ed.]

of Nanking. Once when I was a girl I asked a peasant near my home how many children she had—I'll never forget the implications of her reply.

"I have," she said, "eight mouths to feed." . . .

At this stage Wu Y-feng must have read my mind, for she paused long enough for me to get out the question that I had been longing to ask—the obvious one:

"What about freedom? Intellectual, artistic, political? Will you please"—I was almost painfully earnest by now—"please, tell me, honestly, how much of that must you sacrifice in your new China?"

Wu Y-feng put the tips of her fingers together in a characteristic gesture, and replied, almost fiercely, "Miss Roper, surely you can see that freedom must mean different things in different settings. During a revolution—and long after it—how can the same freedom be expected as in a settled, prosperous country like Australia? You have never known war on your own soil, foreign occupation and mass starvation. And, please note, even so, we don't do too badly. We have our open criticism-and-self-criticism sessions; the draft of our constitution was debated all over China for months before being accepted. In our Nanking Assembly we have a few 'Rightists' who have some freedom to air their views and, as long as they don't advocate violent overthrow of the government, they fare well enough."

Taking a deep breath I came at her again. "Surely, Madame Wu, when you have lived in the United States and know and like many Americans, you cannot accept all this anti-United States agitation—this almost obsessive dislike of 'imperialists'?"

The smile was gone from her eyes, the generous mouth hardened, the voice had an edge. "I used to believe the Americans honestly wanted peace—most of them still do, I hope—but their leaders, their national policy, are aggressive. A peaceful country would not send its biggest fleet to our home waters and keep it off our coast for years; would not put armed forces in bases all round our borders and send planes and missiles over our southern provinces. They would not support a discredited puppet like Chiang Kai-shek and let him keep saying he is going to attack the mainland with

American help. The American people are badly led. How can you expect me to believe that the United States Congress is peaceful?"

Well, I asked for it and got it!

• 4 •

Fairy Tales From the New China

Both of these fairy tales have always been popular with Chinese children; they have been adapted for modern times. What lessons do the children who read these tales receive? Why do you think these children's stories have received the seal of approval from the government? Do these tales differ substantially from the traditional fairy tales? Are these stories a method of brainwashing? Are *Hansel and Gretel* and *Little Red Riding Hood* a method of brainwashing?

THE GOLDEN AXE

Once upon a time there lived a little boy whose name was Chen Ping. He came of a poor family, so poor, in fact, that his father and mother could not support him and he was sent to work for a landlord named Skinflint Wang.

Chen Ping was an honest and hard-working lad. From morning to night he busied himself fetching water, cutting firewood or milling rice. But Skinflint Wang was never satisfied. He kept beating and scolding the boy, accusing him of being lazy or slow, or finding some other fault.

One cold day, Chen Ping set out in the teeth of a bitter wind to collect wood on the mountain top. He carried his axe in his belt and a pole across his shoulder. While crossing a single-plank bridge, his axe slipped out and fell with a splash into the river.

How could he chop wood without an axe? Chen Ping was

Yang Chu (ed.), *The Golden Axe* (Peking: Foreign Languages Press, 1965).

so taken aback that he sat on the bank of the river and wept bitterly.

All of a sudden, an old man with a long white beard appeared before him.

"Well, now! Why are you crying, my boy?" asked the old man.

"Oh grandad! My axe has fallen into the river. I won't be able to chop any wood without it. My master will surely give me a whipping when I go back," answered Chen Ping, wiping away his tears.

"There, there!" replied the old man. "Don't cry any more. I'll get it back for you."

So saying, the old man jumped into the river, and came up with an axe.

"Look! Is this your axe?" he asked.

Chen Ping gazed at the axe in his hand. It was wrought in solid silver, and shone most beautifully in the sunlight. But he shook his head and replied:

"No, grandad, that is not my axe."

The old man jumped into the river again and back on to the bank, with another axe in his hand. It was finely wrought in shining gold, and even more splendid than the first. But Chen Ping still shook his head.

"That's not my axe either, grandad."

Smiling broadly, the old man jumped into the river again. This time he brought back the one Chen Ping had dropped. Chen Ping jumped up happily and said:

"Yes, yes! That's my axe!"

The old man handed him the axe.

"You are a good, honest lad," he said, patting him on the head.

Chen Ping was just about to say "Thank you!" when the old man disappeared.

Chen Ping took the axe and ran towards the mountain. In a remarkably short time, he had cut and chopped a full load of firewood.

Carrying the firewood on his shoulder, he was so happy he sang a little folk-song all the way back to Skinflint's house. But when Skinflint saw him coming, he stared in anger.

"You lazy-bones, why are you back so early?" he shouted.

Chen Ping showed him the load of firewood he had just

collected and told him how the axe had fallen into the river and he had met the old man.

On hearing this story, Skinflint was even more angry.

"You fool!" he snarled. "Why didn't you take the golden axe? Or even the silver one? They're worth much more than this old iron thing! You . . . you really are the biggest dunderhead I've ever come across!"

But even while grumbling and scolding the boy, Skinflint was thinking up a plan.

The next morning he rose very early. Going out into the yard, he picked up an old broken axe and set out toward the mountain as though he were on his way to collect wood. When he reached the bridge, however, he deliberately threw the axe into the river, sat himself on the river bank and cried as loudly as he could.

The old man appeared once more.

"My friend, why do you weep so sadly?" he asked.

Skinflint looked up sharply. "Oh," he thought to himself, "the very old man Chen Ping told me about!" So he opened his mouth and bawled louder than ever.

"Oh, oh, oh!" he sobbed. "My axe fell into the river. I . . . I'm afraid I'll get a beating when I go home. . . ."

The old man laughed.

"Don't cry, I'll get it back for you," he said.

He threw himself into the river and instantly came back with an axe.

"Is this your axe?" he asked.

In fact, it was the very one Skinflint had thrown into the river. But he pulled a long face, shook his head and replied:

"Oh dear, no! Mine is a splendid axe."

The old man pulled out another axe from under the water.

"Look, is this yours?" he asked again.

This time, it was the silver axe. But Skinflint was still dissatisfied.

"No, that's not mine either. Mine was pure gold. You'd better give me that one, and try again. . . ."

The old man threw the silver axe on the bank and once more groped under the water. This time he brought back the golden axe which shone so brightly it dazzled the landlord's eyes. He had hardly reached the river bank when Skinflint snatched the axe from his hands.

"At last! My axe at last!" he shouted joyfully.

By this time, the old man had disappeared.

Beyond himself with joy, Skinflint made his way across the bridge, the golden axe in one hand and the silver axe in the other. Holding them high in the air, he danced and sang:

With the golden axe I'll buy a house,
With the silver axe I'll buy land.
I'll eat with golden chopsticks
And drink soup with a silver spoon.
I'll have golden flowers on my clothes and hat,
And I'll sleep on a gold-embossed bed.
Who is happier than I?
Who is happier than I?

He had hardly sung the last line when his foot slipped and he fell into the river with a loud splash that could be heard from miles away.

Since that day, no one has ever seen him again.

And how about Chen Ping? He returned home and every day went to the mountain to cut wood with his wonderful iron axe. He gathered so much wood that he earned enough to keep his mother and father and himself as well, so they led a very happy life.

THE PROUD GENERAL

Once upon a time, there was a general whose military skill was something quite out of the ordinary. He was so strong he could lift a thousand-catty bronze tripod with one hand.

He was also a skilled archer. He could shoot down a bird on the wing with the greatest of ease. In fact, he was never known to miss.

Naturally, he was held in such fear by his enemies that none dared to invade his territory. So the general became more and more proud.

Now, the general had a toady who did nothing but flatter him. One day, he went so far as to call him "The World's

---

Hua Chun-wu, *The Proud General* (Peking: Foreign Languages Press, 1964).

Greatest Hero." The general was so gratified that he picked up a jar of wine and quaffed it off at one go.

The next morning, he was found lying on the floor dead drunk, still embracing the wine jar. The cock crowed as loud as he could, and the bugler sounded the reveille on the drill-ground. But the general slept on.

From then on, he indulged in a life of dissipation and seemed to lose all interest in the military arts.

Time went by. His spear rusted up and became covered with cobwebs, while mice made a nest among his arrows.

One spring day, the general and his toady went out for a drive in his carriage. The sun shone warmly and the general lay back in his seat feeling pleasantly drowsy.

As they passed through a village, they happened to see a peasant doing weight-lifting. Looking at the weights, the general guessed them to be about ten thousand catties.

He decided to show what he could do. Thinking that he could easily outdo the peasant, he chose a pair that weighed over twenty thousand catties. But, to his great embarrassment, he found he could lift them no higher than his waist.

To save his face, he proposed a contest in archery with the peasant. At that moment a flock of wild geese flew overhead. The general drew his bow with an effort and shot three arrows in succession. They fell far short of the mark and the geese simply dived down and carried them away in their bills.

In spite of this lesson, the general continued to indulge in a life of luxury. On his birthday, he invited many people to a grand banquet.

Just as the festivities were at their height, and the wine was flowing freely, a scout dashed into the hall with the news that the enemy had launched an attack and were only fifty *li* from the city.

The general could not believe his ears. What enemy, he thought, would dare to attack his territory? Not until the actual sound of battle penetrated the hall did it dawn upon him that the scout had spoken the truth. He was utterly flabbergasted.

The guests took panic and began to make for the doors in great confusion. And the toady was well in front of them all.

The general hurried to look for his arms, but there lay his spear all covered with rust and his arrows all in pieces. His guards had scampered off, so he tried to sharpen the spear himself. But scarcely had he put the edge to the whet-stone when the spearhead snapped in two.

The city was occupied and in flames. The battle drums were rolling. In high alarm, the general cried for help. There was no answer but the echo of his own voice.

His mansion was surrounded. A great din of shouting arose here, there and everywhere. As a last hope, he made for a hole under his back wall, and tried to crawl through.

But enemy soldiers were lying in wait the other side of the wall. As he emerged he was ignominiously captured. And this was the end of "The World's Greatest Hero." Nobody knows for certain what happened to him later. But one thing is clear, that a man who is proud will eventually meet with failure.

• 5 •

Poetry From the New China

It was not uncommon for Chinese emperors to be accomplished poets. Therefore, it should not be surprising that Mao Tse-tung is considered one of the finest poets in China today. This poem was written before he came to power, but it is somewhat typical of his style and thematic approach. How does this poem compare to those of the T'ang poets? Is there any ideological content to be found in this poem? Do you think this is a good poem?

It was also not uncommon in traditional China for poets to write pieces in adulation of the rulers. The second poem is in praise of Mao. Do you think this is a good poem? What do you think is the point and purpose of the poem?

What do both of these poems reveal about the new China?

MAO TSE-TUNG

The Snow

All the scenery in the north
Is enclosed in a thousand *li* of ice,
And ten thousand *li* of whirling snow.
Behold both sides of the Great Wall—
There is only a vast confusion left.
On the upper and lower reaches of the Yellow River
You can no longer see the flowing water.
The mountains are dancing silver serpents,
The hills on the plains are shining elephants.
I desire to compare our height with the skies.
In clear weather
The earth is so charming
Like a red-faced girl clothed in white.
Such is the charm of these rivers and mountains,
Calling innumerable heroes to vie with each other in pursuing her.
The emperors Shih Huang and Wu Ti were barely cultured,
The emperors Tai Tsung and Tai Tsu were lacking in feeling,
Genghis Khan knew only how to bend his bow at the eagles.
These all belong to the past—only today are there men of feeling!

Reprinted with permission of Robert Payne, from Robert Payne (ed.), *The White Pony: An Anthology of Chinese Poetry* (New York: The John Day Company, 1947).

HSIANG YANG

Chairman Mao Has Given Me a Gun

Chairman Mao has given me a gun
To guard our red political power;
Clear what I love and hate, firm in my stand,
Holding my course through densest clouds and mist.

Hsiang Yang, "Chairman Mao Has Given Me a Gun," *Chinese Literature*, No. 12 (Peking, 1967).

Chairman Mao has given me a gun
To guard our red political power;
The skies may fall but I shall never falter,
Determined to consolidate proletarian dictatorship.

Chairman Mao has given me a gun
To guard our red political power;
I shall support the Left, make revolution,
Ready to shed my blood or lose my head!

Chairman Mao has given me a gun
To guard our red political power;
If the enemy dare attack
They will meet their doom!

Chairman Mao has given me a gun
To guard our red political power;
All my life I shall follow Chairman Mao
To make our land impregnable for ever.

• 6 •

A Short Story From the New China

This story, recently published in Peking, offers a revealing glimpse into the fabric of contemporary Chinese life, and the attitudes and values that shape it. What values and attitudes are implicit or explicit in this story? What does the story suggest about contemporary China?

KAO YING

The Flood

A man in a dark green raincoat was standing on a jagged rock, overhanging the river, shouting to the owner of a boat

Kao Ying, "The Flood," *Wild Bull Village: Chinese Short Stories* (Peking: Foreign Languages Press, 1965).

anchored on the opposite bank. The rain, driven by a violent wind from the mountain, poured down on him in a steady stream, running off the edges of his green raincoat.

He shouted, "Hey! Hey, over there! I want to cross the river. . . ."

His words were whipped away by the wind, and the only reply was the muffled rolling of thunder in the distance. It was dusk and the Sha River was muddy and dangerously swollen.

He shouted again, but no one appeared on the opposite bank. Obviously, it wasn't a ferry crossing.

Readjusting the pack on his back, he started off with long strides to head upstream to locate the ferry. As he walked he constantly turned his head to look at the fields on the opposite shore. Through the curtain of rain, he perceived a broad, flat valley. Red clay hills could be seen in the distance and behind them towered the hazy outline of the mountains. The heavy downpour which had already lasted many days had caused a flood which cascaded down the mountain into the Sha. The river had overflowed its banks, and submerged nearly half of the dyked ricefields. The newly planted rice seedlings were scattered by the swirling floodwaters. And silt covered some of the fields, raising them above the level of the partition ridges. A small village cowered beside the flood-swollen river. The only sign of life was the wind-blown smoke rising from the kitchen fires. The traveler gazed, frowned at the rain and quickened his pace. The lone man was Chen Hai-min, vice-secretary of the Chengkuan District Party Committee, a man in his late thirties of average height, with a broad face enhanced by a pair of thick, black eyebrows. He was one of several veteran cadres, just dispatched by the county Party committee to help those communes facing flood disaster.

He had shouldered his pack early that morning and, braving the rain, was hurrying to the Shaho People's Commune. Before setting out he had promised the county Party committee that he would do all he could, working with the cadres in the commune, to organize the people, fight the flood and save the 1961 rice crop. He was well aware of the many calamities that had befallen this particular commune: Not a drop of rain had fallen since spring and half the crop had been burnt up. In June the drought was followed by heavy rains which continued for about fifteen days. It now seemed as if the sky had a perpetual leakage, and on the face of things it appeared hopeless to try and save the rice crop in this low valley. But Chen had said: "So long as the people will work with me I have nothing to fear."

All day, he had plodded ahead through rain and mud unmindful of his weariness. He was hurrying on and wishing that he could save the commune with one big effort. He was worried because he could not locate the ferry, and sweat mingled with the rain rolling down his face. As he pressed forward, new doubts assailed his mind: what about the morale of the people in the Shaho People's Commune; had they given up all hope; what were they thinking; how did they feel? These things were important for the crop depended upon the masses and their morale.

As night came on, the clouds seemed to drop lower. He could hear the raindrops beating on the hood of his coat and the dismal howling of the wind. At the turning of the rocky pathway he saw a small hut under a tree. Its thatched roof was black with age, it had no windows, but the door was half open and he caught glimpses of a fire inside. Looking around cautiously, he noticed an empty boat moored to the bank and rocking on the waves. He hurried to the hut.

Three people were seated around a fire burning brightly in the centre of the dirt floor. Two of them were quietly smoking while the third was drying his coat. The only things in the room were a small bed and some long bamboo poles and oars which were leaning against the wall.

"Is this the ferryman's hut?" he asked politely.

A lean old fellow, wearing a white turban, his wiry goatee outthrust as he craned his neck, answered: "What, another night owl! Come on in and sit down. The river is too high to cross yet!"

"But Grandpa, I've urgent business waiting for me!"

"We know that, or you wouldn't be out tramping around in the rain like this, would you?"

The bare-armed young fellow who was seated near the fire drying his clothes began to plead with the old man in a booming voice. "Come on Grandpa Kuo, take us across now. You're the one who is afraid of the wind and water?"

Laughing, the old man patted the young fellow on his broad shoulders and answered: "I'm only thinking what a pity it'd be to lose a fine hunk of meat like you!"

The middle-aged peasant, seated opposite them, looked up

and asked: "Why hurry, Shih Man-tse? Surely you aren't so reckless as to want to cross the river while it is in spate, are you?"

The young fellow did not answer. Flinging his jacket across his deeply tanned glistening shoulders, he rested his chin on his strong arms, and knitting his heavy brows stared moodily into the fire.

Chen Hai-min took off his raincoat, rolled up his trouser legs and sat close to the fire to dry his feet. He began to size up the three beside him, and reached the conclusion that Grandpa Kuo was the boatman and the others were travelers like himself. Just as he was about to say something to them and break the silence, Grandpa Kuo asked:

"Are you on your way to our Shaho People's Commune? On official business, eh?"

"That's right."

"You look as if you used to be a peasant," observed the old man, winking.

"Do you know me?" asked Chen Hai-min, a little surprised.

"Not exactly," answered the old man, shaking his head. Then, smiling as he stroked his goatee, said: "It's your legs that give you away!"

"You're a pretty keen observer!" admitted Chen Hai-min, good humouredly accepting the comment.

Grandpa Kuo knocked his pipe very deliberately on a stone and remarked:

"I was punting boats before you were born and I've met all kinds of people. I find that every man has something special about him and one glance is usually enough to tell me what kind of a person he is. Take legs for example, a peasant's legs are strong and full of knotted veins, but the legs of a townsman are usually thin and flabby. A hard working, honest man goes about fearlessly but a lazy man creeps around like a snail!"

Chen Hai-min burst into hearty laughter, and a dry chuckle forced its way through the lips of the middle-aged peasant.

The old man puffed at his pipe, looked in the direction of the young man who was still staring into the fire and said: "Just take Shih Man-tse for instance, I knew right away that he was worried about the crop; his knitted brows betrayed that." Then looking deliberately at the middle-aged peasant,

Yang Lao-liu, he said: "Now Yang Lao-liu! His easy-going way told me that his pocket is full of cold cash."

Yang Lao-liu, his face flushing, protested: "Grandpa, why are you picking on me today?"

"Because it's you I'm after," the old man admitted uncompromisingly. "While everybody else was trying to cope with the flood and save the paddy fields, you, and only you, went out to peddle firewood."

"The firewood isn't your property, is it?"

"No, it's not mine but the fields belong to us all, you, me and everybody else!"

Irritated, Shih Man-tse raised his head and said: "All right, now stop your fussing! The wind and rain seem to have slackened enough for us to cross. . . . Our team is waiting for me to get things organized so that we can fight the flood."

It was true that the rain had slackened a bit, but the wind was still howling furiously.

Grandpa Kuo fed the fire and said: "Humph, we'd better wait until it blows itself out before we make a move."

All except Chen Hai-min, who was secretly sizing up the others, were gazing into the fire. He, like other Party cadres finding themselves in a new environment, wanted to learn all he could about his new acquaintances. He hoped to find out something about the Shaho Commune from the three seated beside him. Shih Man-tse, low-spirited and scowling, was the first to attract his attention.

He asked him: "Are you a cadre from the production brigade?"

Shih Man-tse didn't answer. The old man replied instead, "He's the leader of the third team in the Yinping Brigade." Chen Hai-min nodded. Then he asked Shih, "How are the rice seedlings doing in your team?"

"Rice seedlings!" exclaimed Shih gruffly. "There are none left! They've all been washed away. . . ." Knitting his brows, he spread out his big hands and added: "There won't be much of a harvest this year! We can forget all about the wheat harvest. Let's talk about the crop that's facing us. When we really needed rain not a drop fell, the maize was as dry as kindling and the sweet potatoes withered away. We waited and longed for rain. Who could have imagined. . . . Curse it! Fate has really been too hard on us!" He clenched his fists and an angry gleam came into his eyes.

"Can't any of the crop be saved?" asked Chen Hai-min.

The effect of his question was like pouring water over a fire. It silenced Shih, who sighed once more, then propped his chin on his hands.

"What's the use of worrying? Times are hard, but come what may, we have government aid to rely on. . . ." began Yang Lao-liu.

"Pah!" interrupted Grandpa Kuo, who spat before continuing, "Am I seeing ghosts again. Shame on you! How can a commune member talk like that? How can we ever build up our country if everyone relies on the government for grain?"

Yang Lao-liu scowled angrily and replied: "You only use your mouth to talk rubbish. Do you want us to think that you're the God with a thousand arms and can save the crop?"

Vexed, Grandpa Kuo rose to his feet and brandishing his pipe in the air he said: "Yang Lao-liu, stop talking nonsense! I'm no God but the masses are! The fields may be flooded with water and the rice seedlings floating about, but we don't have to stand about and just let them rot, do we? Of course everything will be lost if the rest of us act like you and only think of a way to make a fast dollar. It's fortunate for the commune there are only a few people like you!"

"All right, all right, it's no use arguing with you, you're too smart," answered Yang Lao-liu angrily as he turned away.

"Hee, hee," chuckled Grandpa Kuo. "You can't win because you're in the wrong!"

"Brother Yang," interrupted Shih Man-tse. "You have the wrong slant on things. . . ."

A smile of triumph hovered over Grandpa Kuo's face as he turned to Shih, saying: "It was only yesterday, Man-tse, that I told you the rice seedlings could be saved! There isn't a road under the sky that can't be walked along and not a stone in this world that can't be moved. Make up your mind and stop talking about planting maize one minute and setting out sweet potato slips the next. The first and most important thing to do is to save the rice seedlings!"

Chen Hai-min listened attentively. It was almost, he felt, as though he had looked through a number of reports on this commune and found a clue to the solution of its problems. His eyes reflected the glow of the firelight as he nodded in agreement. Grandpa Kuo glanced at him then continued more heatedly:

"You're not the only one I've told. In fact, I've said the same thing to everybody who has crossed the river here and what is more they have all agreed with me. As a team leader you should think of a way out. Now is the time for you to concentrate whatever forces you have. Organize your manpower and put all your draught animals to work on the water wheels. The first thing to do is to drain off the water, repair any breaches in the dyke and build up the dividing ridges. Then straighten up the seedlings that have been dislodged by the rain; replough the fields that are silted over and plant late rice on them. . . ."

Still staring into the fire, Shih mumbled:

"Useless. . . . We won't get anything out of it. . . ."

"It's like trying to dip out water with a sieve. . . ." interrupted Yang Lao-liu.

Ignoring Yang Lao-liu, Chen Hai-min asked Shih:

"Is it really as bad as you say?"

"It certainly is!"

"How much of the crop do you reckon we can save?" he asked.

"At best, only a third."

"All right, then you must save that third," replied Chen Hai-min. He sat on his heels and said: "Suppose we take another look. Since the rectification movement in the communes in the spring, the policy of the Party has been carried out all the way down and the people are more of one mind than ever before. Suppose everyone works energetically and farms more intensively, and applies twice as much fertilizer, how much more do you think you could produce?"

"Twenty percent more at least," interrupted Grandpa Kuo, his chin up and his goatee outthrust.

"I don't understand how you arrive at that figure," said Shih Man-tse, smiling faintly.

Chen Hai-min looked straight at him as he said:

"Well, suppose we count in everything, we'll be assured more than half the usual harvest." Then seeing that Shih Man-tse seemed almost convinced he added enthusiastically, "Comrade, you have to learn to see things in their right perspective. Take note of the loss, but also take the enthusiasm of the masses into account; size up the difficulties but when calculating the results offset them by the conditions in your favour. Your must look ahead. . . ."

"Right!" agreed Grandpa Kuo. "Any man who has ever sailed a boat knows that when navigating you have to look ahead, particularly when you're crossing rapids. If you turn your eyes away, even for one second, you'll be heading for disaster. . . ." Thrusting his lean face closer to Shih Man-tse, he teased: "Your eyes are in the back of your head!" Then, with a quick glance at Yang Lao-liu, he jeered: "There's another type whose eyes are in his behind and all he can see is filth!"

Blushing, Yang Lao-liu asked angrily: "Old Kuo, do I owe you any money, what's the matter with you?"

Grandpa Kuo only clenched his pipe between his teeth and chuckled.

Annoyed, Shih Man-tse waved his hand and said: "Stop talking nonsense and let's get back to the subject!"

Chen Hai-min poked up the fire.

"How much non-irrigated land have you?" he inquired coolly.

"A hundred and eighty *mou* or so."

"That's good!" exclaimed Chen Hai-min with a slapping on his knee. "You can make up for your loss in the paddy by making better use of the dry land. There's still time to plant corn, and even more sweet potatoes, with vegetables to fill in the spare land. Then you can beat the flood, eh?"

"That's just what I think!" agreed Grandpa Kuo, delighted. Shih's frown faded in a questioning manner but he still looked low spirited.

"Nature has really treated us badly," he began. "We're behind with everything! We'll have to save the rice seedlings, drain the water, plant the corn and the land that wasn't flooded, damn it, will have to be weeded." Feeling even more frustrated he continued: "There's too much to do all at once. . . ."

Chen Hai-min laughed and said: "Things can be tackled one by one, can't they?"

"What do you suggest we do first?" asked Shih Man-tse.

"How many people have you got?" Chen Hai-min asked.

"Ninety-odd, counting both major and auxiliary manpower."

"That's plenty!" shouted Chen Hai-min, clapping his hands in his excitement. "First you must round up all the strongest ones and spend three days rescuing the rice seedlings, at the same time a few people should be set to work re-planting them where they have been washed away. While that is going on let the others weed the dry land. When the planting is finished, the group should hurry up and sow late corn and plant sweet potato on the dry land. Last of all, mobilize the commune members to get melons and vegetables planted on every vacant space around their homes, and along the roadside. . . ."

As his words echoed through the room Shih Man-tse's eyes glowed and Grandpa Kuo repeatedly nodded his head. Yang Lao-liu seemed fascinated, even his melancholy face seemed to gain liveliness.

"You sound like an expert who knows what he is talking about!" remarked Grandpa Kuo.

"Well, it's only a suggestion. We must find out what the people think about it," replied Chen Hai-min.

"I'm one of them and I agree!" snapped Grandpa Kuo. He leaned towards Chen Hai-min as he admitted: "I work on the boat but my heart has always been in the fields. Tomorrow I'm going to ask if I can do some field work."

Chen Hai-min answered confidently: "Right! We need everyone out to fight the flood." Turning to Yang Lao-liu he added: "You should keep your mind on the collective work too."

"Of course, of course," replied Yang Lao-liu hurriedly.

The wind had gradually subsided and the rain had stopped unnoticed.

Shih Man-tse was still frowning, and after a brief silence he said:

"The morale of our commune members is high. . . . It's just that our area is hit too hard and we have not enough oxen for the ploughs. I came over here today to try and borrow a few but the people here are all using theirs."

"But we've plenty of them!" announced Chen Hai-min cheerfully.

"Where?" asked Shih Man-tse with a gleam of hope in his eyes. "If we can only borrow them I'll pay double!"

"Several of the communes in the Second District are not hit by the floods at all and they've already agreed to send some oxen to help the Shaho Commune. They'll be here tomorrow!"

Shih Man-tse jumped to his feet and asked: "Is that true?"

"You can take my word for it! When one commune is in trouble others will never stand on one side and refuse to help!" He looked around the small hut, laughed and said: "And here's some more good news. The county Party committee has decided to send some more chemical fertilizer to help the flood-stricken areas."

Shih Man-tse grinned, showing a set of strong, white teeth. Then shaking his fist he shouted: "Hurray! Although nature acts against us it can never crush us!"

Grandpa Kuo stroked his whiskers saying: "Of course, it's as I've always said, so long as we have the Party and the people's communes, a disaster need never worry us overmuch." Knocking the dottle out of his pipe, he went on: "A tiller of the land has to be strong enough to face all difficulties. As for me, I don't believe in going about frowning and sighing. You can't get anything done by looking miserable! You're a team leader. Never mind how terrible things are, you must clench your teeth and bear it, and always look happy when talking with commune members. When they see that you're not worried they'll feel better, too. . . ."

Shih Man-tse threw his jacket around his shoulders saying: "All right, all right. I've heard you say the same thing many a time before. But, please, let's stop talking now and go!"

Grandpa Kuo frowned as he commanded: "You just wait until I finish, young man!" Staring at Chen Hai-min, he went on: "The hardships we're having now aren't half as bad as they were back in the old society. That year when . . . ai . . . I was still so young. . . ."

As he was speaking, a young girl entered the hut. Her clothes were dripping water and as she snatched off her bamboo rain hat, a pair of eyes sparkling beneath a crown of glossy black hair was revealed.

"I wonder who. . . . Oh, it's you, Fen Wa!" exclaimed Grandpa Kuo, hurriedly making room for her by the fire. "Come and get dry by the fire. You mustn't catch cold."

Shih Man-tse inquired: "Why are you out so late? Collecting the facts again?"

Yang Lao-liu shook his head and said: "Fancy girl like you being out on such a night as this. You're not a bit afraid either!"

Wringing out her coat as she squatted by the fire, she answered: "What is there to be afraid of? Are there tigers around here to eat me?"

Chen Hai-min looked at this saucy girl with a quick tongue and assumed that she was probably a clerk to the district Party committee.

Fen Wa had not noticed him, and bursting with news she said: "I have a message for your Shaho Commune. And it's good news, too!"

"Good news?" questioned Shih Man-tse and Grandpa Kuo with one voice.

Rattling away like a string of exploding firecrackers, Fen Wa announced: "The weather station has just announced that the rain will stop tomorrow. And the district Party committee has notified us all to get organized and hurry to save the rice seedlings!"

"This sounds more like it!" exclaimed Shih Man-tse.

Grandpa Kuo winked as he remarked: "I've known all along that it would soon blow over."

"All right, Old Kuo, don't start boasting again. You're always wise after the event! We all know that!" jeered Yang Lao-liu.

"Damn it, Yang Lao-liu, why are you picking on me so much today?" Grandpa Kuo grumbled, disgusted.

"Stop arguing," laughed Fen Wa. "I've some more good news for you."

"All right, tell us then," said Grandpa Kuo. "Some day I'm going to give you a little present, maybe some pears. Eh?"

At this point Fen Wa, who had taken a quick look at Chen Hai-min, turned and asked: "Grandpa, did a stranger cross the river today?"

"Many people crossed the river. How do you expect me to know which one you mean?"

"I don't know who he is either," replied Fen Wa seriously. "But I heard some comrades from the district committee saying that the county Party committee had sent a comrade to the Shaho Commune to take over as Party secretary."

As Chen Hai-min listened a smile played around the corners of his mouth.

Shih Man-tse lifted his eyebrows and said: "This is even better. Another leader for the commune! Good! Has he come yet?"

Grandpa Kuo clenched his pipe between his teeth, cocked

his head birdlike, and remarked: "It looks to me as if the new secretary is sitting right here under our noses!"

Everyone turned to look at Chen Hai-min, who felt a bit embarrassed.

"Are you . . . ?" asked Fen Wa with questioning eyes.

"I'm rather late in getting here," murmured Chen Hai-min.

"Oh, you're not late at all," exclaimed Shih Man-tse, and taking hold of Chen Hai-min's hand he added: "You're right in the nick of time!"

"You're the smartest imp in the Sha River district. How did you guess who he was?" whispered Yang Lao-liu to Grandpa Kuo.

Grandpa Kuo was elated and winking knowingly he said: "Every man has a special air about him that I can spot at a glance." He looked at Chen Hai-min and went on: "Take the Party secretary here, there's something about him that's different from us. . . ."

But Chen Hai-min insisted, "We're all the same. I'm no different from any of you."

"Generally speaking, Party secretaries have a special Party air about them as if they can conquer all the evil spirits in the world."

"That's true!" admitted Yang Lao-liu nodding in approval.

"Well, I'm too silly to be able to distinguish," Fen Wa remarked.

"I'm not boasting," continued Grandpa Kuo. "You tell me, has there ever been any cadre who has crossed this river without my help? So it's I who carry the Party policies over this water. He, he. . . ."

Stamping his feet impatiently, Shih Man-tse shouted: "Grandpa Kuo, you'll have to stop talking for a while, at least long enough to take us across. Come on!"

Roaring with laughter they put on their clothes and shoes and prepared to leave.

Darkness and a slippery road awaited them outside. Grandpa Kuo picked up his small lantern and led the way. The glow from the swinging lantern and the shadows that it cast on the ground wavered to and fro, as they groped their way down the stone steps and walked towards the river. Grandpa Kuo held the boat steady and one after another they jumped in.

The waves were still rolling. . . .

Shih Man-tse took up an oar, spread his legs and dipped the oar in the water.

"The water's still rising!" he shouted.

"Don't worry. The boat will rise with it."

Grandpa Kuo, the last to jump aboard, took a bamboo pole and pushed the boat away from the bank.

As the waves dashed against the sides of it the boat rocked violently, but defying the strong current it moved swiftly towards the opposite bank. Chen Hai-min sat silently in the boat listening to the sound of the waves, the wind, the oars and the heavy panting of old Grandpa Kuo. Unblinkingly he stared at the night scene on the opposite shore, feeling as if his eyes were flickering on and off in unison with the twinkling lights in the sparsely lit village on the opposite bank.

Suddenly he felt that his blood was coursing more strongly through his veins, and his personal worry of a moment ago was now dispersed by a new flow of feeling as he realized that the morale of the people here will never collapse in the face of calamities. Some may become discouraged, but with a little support they too will stand up and fight with the rest! In the little ferry hut he had felt the pulse of the Shaho Commune. It wasn't weak, it was vigorous and strong. . . .

He recalled the words he had said to the county Party secretary the previous day: "So long as the people will work with me, I have nothing to fear."

The surface of the river was churned into a mass of tossing waves.

Fen Wa moved closer to Chen Hai-min and shouted above the roar of the water: "Secretary, listen, on the opposite shore the people are singing. . . ."

"Uh. . . ."

He could not distinguish it clearly, but above the faint sound of folk music wafted on the night air, he was conscious of the sound of the waves, the river and the happiness flowing from the depths of his own heart. . . .

· 7 ·

The Mind of China: Continuity and Change

The following analysis of contemporary Chinese thinking provides an interesting contrast with traditional Chinese thought. To what extent have the efforts of the Communist government eradicated those traditional attitudes and characteristics that hindered radical change and social progress? To what degree do these attitudes continue to persist in China? To what extent does the Chinese government itself reflect the past? This article from *Time* attempts to probe the current Chinese mind to see how the present differs from the past, and how the past continues to shape and influence the present. Can we speak of Mao as now enjoying the Mandate of Heaven as evidence of his supreme virtue? Would it be too much of an exaggeration to suggest that the contemporary Chinese mind represents a synthesis of Confucianism, Marxism, and Maoism?

TIME MAGAZINE (1967)

Viewed against the backdrop of China's past, the Communist regime shows an intricate pattern of change and sameness. . . .

A new generation of scholar-officials interprets the doctrine, which has been put into little red plastic books and spread across the nation for all to memorize. The loyalty to a dynastic ruler has been replaced by adherence to a political party—and to the father figure of Mao himself. Whipping up the old xenophobia and banking on the old lack of individualism, Mao is trying to establish a central regime more stringent than any China has ever known—and, like all past rulers, facing regional opposition. His party cadres travel across country to spy and supervise, as did the imperial secretaries and "censors"; like the Manchus, Mao discourages the use of government officials in their native areas.

Above all, the notion remains that theory can be imposed on reality. Confucious believed that the power of the mind could "move heaven and earth." Mao seems to have a similar belief in that power: the Great Leap Forward can be accomplished, steel can be made in the backyard, revolution can be rendered permanent, if only the will is there. . . . The cult of the right term coincides with the endless Communist name calling and with such moves as changing Peking's Legation Street to Anti-Imperialist Struggle Street.

The Communists used the force of face when they paraded opponents through the streets in dunce caps; reportedly, such humiliation has led many to kill themselves. . . .

Yet the breaks with the past are at least as significant as the parallels. Both Sun Yat-sen and Chiang Kai-shek fought in some measure against the Confucian tradition, passivity and family loyalties. Mao is continuing the fight more ruthlessly. Where the old China put soldiers at the bottom of the social order, Red China glorifies them. A streak of neo-puritanism now replaces the older hedonism. The family is under heavy attack. One effective campaign involved a marriage-reform law, which was aimed at female equality. The People's Communes, with their central mess halls, were intended to subordinate family loyalties to the state. No longer is a son punished for informing against his father; on the contrary, he is ordered to do so. Ancestor worship is also being stamped out; thousands of ancestral cemeteries have been dug up. Children are not taught the five relationships of Confucius, but learn the five loves instead: "love of country, of the people, of work, of science, of the people's property."

How successful the Communists are in changing the old thought patterns, no one can say. Until its recent easing, the Red Guards' roving revolution suggested turmoil that reached the roots of the nation. Mao may be gambling with the Mandate of Heaven—or of history. Endurance is the greatest Chinese virtue. The Chinese express it by saying: "We know how to *ch'ih-ku*—to eat bitterness." Without doubt the bitterness of Communist rule will profoundly change China. In the process, China will also change Communism.

• 8 •

The Economic Situation

When the Communists completed their victory in the civil war in late 1949, the Chinese economy was in a chaotic state. Almost two decades of war with Japan and civil war had left their mark. With this chaos came the inheritance of China's traditional economic situation: scarcity of land and capital, abundance of labor. Thus the first task for the new government was one of reconstruction and rehabilitation. By 1952 the inflation had ended, industrial production had reached prewar levels, redistribution of land—with the goal of ending landlordism—had begun, and major social reforms were under way.

China's first Five Year Plan went into effect in 1953. Its aims were the gradual collectivization of agriculture, the socialization of industry (with emphasis on production in heavy industry), and continued social reform. Its execution was to a large extent dependent on aid from the Soviet Union in the form of loans, and assistance from technical advisers. While the results cannot be ascertained with any degree of precision, it appears that they were successful. (Domestic peace must be counted as a major factor.) Landlordism was ended, and cooperatives, modeled somewhat after the Soviet *kolkhoz*, were established. Food production rose to at least subsistence conditions, but shortages continued to exist in urban areas as the industrial sector expanded and the population of these cities increased. All the basic industries came under state control. There was considerable advancement in the areas of education, social and health insurance, and social equality.

In spite of a lack of coordination in planning, and in spite of shortages in food and consumer goods, the Chinese leaders and planners were buoyed up by the results of the plan, and projected truly revolutionary goals in their next plan. (This irritated the Russian advisers who argued that the Chinese were not yet ready for the final leap toward complete socialism.) The second plan, known as the Great Leap Forward, had as its professed general aim, the communization of China. A breakthrough in agriculture was planned in order to sustain rapid industrialization. The commune system was designed as the major medium for this radical change. The commune, a multifaceted, decentralized unit, was intended to combine both primitive and modern economic techniques and to take the initiative in political, military, and cultural activities.

The results of the Great Leap were not up to the Chinese expectations. (The government stopped issuing economic statistics shortly after the plan went into effect.) Nature did not cooperate—1959 to 1961 were years of drought. Apparently there was some resistance from the peasants toward the extreme measures employed in the commune system. It was at this time that the Soviet Union began to withdraw its assistance. These factors, combined with serious errors on the part of the planners—both economic and political—prevented the Great Leap from succeeding. Whether it was as great a disaster as some observers have indicated remains an open question.

Since 1962 the Chinese have deliberately slowed the pace of change, although the ultimate goals remain substantially the same. The communes continue to function, though in somewhat altered form. Most reports indicate that recovery from the setbacks of the Great Leap has already been accomplished, and that economic growth, while uneven, continues. However, it is possible that the disturbances caused by the Cultural Revolution have led to some disruption.

Walter Galenson describes some of the obstacles involved in obtaining and interpreting economic statistics on Chinese economic growth. Following are some statistics on economic growth in China. When studied they should yield some insight into what has happened to the Chinese economy since the Communists have come into power. What tentative conclusions on economic growth can you come to from studying the charts on China's international trade? What insight can you garner from the chart on population growth that relates to economic problems?

WALTER GALENSON

The Obstacles to Study

The overwhelming problem that faces all students of the contemporary Chinese economic scene is the blackout of economic statistics imposed by the Chinese authorities in 1960, and continued ever since. For over six years, scarcely a significant figure relating to the national economy, regional economies, sectors of the economy, or branches of industry has been published. There has been no public announcement of the magnitude of steel or coal production, of machinery output, of the size of harvests. The routine information which we ordinarily find in annual statistical yearbooks and allied publications is completely unavailable for China on a current basis. . . .

Most books, journals, and newspapers have been embargoed, so effectively that they are not even available in Hong Kong. Those few that still come through contain almost no economic data. There is an occasional statement about the success of an individual enterprise in raising its output, and a few percentage increase claims have been released (for example, that in the first eight months of 1966, steel output was 20 percent higher than in the corresponding period of 1965). Visitors have been given an odd figure or two. But there is nothing of a systematic character; not even plan targets. Indeed, we do not know whether China is actually operating under a Five Year Plan.

A substantial quantity of statistics was published up to 1958, culminating in the issuance of a retrospective statistical handbook in 1959, entitled *Ten Great Years*. While this was a slender volume compared with the *Statistical Abstract of the United States* or the Soviet *Narodnoye Khozyaistvo,* it is absolutely fundamental to any study of the period. The flow of material began to dry up in 1959, slowed to a tiny trickle in 1960, and then stopped.

The quality of the data is another matter. . . .

Economic decentralization and the inauguration of the

Walter Galenson, "The Current State of Chinese Economic Studies," *An Economic Profile of Mainland China*, Joint Economic Committee, Congress of the United States, 90th Cong., 1st Sess. (Washington, D.C.: Government Printing Office, 1967), I, 3-7.

Great Leap Forward wreaked havoc with the statistical system. Reality gave way to wishful thinking at all echelons of the economy. A good example is provided by the agricultural statistics for 1958: The output of grain was announced initially at 375 million tons, presumably on the basis of crop reports from around the country. This was later scaled down to 250 million tons, a reduction of one-third, and there is considerable doubt about the validity of the lower figure. Exaggeration extended to all sectors of the economy. The claimed *increment* in coal output for 1958 was greater than total coal output in 1957. The volume of railroad freight traffic was reported to have doubled during 1958 and 1959. Pig iron production was supposed to have risen from 5.9 million tons in 1957 to 20.5 million tons in 1959. It is abundantly clear that official data for 1958, 1959, and 1960 (there are relatively few data for the last year) cannot be used without extremely close scrutiny. . . .

American economists are barred from the mainland, and apart from the possible value of contact with refugees, they are just as well off working at home as in Hong Kong or other areas contiguous to China. The few non-Communist economists who have been allowed to visit China have come back with little but fleeting impressions. The number of foreign businessmen visiting China is on the increase, and they are probably the best available source of information on technology there. But their experience is usually quite limited, and does not often permit generalization.

The same is true of those who manage to leave China with or without permission of the regime. . . .

Another very formidable barrier to the study of China is language. While a great deal of current information is available in translation, there is simply no substitute for the ability to read original sources. A paragraph, or even a sentence, in a specialized journal or a secondary newspaper may contain the key to a problem. A research assistant can be very helpful, but he can never be an adequate substitute for personal study of original material.

For the purposes of the economic analyst, Russian or the languages of Eastern Europe can be mastered in a relatively short time. Chinese is another story. People have different experience with learning it, but even after several years of intensive study, the degree of facility attained is generally not great. Many non-Chinese specialists with years of experience are still forced to lean heavily on Chinese research assistants.

Direction of Chinese Communist international trade, 1950–65

[In millions of U.S. dollars]

	Total international trade			Trade with Communist countries			Trade with Free World		
Year	Total	Exports	Imports	Total	Exports	Imports	Total	Exports	Imports
1950....	1,210	620	590	350	210	140	860	410	450
1951....	1,895	780	1,115	975	465	510	920	315	605
1952....	1,890	875	1,015	1,315	605	710	575	270	305
1953....	2,295	1,040	1,255	1,555	670	885	740	370	370
1954....	2,350	1,060	1,290	1,735	765	970	615	295	320
1955....	3,035	1,375	1,660	2,250	950	1,300	785	425	360
1956....	3,120	1,635	1,485	2,055	1,045	1,010	1,065	590	475
1957....	3,025	1,595	1,430	1,935	1,065	870	1,090	530	560
1958....	3,735	1,910	1,825	2,350	1,250	1,100	1,385	660	725
1959....	4,265	2,205	2,060	2,960	1,595	1,365	1,310	615	695
1960....	3,975	1,945	2,030	2,605	1,320	1,285	1,370	625	745
1961....	3,015	1,525	1,495	1,680	965	715	1,335	560	775
1962....	2,675	1,525	1,150	1,410	920	490	1,265	.605	660
1963....	2,755	1,560	1,200	1,245	820	425	1,510	740	770
1964....	3,245	1,770	1,475	1,125	730	395	2,120	1,040	1,080
1965....	3,695	1,955	1,740	1,125	645	480	2,570	1,310	1,260

Robert L. Price, "International Trade of Communist China, 1950-65," *An Economic Profile of Mainland China*, Joint Economic Committee, Congress of the United States, 90th Cong., 1st Sess. (Washington, D.C.: Government Printing Office, 1967), II, 584, 600.

Communist China—Trade with countries of the Free World, 1961–64

[In millions of U.S. dollars]

	1961	1962	1963	1964
Exports	560	605	740	1,040
Total, industrial West	222	210	265	415
Western Europe	181	149	172	229
Of which—				
United Kingdom	73	50	47	59
West Germany	35	32	34	49
France	13	15	19	28
Italy	10	12	19	21
Japan	29	44	71	150
Australia, Canada, and New Zealand	12	17	22	36
Total, less developed countries	223	259	304	371
South and southeast Asia	165	194	226	270
Of which—				
Burma	21	27	25	34
Ceylon	21	20	32	39
Indonesia	40	46	34	38
Malaya and Singapore	54	64	90	95
Pakistan	3	4	6	17
Middle East	27	32	42	45
Africa	29	31	34	54
Latin America	2	2	1	2
Hong Kong	115	138	170	253
Imports	775	660	770	1,080
Total, industrial West	602	473	582	684
Western Europe	234	170	184	196
Of which—				
United Kingdom	52	28	35	56
West Germany	46	36	18	20
France	41	51	67	43
Italy	38	23	21	20
Japan	17	40	66	160
Australia, Canada, and New Zealand	350	263	332	328
Total, less developed countries	174	186	188	394
South and southeast Asia	109	100	94	131
Of which—				
Burma	40	20	13	18
Ceylon	16	33	22	25
Indonesia	32	40	37	68
Malaya and Singapore	9		6	1
Pakistan	10	2	12	13
Middle East	27	30	34	54
Africa	28	22	54	54
Latin America	9	34	7	155
Of which Argentina	5	33	4	112
Hong Kong	1	2	2	2
Total, Free World	1,335	1,270	1,510	2,120

*Model of China's population growth**

Mid-year	Life expectancy (years)	Number of women, aged 15 to 44 (millions)	Annual births per 1,000 women, aged 15 to 44	Population (millions)			
				0 to 14	15 to 59	Over 59	Total
1948				181	317	37	535
	40.0	119	196				
1953				209	331	43	583
	50.0	124	200				
1958				254	351	49	654
	40.0	130	176				
1963				270	368	52	690
	50.0	142	195				
1968				298	412	58	768
	52.5	163	173				
1973				319	466	64	849
	55.0	184	145				
1978				343	510	72	925

Edwin F. Jones, "The Emerging Pattern of China's Economic Revolution," *An Economic Profile of Mainland China*, Joint Economic Committee, Congress of the United States, 90th Cong., 1st Sess. (Washington, D.C.: Government Printing Office, 1967), I, 93.

* This model ages and reverse-ages the 1953 census population, employing U.N. life table values and assuming life expectancies and fertilities appropriate to obtain the total population estimated or projected by Peking.

POPULATION DENSITIES IN MAINLAND CHINA: 1953

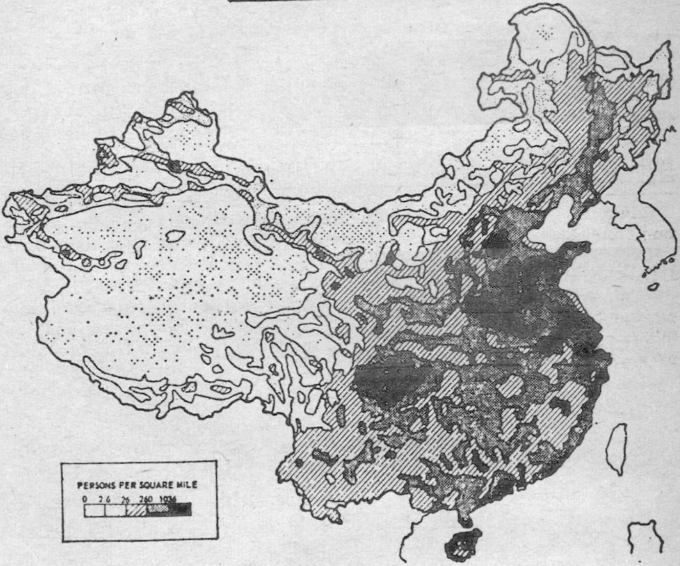

JOHN S. AIRD, "POPULATION GROWTH AND DISTRIBUTION IN MAINLAND CHINA," **AN ECONOMIC PROFILE OF MAINLAND CHINA,** JOINT ECONOMIC COMMITTEE, CONGRESS OF THE UNITED STATES, 90TH CONG., 1ST SESS. (WASHINGTON, D.C.: GOVERNMENT PRINTING OFFICE, 1967) II, 371.

• 9 •

The Dragon and the Bear: Sino-Soviet Relations

The hostility that has erupted in the last few years between China and the Soviet Union should not have surprised as many Westerners as it did. Much of what is today Russian territory in Siberia was taken away from China in early modern times. The Chinese and the Russians have a long history of border disputes. The infant Chinese Communist Party was almost sacrificed to Russian interests. During the war with Japan, the Russians recognized Chiang as the sole leader of China, and urged the Communists to cooperate with him, rather than the other way around. After the war, the Russians hedged before throwing full support to Mao—apparently not until it was entirely clear that the Kuomintang was doomed to fail. Thus there is ample evidence to suggest that the two Communist nations could not long remain allied.

The first reading presents the text of the Chinese–Soviet friendship treaty. What do you think were the motivations for each partner's acceptance of this pact? The second selection outlines the Chinese reasons for their growing distrust of Khrushchev and the Russians. Do you think this document sufficiently explains the rift? The third selection is a letter from the Chinese declining an invitation to attend the annual congress in Russia. What does this letter reveal about the quarrel?

THE USSR–CHINA FRIENDSHIP TREATY

TEXT OF COMMUNIQUE

In the course of a recent period, negotiations have taken place in Moscow between J. V. Stalin, Chairman of the Council of Ministers of the U. S. S. R., and A. Y. Vishinsky,

U. S. S. R. Minister of Foreign Affairs, on the one hand and Mr. Mao Tze-tung, Chairman of the Central Government of the Chinese People's Republic and Mr. Chou En-lai, Premier of the State Administrative Council and Foreign Minister of the People's Republic, on the other hand, during which important political and economic problems on relations between the Soviet Union and the Chinese People's Republic were discussed.

The negotiations, which took place in an atmosphere of cordiality and friendly mutual understanding, confirmed the striving of both sides to strengthen in every way and to develop relations of friendship and cooperation between them as well as their desire to cooperate for the purpose of guaranteeing general peace and the security of the nations. The negotiations were ended by the signing in the Kremlin Feb. 14 of:

1. A Treaty of Friendship, Alliance and Mutual Aid between the Soviet Union and the Chinese People's Republic.
2. Agreements on the Chinese Changchun railway, Port Arthur and Dalny [Dairen], under which, after the signing of the peace treaty with Japan, the Chinese Changchun railway will pass into complete ownership of the Chinese People's Republic, while Soviet troops will be withdrawn from Port Arthur.
3. Agreements by which the Government of the U. S. S. R. will give to the Government of the Chinese People's Republic a long term economic credit for payments of deliveries of industrial and railway equipment from the U. S. S. R. . . .

A Treaty Regarding Friendship, Alliance and Mutual Aid Between the Soviet Socialist Republics and the Chinese People's Republic. . . .

The high contracting parties will not conclude any alliance directed against the other high contracting party, nor will they participate in any coalition, or in actions or measures directed against the other party.

The high contracting parties will cooperate with each other in all important international questions touching on the mutual

REPRINTED WITH PERMISSION, FROM ED VALTMAN, THE HARTFORD TIMES.

interests of the Soviet Union and China, being guided by the interest of strengthening peace and universal security.

The high contracting parties undertake, in the spirit of friendship and cooperation and in accordance with the principles of equality, in the joint interest and likewise with joint respect for state sovereignty and territorial integrity and non-intervention in the internal affairs of the other country to develop and strengthen economic and cultural ties between the Soviet Union and China, and to render each other every possible economic aid, and realize the necessary economic cooperation.

Done in this city of Moscow, Feb. 14, 1950, in duplicate, each in the Russian and Chinese languages, both texts have equal force.

CENTRAL COMMITTEE OF THE CHINESE COMMUNIST PARTY

1963

THE DIFFERENCES BEGAN WITH THE TWENTIETH CONGRESS OF THE CPSU

There is a saying, "It takes more than one cold day for the river to freeze three feet deep." The present differences in the international communist movement did not, of course, begin just today. . . .

The truth is that the whole series of differences of principle in the international communist movement began more than seven years ago.

To be specific, it began with the 20th Congress of the CPSU in 1956.

The 20th Congress of the CPSU was the first step along the road of revisionism taken by the leadership of the CPSU. From the 20th Congress to the present, the revisionist line of the leadership of the CPSU has gone through the process of emergence, formation, growth and systematization. . . .

From the very outset we held that a number of views advanced at the 20th Congress concerning the contemporary

From *The Origin and Development of the Differences Between the Leadership of the CPSU and Ourselves* (Peking: Foreign Language Press, 1963).

international struggle and the international communist movement were wrong, were violations of Marxism-Leninism. In particular, the complete negation of Stalin on the pretext of "combating the personality cult" and the thesis of peaceful transition to socialism by "the parliamentary road" are gross errors of principle.

The criticism of Stalin at the 20th Congress of the CPSU was wrong both in principle and in method. . . .

In his report to the 20th Congress, under the pretext that "radical changes" had taken place in the world situation, Khrushchov put forward the thesis of "peaceful transition." . . .

Khrushchov declared: "We want to be friends with the United States and to co-operate with it for peace and international security and also in the economic and cultural spheres." This wrong view later developed into the line of "Soviet-U.S. co-operation for the settlement of world problems."

Distorting Lenin's correct principle of peaceful coexistence between countries with different social systems, Khrushchov declared that peaceful coexistence was the "general line of the foreign policy" of the U.S.S.R. This amounted to excluding from the general line of foreign policy of the socialist countries their mutual assistance and co-operation as well as assistance by them to the revolutionary struggles of the oppressed peoples and nations, or to subordinating all this to the policy of so-called "peaceful coexistence."

The facts of the past seven years have amply proved that the differences between the Chinese and Soviet Parties and within the international communist movement have arisen solely because the leadership of the CPSU has departed from Marxism-Leninism. . . .

The facts of the past seven years have amply proved that the present differences within the international communist movement are differences between the line of adhering to Marxism-Leninism and the line of clinging to revisionism, between the revolutionary line and the non-revolutionary and counter-revolutionary line, between the anti-imperialist line and the line of capitulation to imperialism. They are differences between proletarian internationalism and great-power chauvinism, sectarianism and splittism.

The facts of the past seven years have amply proved that

the road taken by the leadership of the CPSU is the course of allying with imperialism against socialism, allying with the United States against China, allying with the reactionaries of all countries against the people of the world.

March 22, 1966

The Central Committee of the
Communist Party of the Soviet Union

Dear Comrades,

The Communist Party of China has received the letter of the Central Committee of the Communist Party of the Soviet Union dated February 24, 1966, inviting us to send a delegation to attend your Twenty-third Congress as guests.

In normal circumstances, it would be considered an indication of friendship for one Party to invite another fraternal Party to send a delegation to its congress. But around the time you sent this invitation, you distributed an anti-Chinese document in the Soviet Union both inside and outside the Party and organized a whole series of anti-Chinese reports from top to bottom, right down to the basic units, whipping up hysteria against China. . . .

Russia is the native land of Leninism and used to be the centre of the international working class movement. After Stalin's death, the leaders of the CPSU headed by Khrushchov gradually revealed their true features as betrayers of Lenin and Leninism. . . .

Over the last ten years, we have made a series of efforts in the hope that you would return to the path of Marxism-Leninism. Since Khrushchov's downfall, we have advised the new leaders of the CPSU on a number of occasions to make a fresh start. We have done everything we could, but you have not shown the slightest repentance.

Since coming to power, the new leaders of the CPSU have gone farther and farther down the road of revisionism, splittism and great-power chauvinism. . . . Far from publicly retracting the anti-Chinese Open Letter of July 1963 and the

---

From "Letter of Reply Dated March 22, 1966 of The Central Committee of The Communist Party of China to The Central Committee of The Communist Party of The Soviet Union" (Peking: Foreign Language Press, 1966).

anti-Chinese report and resolution of February 1964, you have intensified your activities against China by more insidious tactics. Despite the tricks you have been playing to deceive people, you are pursuing U.S.-Soviet collaboration for the domination of the world with your whole heart and soul. In mouthing a few words against U.S. imperialism and in making a show of supporting anti-imperialist struggles, you are conducting only minor attacks on U.S. imperialism while rendering it major help. In following this tactic you very well know what you are up to, and so does U.S. imperialism. . . . You have worked hand in glove with the United States in a whole series of dirty deals inside and outside the United Nations. In close co-ordination with the counter-revolutionary "global strategy" of U.S. imperialism, you are now actively trying to build a ring of encirclement around socialist China. Not only have you excluded yourselves from the international united front of all the peoples against U.S. imperialism and its lackeys, you have even aligned yourselves with U.S. imperialism, the main enemy of the people of the world, and the reactionaries of all countries in a vain attempt to establish a Holy Alliance against China, against the people, against the national liberation movement and against the Marxist-Leninists.

The Central Committee of the
Communist Party of China

· 10 ·

The Dragon and the Eagle: Sino-American Relations

China and the United States do not maintain diplomatic relations. For a fleeting moment after the Communists came into power, an effort was made at establishing normal relations. But the Korean War, which broke out in 1950—with American and Chinese troops fighting each other, and resulting in a security treaty between the United States and Taiwan—erased any early opportunity for coming to terms. America's

"Let's Be Reasonable"

REPRINTED WITH PERMISSION OF W.C.C. PUBLISHING CO., FROM N.Y. HERALD TRIBUNE.

increasing involvement in Asia, as symbolized by the Vietnam War, and China's angry denunciations of United States policy have increased tensions and, according to some observers, have put the two powers on a collision course.

Dean Rusk, American Secretary of State from 1961 to 1968, gives the official position of the United States. Do you find Rusk's arguments convincing? Myra Roper records Vice-Premier Chen Yi's statement of Chinese policy. Do you find Chen's arguments convincing? Who do you think is closer to the truth? Does either of these views contain misconceptions?

DEAN RUSK

WHAT DOES PEIPING WANT?

First, the Chinese Communist leaders seek to bring China on the world stage as a great power. They hold that China's history, size, and geographic position entitle it to great-power status. They seek to overcome the humiliation of 150 years of economic, cultural, and political domination by outside powers.

Our concern is with the way they are pursuing their quest for power and influence in the world. And it is not only our concern but that of many other countries, including in recent years the Soviet Union. . . .

Peiping's use of power is closely related to what I believe are its second and third objectives: dominance within Asia and leadership of the Communist world revolution, employing Maoist tactics. Peiping is striving to restore traditional Chinese influence or dominance in South, Southeast, and East Asia. Its concept of influence is exclusive. . . .

DIRECT AGGRESSION

Peiping has not refrained from the use of force to pursue its objectives. Following Korea, there were Tibet and the attacks on the offshore islands in the Taiwan Straits. There have been the attacks on India. It is true that, since Korea, Peiping has moved only against weaker foes and has carefully avoided situations which might bring it face to face with the United

---

Dean Rusk, *United States Policy Toward Communist China,* Department of State Publication 8078 (Washington, D.C.: Government Printing Office, 1966).

States. It has probed for weaknesses around its frontier but drawn back when the possibility of a wider conflict loomed. . . .

MAO'S DOCTRINE OF WORLD REVOLUTION

As I have said, the Chinese Communist leaders are dedicated to a fanatical and bellicose Marxist-Leninist-Maoist doctrine of world revolution. Last fall, Lin Piao, the Chinese Communist Minister of Defense, recapitulated in a long article Peiping's strategy of violence for achieving Communist domination of the world. This strategy involves the mobilization of the underdeveloped areas of the world—which the Chinese Communists compare to the "rural areas"—against the industrialized or "urban" areas. It involves the relentless prosecution of what they call "people's wars." The final stage of all this violence is to be what they frankly describe as "wars of annihilation."

It is true that this doctrine calls for revolution by the natives of each country. In that sense it may be considered a "do-it-yourself kit." But Peiping is prepared to train and indoctrinate the leaders of these revolutions and to support them with funds, arms, and propaganda, as well as politically. It is even prepared to manufacture these revolutionary movements out of whole cloth. . . .

WORDS VERSUS ACTIONS

Some say we should ignore what the Chinese Communist leaders say and judge them only by what they do. It is true that they have shown, in many ways, that they have a healthy respect for the power of the United States.

But it does not follow that we should disregard the intentions and plans for the future which they have proclaimed. To do so would be to repeat the catastrophic miscalculation that so many people made about the ambitions of Hitler—and that many have made at various times in appraising the intentions of the Soviet leaders. . . .

CHINESE COMMUNIST FEAR OF ATTACK

At times the Communist Chinese leaders seem to be obsessed with the notion that they are being threatened and encircled. We have told them both publicly and privately, and I believe have demonstrated in our actions in times of crisis and even under grave provocation, that we want no war with Communist China. . . .

How much Peiping's "fear" of the United States is genuine and how much it is artificially induced for domestic political purposes only the Chinese Communist leaders themselves know. I am convinced, however, that their desire to expel our influence and activity from the western Pacific and Southeast Asia is not motivated by fears that we are threatening them. . . .

CHINA AS A GREAT POWER

We expect China to become some day a great world power. Communist China is a major Asian power today. In the ordinary course of events, a peaceful China would be expected to have close relations—political, cultural, and economic—with the countries around its borders and with the United States.

It is no part of the policy of the United States to block the peaceful attainment of these objectives.

ELEMENTS OF FUTURE POLICY

What should be the main elements in our policy toward Communist China?

We must take care to do nothing which encourages Peiping—or anyone else—to believe that it can reap gains from its aggressive actions and designs. It is just as essential to "contain" Communist aggression in Asia as it was, and is, to "contain" Communist aggression in Europe.

At the same time, we must continue to make it plain that, if Peiping abandons its belief that force is the best way to resolve disputes and gives up its violent strategy of world revolution, we would welcome an era of good relations.

CHEN YI

(quoted by Myra Roper)

He dealt immediately, and more in sorrow than in anger, with the idea that China was warlike and encouraging others to be so; that this was a travesty, he said, was clearly shown by China's steadfast refusal to reclaim her alienated territories by force. Taiwan, Hong Kong and Macao were indubitably part of China, but none had been threatened by military attack and China had not attempted to reclaim its Indian border territories until Indian forces moved into them. . . . As for encouraging revolutions in Asia or elsewhere, he stressed that China was the great friend of all oppressed people, that it gave support and encouragement to Afro-Asian and Latin American revolts, but that this was never armed support. . . .

He went on to say that nothing was farther from China's intentions than overrunning neighbouring countries. This would be palpably illogical; China had hitherto failed to develop her own extensive resources because of feudal control and foreign exploitation but full development was now planned and would more than absorb her population. For example, western provinces which now carry some sixty million people could well carry two hundred million and still be less crowded than Hopei. . . .

He moved on logically to what he called the great slander—that China was not afraid of the atomic bomb and would sacrifice untold millions of her people with equanimity. The Chinese feared the bomb as much as the next man, he argued, but they needed it themselves as a defence weapon. . . .

Chen Yi made it clear that China resents any implication by the Soviet Union or anyone else that she has a subordinate role in the Communist world; and indeed national pride is as important in the new China as it always was in the old. It is the prime motivating factor today, and though the breach with Russia was ostensibly caused by Khrushchev's abandonment of Marxist-Leninist principles of international Communism, Chinese nationalism played a vital part. This was underlined when Chen Yi moved on to answer our question on China's seeming isolation after her break with both the USSR and India. As we expected, he denied any isolation. "China has friends all over the world, diplomatic relations with forty countries will soon increase to sixty and it will be realized that those who isolate China isolate themselves, for China is a great power."

Here Chen Yi paused to pose and answer his own question. Asking if China could fairly call herself a great power when she was still poor and, by Western standards, backward, he explained that she would not be backward for long for she had immense, untapped natural resources, a vast population ready to work hard and, above all, a policy which they all knew to be the correct one—"our strength is in the rightness of the Party's policy." . . .

Recently Mr. Rusk had been having a go at China; how could he believe that this country would be bullied and vilified and not defend herself? "How does the United States think that we can ease tension? Where do we start? By removing military bases which we haven't got? Have we one on Taiwan (Formosa) or in Hong Kong, or have we a blockade on the United States to lift?" . . .

"The trouble with the United States," he commented, "is that she will act the big boss, indulge in great power chauvinism and want to dictate where she assists. We don't receive her assistance and get by better than Taiwan which has it." . . .

• 11 •

China and the United Nations

(See updated supplement on recent events, page 311.)

China has a seat in the United Nations, but it is the government of Chiang Kai-shek on Taiwan that has this vote. Since 1950 the United Nations has voted to deny mainland China a seat. The debate has been heated, the vote has fluctuated, but the result has been consistent. Keeping China out of the United Nations has been a cornerstone of American policy since the Korean War. This aspect of American policy has been severely criticized at home and abroad, and the United States has shown some interest recently in some of the alternatives suggested. However, the official policy has remained steadfast. The entire debate may be academic: the Chinese leaders have maintained hostility toward the policies of the United Nations, and have not displayed any enthusiasm for joining. How can you account for this aspect of Chinese policy?

Adlai Stevenson, American ambassador to the United Nations from 1961 to 1965, states the official American position. Do you find his arguments convincing? Next is a chart giving the voting statistics on admitting China, followed by

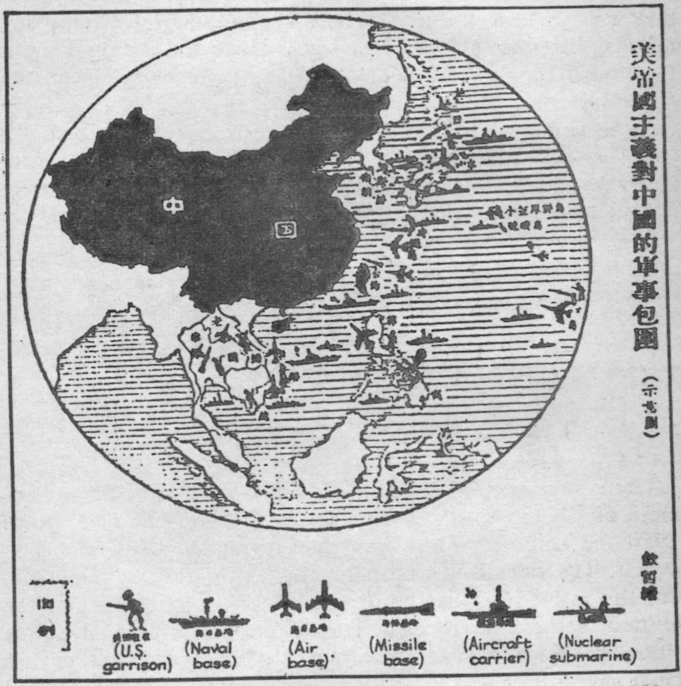

This map was prepared in China. Assuming the information in this map reasonably accurate, how would China and the United States differ in their interpretation?

Bird's Eye View

REPRINTED WITH PERMISSION, FROM ROY JUSTUS, THE MINNEAPOLIS STAR.

Do you think this is an accurate view of United States-China policy?

the actual voting on the 1969 resolution. Can you detect any pattern in these figures? Does there seem to be any particular alignment? The next two readings are excerpts from the hearings of the Senate Foreign Relations Committee in 1966, held to reevaluate American policy. A. Doak Barnett, professor at Columbia, argues for a change in policy. Former Congressman Walter Judd, once a medical missionary to China, argues for maintenance of the present policy. With whom do you agree?

ADLAI STEVENSON

The United States believes, as we have believed from the beginning, that the United Nations would make a tragic and perhaps irreparable mistake if it yielded to the claim of an aggressive and unregenerate "People's Republic of China" to replace the Republic of China in the United Nations. I realize that we have sometimes been charged with "unrealism"—and even with "ignoring the existence of 600 million people." . . .

No country is more aware of their existence. I think it could be said with more justice that it would be dangerously unrealistic if this Assembly were to bow to the demands of Peiping to expel and replace the Republic of China in the United Nations; it would be ignoring the warlike character and aggressive behavior of the rulers who dominate 600 million people and who talk of the inevitability of war as an article of faith and refuse to renounce the use of force. . . .

Into the international sphere the Chinese Communists have carried . . . qualities of arrogance, regimentation, and aggression. . . . It was the supreme leader of Chinese communism, Mao Tse-tung, who summed up his world outlook over twenty years ago in these words: "Everything can be made to grow out of the barrel of a gun." And again: "The central duty and highest form of revolution is armed seizure of political power, the settling of problems by means of war. This Marxist-Leninist principle is universally correct, whether in China or in foreign countries; it is always true." . . .

There are some who acknowledge the illegal and aggressive conduct of the Chinese Communists but who believe that the

---

"Statement by Ambassador Adlai Stevenson, U.S. Representative to the General Assembly on December 1, 1961," U.S. Department of State *Bulletin* (Washington, D.C., January 15, 1962).

United Nations can somehow accommodate this unbridled power and bring it in some measure under the control, or at least the influence, of the community of nations. They maintain that this can be accomplished by bringing Communist China into participation in the United Nations. By this step, so we are told, the interplay of ideas and interests in the United Nations would sooner or later cause these latter-day empire-builders to abandon their warlike ways and accommodate themselves to the rule of law and the comity of nations.

This is a serious view, and I intend to discuss it seriously. Certainly we must never abandon hope of winning over even the most stubborn antagonist. But reasons born of sober experience oblige us to restrain our wishful thoughts. . . .

My first point is that the step advocated, once taken, is irreversible. We cannot try it and then give it up if it fails to work. . . .

Secondly, there are ample grounds to suspect that a power given to such bitter words and ruthless actions as those of the Peiping regime, far from being reformed by its experience in the United Nations, would be encouraged by its success in gaining admission to exert, all the more forcefully, by threats and maneuvers, a most disruptive and demoralizing influence on the Organization at this critical moment in its history.

Thirdly, its admission, in circumstances in which it continues to violate and defy the principles of the charter, could seriously shake public confidence in the United Nations—I can assure you it would do so among the people of the United States—and this alone would significantly weaken the Organization. . . .

The issue we face is, among other things, this question—whether it is right for the United Nations to drive the Republic of China from this Organization in order to make room for a regime whose appetite seems to be insatiable. It is whether we intend to abandon the charter requirement that all United Nations members must be peace-loving. . . .

The root of the problem lies, as it has lain from the beginning, in the hostile, callous, and seemingly intractable minds of the Chinese Communist rulers. Let those members who advocate Peiping's admission seek to exert upon its rulers whatever benign influence they can, in the hope of persuading them to accept the standards of the community of nations.

VOTE ON COMMUNIST CHINA IN THE U.N.

Year	Membership	For	Against	Abstentions	Absent
1950	59	16	33	10	0
1951	60	11	37	4	no roll call
1952	60	7	42	11	0
1953	60	10	44	2	4
1954	60	11	43	6	0
1955	60	12	42	6	0
1956	79	24	47	8	0
1957	82	27	48	6	1
1958	81	28	44	9	0
1959	82	29	44	9	0
1960	98	34	42	22	0
1961	104	36	48	20	0
1962	110	42	56	12	0
1963	111	41	57	12	1
1964	no vote taken				
1965	117	47	47	20	3
1966	121	46	57	17	1
1967	122	45	58	17	2
1968	126	44	58	23	1
1969	126	48	56	21	1

The vote in 1969—For: Afghanistan, Albania, Algeria, Bulgaria, Burma, Burundi, Byelorussia, Cambodia, Ceylon, Congo (Brazzaville), Cuba, Czechoslovakia, Denmark, Ethiopia, Finland, France, Ghana, Guinea, Hungary, India, Iraq, Kenya, Libya, Mali, Mauritania, Mauritius, Mongolia, Morocco, Nepal, Nigeria, Norway, Pakistan, Poland, Romania, Somalia, Southern Yemen, Sudan, Sweden, Syria, Tanzania, Uganda, Ukraine, United Arab Republic, United Kingdom, U.S.S.R., Yemen, Yugoslavia, Zambia.

Against: Argentina, Australia, Barbados, Bolivia, Botswana, Brazil, Cameroon, Central African Republic, Chad, China, Colombia, Congo (Kinshasa), Costa Rica, Dahomey, Dominican Republic, El Salvador, Gabon, The Gambia, Greece, Guatemala, Haiti, Honduras, Ireland, Israel, Ivory Coast, Japan, Jordan, Lesotho, Liberia, Luxembourg, Malagasy Republic, Malawi, Malaysia, Malta, Mexico, New Zealand, Nicaragua, Niger, Panama, Paraguay, Peru, Philippines, Rwanda, Saudi Arabia, Senegal, Sierra Leone, South Africa, Spain, Swaziland, Thailand, Togo, Turkey, United States, Upper Volta, Uruguay, Venezuela.

Abstentions: Austria, Belgium, Canada, Chile, Cyprus, Ecuador, Equatorial Guinea, Guyana, Iceland, Iran, Italy, Jamaica, Kuwait, Laos, Lebanon, Maldive Islands, Netherlands, Portugal, Singapore, Trinidad and Tobago, Tunisia.

Absent: Indonesia.

John C. Kimball (ed.), *Issues in United States Foreign Policy, No. 4—Communist China*, United States Department of State Publication 8499, East Asian and Pacific Series 173, Office of Media Services, Bureau of Public Affairs, (Washington, D.C.: Government Printing Office, December, 1969).

A. DOAK BARNETT

On Relations With China

I would like, right at the start, to state my own belief that there is a need for basic changes in the overall United States posture toward Communist China. For almost seventeen years we have pursued a policy that might best be characterized as one aimed at containment and isolation of Communist China.

In my view, the element of containment—using this term in a very broad sense to include both military and nonmilitary measures to block threats posed by China to its neighbors—has been an essential part of our policy and has been, in some respects at least, fairly successful. Our power has played to Communist China's power in Asia, and we have contributed significantly to the task of gradually building stable non-Communist societies in areas that lie in China's shadow. But the U.S. attempt to isolate Communist China has been, in my opinion, unwise and, in a fundamental sense, unsuccessful, and it cannot, I believe, provide a basis for a sound, long-term policy that aims not only at containing and restraining Chinese power but also at reducing tensions, exerting a moderating influence on Peking, broadening the areas of non-Communist agreement on issues relating to China, and slowly involving Communist China in more normal patterns of international intercourse.

I strongly believe, therefore, that the time has come—even though the United States is now engaged in a bitter struggle in Vietnam—for our country to alter its posture toward Communist China and adopt a policy of containment but not isolation, a policy that would aim on the one hand at checking military or subversive threats and pressures emanating from Peking, but at the same time would aim at maximum contacts with and maximum involvement of the Chinese Communists in the international community. . . .

We should press in every way we can to encourage non-official contacts. We should, instead of embargoing all trade

Hearings on U.S. Policy with Respect to Mainland China, Joint Committee on Foreign Relations, Congress of the United States, 89th Cong., 2nd Sess. (Washington, D.C.: Government Printing Office).

with the China mainland, restrict only trade in strategic items and encourage American businessmen to explore other opportunities for trade contacts. And within the United Nations we should work for the acceptance of some formula which would provide seats for both Communist China and Nationalist China. In taking these steps, we will have to do so in full recognition of the fact that Peking's initial reaction is almost certain to be negative and even hostile and that any changes in our posture will create some new problems. But we should take them, nevertheless, because initiatives on our part are clearly required if we are to work, however slowly, toward the long-term goal of a more stable, less explosive situation in Asia and to explore the possibilities of trying to moderate Peking's policies. . . .

WALTER JUDD

For Isolation

Communist governments and their fronts are waging war against free peoples worldwide. . . .

Mr. Chairman, no great expansionist movement has ever stopped until it was checked. Our choice—with Red China just as it was with Japan and Hitler—is not between checking and not checking. The choice is whether to check early, while we can, and with allies—or try to check the aggression later when it is stronger, closer, and we have fewer and weaker friends and allies.

From what I have seen in the press, most of the changes in American policy toward Communist China proposed by various witnesses before this committee appear to be based on certain assumptions which do not seem to me to be justified:

1. That the Communist regime now in control of China mainland is here to stay.

But the same was said of Hitler, of Khrushchev, of Sukarno, of Nkrumah. People are not so sure now that Castro will last forever. Despots generally appear invincible—"until the last five minutes."

2. That the United States is stubbornly keeping Red China

Hearings on U.S. Policy with Respect to Mainland China, Joint Committee on Foreign Relations, Congress of the United States, 89th Cong., 2nd Sess. (Washington, D.C.: Government Printing Office).

isolated and therefore we are responsible for its hostility and belligerence. The reverse is the truth; . . .

The cause of Red China's hostility is not its isolation, but the Communist doctrine of the necessity for use of armed force to achieve world revolution. To remove China's isolation now would prove that the doctrine is correct and should be adhered to by them even more tenaciously.

3. That there is a better hope of getting Red China to change its attitudes and activities by giving in to it on matters like diplomatic recognition, trade, and admission to the United Nations than by resolute continuance of the policy of containment as long as Red China refuses to act like a responsible member of civilized society.

4. That changing our policy vis-à-vis Red China might start an evolutionary process there.

But, of course, it might just as easily reduce the chances of such an evolutionary process. Everybody desires and hopes for "evolution" in Red China. The debate should be over what measures are most likely to produce it.

For example (a) giving Red China greater prestige, influence, entree; that is, making it stronger? Or keeping it as weak and isolated as possible? . . .

• 12 •

The American Public Gives Its Views

Here are the results of some national polls that quizzed a scientific sampling of the American public on a variety of issues relating to China. How would you answer each of the questions in the polls? How would you interpret the results of these findings? Do you think the results would appreciably change if these polls were conducted today?

POLLS REVEAL HOW AMERICANS FEEL ABOUT COMMUNIST CHINA
. . . About U.S. Recognition and UN Admission

Do you think Communist China should or should not be admitted as a member of the United Nations? (Gallup Poll)

	Should %	Should not %	No opinion %
1966	25	56	19
1965	22	64	14
1964	20	57	23
1961	18	65	17
1958	17	66	17
1957	13	70	17
1956	11	74	15
1955	10	67	23
1954	8	79	13
1950	11	58	31

If Communist China is admitted to the United Nations, do you feel we should pull out of the United Nations or remain in? (Harris Survey)

	June 1967 %	June 1966 %	Nov. 1964 %
U.S. remain in	76	78	77
U.S. pull out	9	7	7
Not sure	15	15	16

Would you favor the admission of Communist China if it would improve U.S.-Communist China relations? (Gallup Poll)

	1966 %
Favor	55
Oppose	30
No opinion	15

Note: Where more than one poll was taken in a year, the figures shown are from the latest poll in that year.

Do you favor or oppose diplomatic recognition by the United States of Communist China?

Do you favor or oppose admitting Communist China to the United Nations?

It has been suggested that both Communist China and Nationalist China be made members of the United Nations, as two different countries. Would you favor or oppose this as a solution? (Harris Survey)

	1967	1966
	%	%
Recognize Red China	55	57
Admit China to the UN	30	37
Favor two-China UN policy	53	55

(Table shows affirmative answers to three different questions, thus adds up to more than 100%.)

Suppose a majority of the members of the United Nations decide to admit Communist China to the United Nations. Do you think the United States should go along with the UN decision or not? (Gallup Poll)

	1966	1965	1964	1961
	%	%	%	%
Should	53	49	42	46
Should not	33	35	44	38
No opinion	14	16	14	16

. . . ON WAR, TREATIES AND THE ATOM BOMB

It has been argued that if we remain stronger militarily, we can keep Red China from using the atom bomb. Do you tend to agree with that, or do you think war with China is inevitable? (Harris Survey)

	Nov. 1964
	%
Keeping strong will avoid war	72
War inevitable	9
Not sure	19

The argument has been made that one way to avoid war with Red China is to try to sit down and reason with her that war would destroy China as well as the rest of the world. Do you think that such reasoning might work or do you think it is not likely to work? (Harris Survey)

	Nov. 1964 %
Reasoning might work	43
Reasoning won't work	43
Not sure	14

Communist China now has the atom bomb. Do you think we should try to negotiate an atomic test-ban treaty with the Chinese, as we have with the Russians, or are you against such negotiations with Communist China? (Harris Survey)

	June 1966 %
Favor treaty	61
Oppose	21
Not sure	18

Our country has a defensive treaty alliance with Chiang Kai-shek and Nationalist China (Formosa). Should we continue or end this defensive alliance? (Harris Survey)

	June 1966 %
Continue defense treaty	65
End treaty	6
Not sure	29

. . . On Comparing Russia and China

If trouble ever broke out between the U.S. and China, do you think Russia would be more likely to be on our side or on China's side? (Gallup Poll)

	March 1967 %	March 1965 %
On side of U.S.	48	18
On side of Red China	37	59
No opinion	15	23

(The striking differences in the more recent poll to those of the previous poll when a similar question was asked, obviously reflect a strong reaction to the intensified split between Russia and China.)

Looking ahead to 1970, which country do you think will be the greater threat to world peace—Russia or Communist China? (Gallup Poll)

	1967	1964	1963	1961
	%	%	%	%
Red China	71	59	47	32
Russia	20	20	34	49
No opinion	9	21	19	19

. . . On China and the Vietnam War

If the North Vietnamese show signs of giving in, do you think Communist China will or will not send many troops to help North Vietnam? (Gallup Poll)

	Will	Will not	No opinion
	%	%	%
December 1967	49	36	15
June 1966	38	35	27

• 13 •

China and the Third World

Regardless of what the Soviet Union desires, what the United States thinks, or the United Nations does, the Chinese are determined that the Middle Kingdom shall be granted a seat of equality among the nations of the world, if not actually restored to its position of preeminence. Already, one of the major Chinese exports is the cult of Mao. Revolutionaries and Communist Party members—they are not necessarily synonymous—in most underdeveloped countries have avidly devoured his works and seek to use the Chinese experience as a model for their own activities. China certainly has not discouraged these activities, although material aid has necessarily been minimal. (The cult has even spread to the "have" nations. Witness the student movements in France, Italy, Germany, and the United States. What is the appeal of Maoism to these groups?)

Lin Piao, leader of the Chinese People's Liberation Army, and vice-chairman of the central committee (and the successor to Mao, according to most educated guesses), discusses the struggle between the "world country" and the "world city." This particular address was interpreted by several American spokesmen as additional evidence of China's determination to use aggression to achieve world conquest. Would you agree? Do you think Lin's analysis is correct? What do you think is the appeal of Maoism in underdeveloped countries? Can the Chinese experience be repeated elsewhere?

LIN PIAO

What should the oppressed nations and the oppressed people do in the face of wars of aggression and armed suppression by the imperialists and their lackeys? Should they submit and remain slaves in perpetuity? Or should they rise in resistance and fight for their liberation?

Comrade Mao Tse-tung answered this question in vivid terms. He said that after long investigation and study the Chinese people discovered that all the imperialists and their lackeys "have swords in their hands and are out to kill. The people have come to understand this and so act after the same fashion." This is called doing unto them what they do unto us.

In the last analysis, whether one dares to wage a tit-for-tat struggle against armed aggression and suppression by the imperialists and their lackeys, whether one dares to fight a people's war against them, means whether one dares to embark on revolution. This is the most effective touchstone for distinguishing genuine from fake revolutionaries and Marxist-Leninists.

In view of the fact that some people were afflicted with the fear of the imperialists and reactionaries, Comrade Mao

From Lin Piao, *Long Live the Victory of People's War!* (Peking: Foreign Language Press, 1966).

Tse-tung put forward his famous thesis that "the imperialists and all reactionaries are paper tigers." He said,

> All reactionaries are paper tigers. In appearance, the reactionaries are terrifying, but in reality they are not so powerful. From a long-term point of view, it is not the reactionaries but the people who are really powerful.

The history of people's war in China and other countries provides conclusive evidence that the growth of the people's revolutionary forces from weak and small beginnings into strong and large forces is a universal law of development of class struggle, a universal law of development of people's war. A people's war inevitably meets with many difficulties, with ups and downs and setbacks in the course of its development, but no force can alter its general trend towards inevitable triumph. . . .

Why can the apparently weak new-born forces always triumph over the decadent forces which appear so powerful? The reason is that truth is on their side and that the masses are on their side, while the reactionary classes are always divorced from the masses and set themselves against the masses.

This has been borne out by the victory of the Chinese revolution, by the history of all revolutions, the whole history of class struggle and the entire history of mankind. . . .

Comrade Mao Tse-tung's theory of people's war solves not only the problem of daring to fight a people's war, but also that of how to wage it.

Comrade Mao Tse-tung is a great statesman and military scientist, proficient at directing war in accordance with its laws. . . .

It must be emphasized that Comrade Mao Tse-tung's theory of the establishment of rural revolutionary base areas and the encirclement of the cities from the countryside is of outstanding and universal practical importance for the present revolutionary struggles of all the oppressed nations and peoples, and particularly for the revolutionary struggles of the oppressed nations and peoples in Asia, Africa and Latin America against imperialism and its lackeys.

Many countries and peoples in Asia, Africa and Latin America are now being subjected to aggression and enslavement on a serious scale by the imperialists headed by the United States and their lackeys. The basic political and economic conditions in many of these countries have many similarities to those that prevailed in old China. As in China, the peasant question is extremely important in these regions. The peasants constitute the main force of the national-democratic revolution against the imperialists and their lackeys. In committing aggression against these countries, the imperialists usually begin by seizing the big cities and the main lines of communication, but they are unable to bring the vast countryside completely under their control. The countryside, and the countryside alone, can provide the broad areas in which the revolutionaries can manoeuvre freely. The countryside, and the countryside alone, can provide the revolutionary bases from which the revolutionaries can go forward to final victory. Precisely for this reason, Comrade Mao Tse-tung's theory of establishing revolutionary base areas in the rural districts and encircling the cities from the countryside is attracting more and more attention among the people in these regions.

Taking the entire globe, if North America and Western Europe can be called "the cities of the world," then Asia, Africa and Latin America constitute "the rural areas of the world." Since World War II, the proletarian revolutionary movement has for various reasons been temporarily held back in the North American and West European capitalist countries, while the people's revolutionary movement in Asia, Africa and Latin America has been growing vigorously. In a sense, the contemporary world revolution also presents a picture of the encirclement of cities by the rural areas. In the final analysis, the whole cause of world revolution hinges on the revolutionary struggles of the Asian, African and Latin American peoples who make up the overwhelming majority of the world's population. The socialist countries should regard it as their internationalist duty to support the people's revolutionary struggles in Asia, Africa and Latin America.

MASTER STROKE

REPRINTED WITH PERMISSION, FROM DAVID MYERS, EVENING NEWS, LONDON.

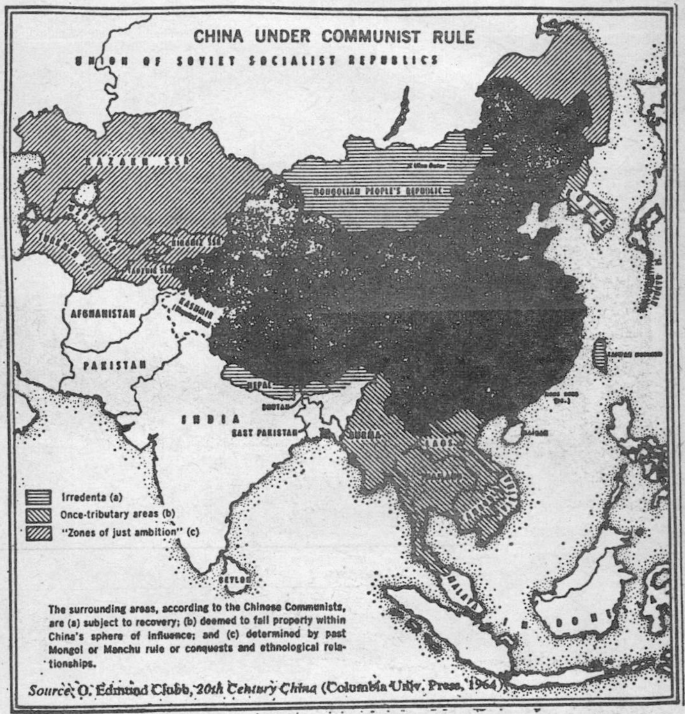

The surrounding areas, according to the Chinese Communists, are (a) subject to recovery; (b) deemed to fall properly within China's sphere of influence; and (c) determined by past Mongol or Manchu rule or conquests and ethnological relationships.

Source: O. Edmund Clubb, *20th Century China* (Columbia Univ. Press, 1964).

REPRINTED WITH PERMISSION, FROM O. EDMUND CLUBB, **TWENTIETH CENTURY CHINA** (NEW YORK: COLUMBIA UNIVERSITY PRESS, 1964).

This map illustrates what China considers to be her rightful territorial integrity, or what others would argue to be her territorial ambitions. Should these areas of Asia be considered China's legitimate sphere of influence?

NEW TOOTH

• 14 •

The Great Proletarian Cultural Revolution

One of the major achievements upon which the Chinese Communists have prided themselves has been the restoration of internal peace and order after decades of foreign aggression and civil war. However, since the summer of 1966 there has been a vast internal upheaval which, if not threatening the government itself, has led to the breakdown of order and to serious questioning and reevaluation of the direction in which Chinese society was developing. This has become known as the Great Proletarian Cultural Revolution. The movement, led by students known as Red Guards—the protectors of the ideologically pure—developed into a defense of Maoism, indicating perhaps an internal power struggle.

Several factors were involved: the deterioration of relations with the Soviet Union; the Vietnam War; the cooling of revolutionary zeal; the entrenchment of the bureaucracy; the approach to socialism. Loyalty to Mao was the rallying cry of the Red Guards, and they leveled their attacks against anyone and anything that appeared to be ancient, foreign, or bourgeois. There was some evidence to indicate that in their enthusiasm to vilify everything that was non-Maoist, the students went beyond the limits that Mao himself considered desirable. Their emphasis settled on the cultural institutions that reached the masses of the population: the schools; the theater; the movies; popular literature and music.

The first two readings, taken from the *Peking Review*, exemplify the emphasis on Mao in the popular culture of China. How would you interpret these obviously propagandistic articles? What do they reveal about the current scene in China? In the last reading, Professor A. Doak Barnett presents a perceptive analysis of the Cultural Revolution, and of its significance for the future of China.

PEKING REVIEW

Quotations from Chairman Mao Set to Music (January 6, 1966)

A new revolutionary song movement is in full swing throughout the country. More and more people are singing scores of new songs made up of texts from Chairman Mao's quotations set to music. The new songs, composed by revolutionary musicians during the current great cultural revolution, are being sung by the masses with rousing revolutionary fervour. . . .

To meet this revolutionary mass demand, revolutionary composers already before National Day last year, began to set quotations from Chairman Mao to music. Scores of these songs are already popular favourites. People say: "Singing Chairman Mao's quotations helps us to remember his words. With revolutionary hearts serving the people, we throw away self-interest and promote the public good for the sake of the revolution." "While we sing these new songs, a red sun rises in our hearts." . . .

. . . The workers sing them everyday, and every worker sings, and the revolutionary spirit of the workers grows. They take firm hold of revolution and promote production. Many examples of mutual help, and of help gladly given are told in the works. The workers say: "Of all songs, we like to sing songs of Chairman Mao's quotations best." "Singing these songs is as good as attending a political class on creatively studying and applying Chairman Mao's works." They have also sent articles to the press describing the inspiration they have got from singing these songs.

. . . At a recent commune meeting, a choir of nine elderly women members sang some of these and other revolutionary songs. All of them are illiterate, but they ardently love Chairman Mao and his writings and are determined to bear in mind Chairman Mao's teachings. This is why they got the young people to teach them the songs of Chairman Mao's quotations. At the start someone laughed at them: "You're old, short of breath and toothless; you lisp and you still want

From "Quotations from Chairman Mao Set to Music," *Peking Review* (Peking, January 6, 1966).

to sing?" Undaunted and resolute, however, they mastered many songs. As they said: "We led a miserable life in the old society. We never even sang a song when we were young girls. It is only because Chairman Mao and the Communist Party have liberated us that we can sing songs at our age now. We must study Chairman Mao's writings and follow his teachings better!"

THE WORDS OF TWO SONGS ARE:

All reactionaries are paper tigers. In appearance, the reactionaries are terrifying, but in reality they are not so powerful. From a long-term point of view, it is not the reactionaries but the people who are really powerful.

* * *

We must have faith in the masses and we must have faith in the Party. These are two cardinal principles. If we doubt these principles, we shall accomplish nothing.

Mao Tse-tung's Thought in Command of Our Battle (September 13, 1966)

It was late at night on June 21 [1966]. Chang Yung-ching, the deputy leader of the No. 1 squad who had refused to leave his work despite illness, once again studied Chairman Mao's brilliant work "Serve the People" before he went to the well site to take over his shift. On the top of the page he printed in a clear hand: "Every one of us revolutionaries should serve the people whole-heartedly as long as he lives." Then he changed into his work-clothes, put on his aluminum helmet and strode to the brightly lit well site.

After looking at the manometer, he told the comrades in a quiet but determined voice: "This is the first wildcat (exploratory well) drilled on a new geological structure, and we do not have all the information about the formations. Pressure has risen rapidly tonight. We must remain at our posts and be responsible to the Party and the people without any reservation whatever. . . ."

As he finished speaking, and they were carrying out the shut-in well pressure test and getting ready for the open flow

---

From "Mao Tse-tung's Thought in Command of Our Battle," *Peking Review* (Peking, September 30, 1966).

test, an imported seamless pipe on the side of the well-head suddenly burst and there was an earth-shaking explosion.

The big natural gas field was threatened with destruction.

Red-hot fire can melt steel and rock but it cannot burn out the red hearts of the oil workers who are loyal to Chairman Mao, to Mao Tse-tung's thought, to the Party and the people.

At this critical point, the comrades working at the well site, who were faced with the sudden attack by the blazing inferno, completely disregarded the threat to their own safety. No one thought of death. There was no change of expression and no quickening of the pulse as they fought the fire. All that was in their minds was how to put out the fire, save the gas well and safeguard state property. . . .

No. 3 valve was right in the centre of the sea of fire. With this valve shut, the source of the gas could be cut off and the fire put out.

Armed with Mao Tse-tung's thought, comrades of the No. 32111 Drilling Team deliberately went, so to speak, into tiger-infested mountains, knowing there would be tigers, and rushed into the sea of fire, knowing they would get burnt. When one fell, more charged forward in his wake. . . .

Hsu Kuang-yi, a new hand who had come from a village only six months earlier, was felled by the poisonous gas fumes after battling for two minutes. Hu Teh-ping carried him out on his back. The moment Hsu came to, he jumped up and again dashed to the fire site. He seemed to have heard *the loving voice of our great leader: "Young fellow, charge! Be resolute and unafraid of sacrifice, you will surmount every difficulty to win victory."*

Hu Teh-ping also fainted at this time. When he came to and saw that his comrades, one group after another, were rushing in, he was filled with strength. He sprang up and joined his comrades and dashed into the roaring flames to turn the wheel of the No. 3 valve. He thought:

"It is now the moment of putting myself to the test, the moment the Party needs me most! While a man's life is precious, the Party's cause is even more so. I am going to shut this valve as long as I can move. To stick it out one more second, to turn the valve once more means one more contribution to putting out the fire!" . . .

Mou Mao-hsiu, a worker's wife, was rushing water to the fire when suddenly someone shouted to her: "Your husband

Heng Szu-shu is injured!" She abruptly recalled what her husband had told her that morning before going to work: "We're out for the 'gas tiger' today! If anything should happen, remember to save the state's property first." Without the state's interests, she continued in her mind, there can be no personal interests. She just could not dash off to see her husband and stayed on to carry water.

A little later, somebody urgently cried out again: "Mou Mao-hsiu! Mou Mao-hsiu! Hurry up and go to your husband! He's hurt badly!"

Mou Mao-hsiu's heart throbbed, the water almost spilt out of the container she was holding. She thought to herself: Should I go? At this moment, she saw some of the injured men pick themselves up from the ground and rush in front of her to the fire. Such heroism sustained her, and she became calm. "No, I cannot leave my post. *Wherever there is struggle there is sacrifice.*" . . .

After a thirty-minute life-and-death struggle, the big fire was finally put out by heroes who had been armed with Mao Tse-tung's invincible thought and who gave their own lives and blood and used the collective bravery and wisdom to protect vital state property. They had made an imperishable contribution to the Party and the people.

After the fire, deputy team leader Peng Chia-chih, walking through the crowds and the smoke-clouded well site, shouted: "Comrades of Team 32111, fall in!"

Behind the broken derrick, by the side of the burnt-down pump room, heroes walked out and lined up in rows. They looked like a rock on the sea coast, standing there proudly at the well site. When they thought of their fallen and injured class brothers, tears welled up. Yet sadness immediately turned into militant strength.

"Comrades, we have won!"

"We have beaten the fire!"

The heroic acts of these brave men and women who protected state property give the people boundless pride and encouragement. The brilliance of their Communist ideas reddens the surrounding high peaks, and brightens the blue sky overhead!

A. DOAK BARNETT

. . . [The] forces are increasingly complex, but in oversimplified terms one can differentiate between two poles in a spectrum of opinion, and these appear to be exerting pressures in very different directions.

On the one side are those who still have great faith in the effectiveness of ideological and political mobilization of the sort that served the Party well in earlier years. Mao himself clearly persists in this faith, as do many other top leaders. On the other side, however, there now appear to be persons at all levels in the regime who, after struggling for years with the practical problems of administration and development, incline toward a more pragmatic, less dogmatic, and less ideological approach to problems. These men, who are undoubtedly most strongly represented among China's economic administrators, technical-bureaucrats, and specialists of all sorts, are the ones who tend to be skeptical of visionary "upsurges" and seemingly favor relatively pragmatic, realistic, and moderate policies.

Men in the first category insist that it is essential to maintain a high state of tension and ideological fervor in China in order to sustain revolutionary momentum and ensure a rapid pace of change. They fear that otherwise, over time, the revolution will be gravely weakened by erosion and might fundamentally change its character.

Those in the second category seem prepared—in relative terms at least—to acknowledge that the present problems of modernization and development differ from the earlier problems of revolutionary struggle. They apparently recognize that effective management, scientific and technical skills, and economic incentives are required for success in economic development and modernization, and that organizational mobilization and ideological indoctrination are not enough to do the job. At least some of them seem prepared to recognize that change will, of necessity, have to take place at a more gradual rate than was possible in earlier years. . . .

To date, in the interplay of forces that has taken place in

Reprinted with permission of Princeton University Press, from A. Doak Barnett, *China After Mao: With Selected Documents* (Princeton, N.J., 1967).

China in recent years, while Mao and other militant Maoists have successfully insisted on pushing toward increasing radicalization of the regime's political line, the pragmatists—who doubtless include some of China's leading administrators and technical-bureaucrats—have apparently been successful in demanding that economic policies must take account of economic realities. So far, at least, they seem to have insisted successfully that at least minimum economic incentives must be provided to the people, and that visionary big pushes are not feasible under existing conditions—even though this probably does mean acceptance of a fairly moderate rate of economic growth for the immediate future. . . .

The dilemmas and policy choices facing Peking's leaders in the economic field are really only one facet of an even more fundamental question that relates to virtually every aspect of society and is crucial to the future course of developments in China. The Chinese Communists, with their genius for coining slogans, have summed this up as the "red and expert" problem. The regime's aim has been to create a new generation that would be both "red and expert" or, to translate this slogan into more familiar terms, both ideologically motivated, loyal servants of the revolution and technically proficient specialists capable of performing the varied and complex tasks required in a modernizing society. While both "redness" and "expertness" are recognized to be important, however, Mao and the leaders who are now dominant clearly insist on "redness" above all, and if faced with a choice, they would prefer "reds" who are not "expert" to "experts" who are not "red." They have a deep, and well-justified, apprehension that specialization and technical expertise may tend to undermine the kind of commitment to ideological dogma that they believe to be necessary to continue the sort of revolution which they think China must undergo. . . .

Mao's idealized conception of the sort of man required to keep up the revolutionary struggle is one who is wholly obedient to Party discipline, loyal and dedicated to the regime's goals, self-sacrificing and unconcerned about his personal welfare, and always willing to place the good of the revolution as a whole—as defined by the Party's leaders—above parochial interests or specialized concerns. The irony of the situation, however, is that the process of modernization requires, and helps to create, specialists who tend to value professional competence over ideological commitment and who are likely to push for at least some policies of a kind that the present top leaders in China call "revisionist." . . .

Because of his unique position, Mao himself has been able in recent years to make the crucial decisions on strategy and policy, both at home and abroad. He has been able to impose his own views and to carry along the rest of the leadership, the Party, and the country with him. But no individual after Mao is likely to be able to do this in the same fashion.

In a fundamental sense perhaps the basic choice that will confront Mao's successors will be whether to continue pursuing paths already charted, to adhere to Mao's prescribed course of action, and to try to preserve the character of the revolution and the regime unchanged, or to move in new directions, adapting to evolving conditions and needs, and responding primarily to the imperatives of modernization rather than to the requirements of ideological dogma, even if this demands major changes in the patterns of organization and action that have guided the Chinese Communist regime in the past.

Mao himself is obviously determined to do all he can to ensure continuity in the future. The current upheaval in China can be viewed in one sense as a final apocalyptic effort by Mao—or at least by men who share his vision—to ensure that his successors resist the pressures to move the Chinese revolution in new directions.

• 15 •

The Other China

This section has up to this point concentrated exclusively on events in mainland China. However, approximately one hundred miles to the east across the Straits of Formosa lies the island of Taiwan, the home of the government of the Republic of China. Chiang Kai-shek claims that his is the legitimate and true government of China which represents the

'WELL, I CAN TELL YOU THIS--SOMETHING'S BURNING!'

REPRINTED WITH PERMISSION, FROM OLIPHANT, DENVER POST.
DISTRIBUTED BY LOS ANGELES TIMES SYNDICATE.

aspirations of the Chinese people. The United States has supported this position with official recognition, a security treaty, and military and economic aid.

This bulletin of the United States Department of State outlines and explains this position. Included is information on economic growth in Taiwan. Why do you think economic growth in Taiwan has been proportionally greater than that on the mainland? Would you dispute any of the points raised in this article?

UNITED STATES DEPARTMENT OF STATE

Background Notes: Republic of China

The Government of the Republic of China moved to Taipei on December 8, 1949. The United States Government recognizes it as the only legal Government of China, entitled to represent China in all international bodies and activities. Chiang Kai-shek has been President of the Republic of China since 1948, except for a brief period of semiretirement in 1949. He has been free China's foremost statesman and military leader since 1927. . . .

POLITICAL CONDITIONS

Taiwan lives constantly under the threat of Communist attack. Because of its strategic position between the Philippines and Okinawa, it is important to the United States that it be retained in friendly hands. The Chinese Government based on Taiwan stands as a symbol of hope to millions of Chinese on the mainland of China and as an alternate focus for the allegiance of the 12 million overseas Chinese throughout Southeast Asia.

Political conditions on Taiwan are relatively stable. The population is strongly anti-Communist. During the 1958 crisis in the Taiwan Strait the people displayed high morale and showed no disposition to bend to Communist threats or to be affected by Communist propaganda designed to weaken the Republic of China's alliance with the United States. Friction

---

Background Notes: Republic of China, Department of State Publication 7791, Revised April 1967. Office of Media Services, Bureau of Public Affairs, U.S. Department of State.

between the native Taiwanese and the Chinese from the mainland, which constituted a serious problem in the early years after the Japanese surrender, has been reduced. . . .

ECONOMY

Taiwan is in transition from a basically agricultural economy to an industrialized economy. In 1965 industry surpassed agriculture in its contribution to the gross national product for the first time, and incomplete figures for 1966 show that this trend is being maintained and even strengthened.

This substantial economic progress has been due to effective use of large amounts of U.S. aid, to an enterprising and highly skilled population, and to a government which has planned and facilitated economic development in the private sector. Gross national product in real terms has increased by over 7 percent per year for the last 12 years, and the increase in real per capita income has averaged approximately 3.6 percent annually. . . .

INDUSTRY

While the rate of growth in the highly developed agricultural sector has been good—almost 6 percent annually during the last 10 years—the development of industry has been far more striking. Industrial production has increased by an average of over 12 percent per year during the same period. Manufacturing now offers the best opportunities for employment and higher standards of living. Industries which have grown rapidly in recent years include electronics, textiles, plywood, fertilizer, chemicals, cement, glass, plastics, and food processing. Major emphasis has been placed on expansion of electric power, which has been hard put to keep pace with the growing demand from industry. Several new hydroelectric and thermal plants, partly financed by U.S. aid, have been completed or are under construction.

AGRICULTURE

Agriculture, still an important sector of the economy, is more intensive than in any other country in the world except Japan. Although only one-fourth of the land in Taiwan is arable, virtually all of this is cultivated and most of it produces two or three crops per year. . . .

U.S. AID

Close and effective cooperation between the U.S. AID Mission and the Chinese Government has made possible long-range planning within the framework of five 4-year development plans and a 10-year long-term development plan to industrialize Taiwan.

Although military expenditures necessitated by security and political factors have had a braking effect, the pace of economic development has made it possible for the United States to phase out its aid program. In May 1963 it was announced that a gradual step-by-step reduction of American aid would begin. No new programs were undertaken in 1964 and the AID Mission to China was closed July 1, 1965. Aid in the form of surplus agricultural commodities is to continue, as will the military assistance program. . . .

MILITARY SPENDING

The Republic of China supports perhaps the heaviest defense burden in the world, in relation to its population and national income. This burden absorbs resources which could well be used for economic investment to meet the needs of the island's rapidly growing population.

FOREIGN RELATIONS

Since December 1949, when the Government of the Republic of China moved to Taipei, its foreign policy has been guided by three dominant considerations:

1. The Government is mortally threatened, politically and militarily, by the Chinese Communist regime on the mainland.

2. The Government is situated in a territory without resources adequate to carry the extraordinary military defense burden it has assumed.

3. The Government sees itself as the legitimate Chinese Government and is dedicated to eventual recovery of all of China. . . .

U.S. POLICY

The United States recognizes the Government of the Republic of China as the only legitimate Chinese Government.

It supports the GRC's rightful place in the United Nations and other international organizations.

Since the beginning of the Korean War it has been United States policy to assist the Chinese Government in defending Taiwan and the Pescadores against Communist attack. To carry out this mission the 7th Fleet was directed by President Truman on June 27, 1950, to repel any attack on Taiwan by the Chinese Communists. On March 3, 1955, a mutual defense treaty between the United States and China came into effect. Under the terms of this treaty the United States is committed formally to the defense of Taiwan and the Pescadores; . . .

• 16 •

The Future

Professor Dun J. Li summarizes what the past has meant to the Chinese, and how that experience continues to shape the present. In conclusion, he poses the questions that must be asked about the future of China, and that the Chinese must answer about themselves.

DUN J. LI

For the past two thousand years the basic economic problem of China has been too little arable land and too many people, as we have said repeatedly in this book. While all Chinese might be said to have been poor, poverty became more unbearable when the limited amount of land was concentrated in the hands of a comparative few. Those few who owned land were the gentry class which provided the country with scholars and government officials; those who owned little or only a small amount of land were the peasants and they constituted the overwhelming majority of the Chinese people. Though

---

social mobility was great, at any given time the dividing line between gentry-scholars and peasants was nevertheless distinct. Since most government officials came from gentry families, the socio-economic relationship between gentry-scholars and peasants corresponded fairly well with the political relationship between rulers and the ruled. Though a typical landlord might not own more than ten acres of land, the fact that most of his fellow villagers owned little or nothing was a constant source of frustration and discontent. . . . The problem became more acute as population continued to grow throughout the last three centuries. While in power on the mainland, the Nationalist regime attempted to carry out a mild form of land reform, and the result, as we have noted before, was almost nil. Rural discontent continued and was intensified during and shortly after the Sino-Japanese War. It was ruthlessly and successfully exploited by Mao Tse-tung and his comrades.

The Communists came to power by riding on rural discontent, and authoritarian as the government is, its continuance in power ultimately depends upon the peasants' continuous support, or more correctly, the absence of withdrawing such support. If the history of the past 3,500 years indicates anything, the peasants revolt only as a last resort. Used to suffering, they prefer to suffer more instead of launching a bloody rebellion. In practical terms, it means that they revolt only when they are hungry. Freedom and democracy, the noble ideas that inspire many men to rise in anger against tyranny, do not impress a Chinese peasant who, used to authoritarian government, is more concerned with a practical need: food. As far as he is concerned, a good government is a government that leaves him enough to eat after he has paid his taxes.

To provide enough food for so many people out of a limited amount of land, the People's Republic introduced a series of rural reforms, including the commune which was in fact a desperate attempt to solve economic problems at the expense of social and human values. Despite the recent setback it is expected that continuous efforts will be made to increase food production. Improvements in irrigation and flood control, the use of better and more fertilizers, and rigid insect control will be emphasized. Meanwhile, much hope is placed upon continuous industrialization to absorb surplus population from rural areas and to produce industrial goods to be shipped abroad in exchange for much needed food. If industrialization cannot reduce the pressure of population or alleviate the shortage of food, birth control will be the next logical step, a step which every Chinese regime, including that of the Communists, has been extremely reluctant to take. Should all these measures fail and when millions of people are starving at home, the temptation of the rich rice-producing areas in Southeast Asia will become irresistible. However, any overt act on the part of Communist China will not only antagonize the entire world but will perhaps bring immediate retaliation from the Western powers against mainland China. . . . Communist China will perhaps prefer trade to obtain what it needs from the food-producing countries in Southeast Asia.

Chinese nationalism in its modern sense can be dated from the Opium War. For more than one century it has been one of the most dynamic forces in shaping the national life. The Chinese are a proud people, conscious of their cultural heritage and identifying themselves with a glorious past. The humiliations which they have suffered during the past century contrast sharply with the position which they once occupied as a center of power and of a great civilization. . . . Without taking into consideration Chinese nationalism, it is difficult to explain why many intellectuals, all of bourgeois and gentry background, swarmed to the standard of Mao Tse-tung. Mao, a crafty politician, exploited their nationalist sentiments as effectively as he had exploited the economic discontent of the peasants. When he declared that China had stood up, he was echoing the wishes of millions of Chinese. . . .

To the outside world, the most important question is: into what kind of action will Chinese nationalism be translated, now that it is directed by the Communists? Will it be aimed at the fulfillment of China's legitimate aspirations or will it develop into a mass force of aggression? If it is the former, the outside world can learn to live with it. If it is the latter, it is no longer genuine nationalism; it becomes imperialism, the same "crime" which Communist China has accused the Western powers and Japan of having committed against China during the past one hundred years.

PART FIVE

SUPPLEMENT ON CONTEMPORARY CHINA

Since this book first went to press, dramatic changes have taken place within China, and in relations between China and other nations, especially the United States. The return of some semblance of political unity after the upheaval of the Cultural Revolution, the increasing moderation of political rhetoric, the admission into the United Nations, the Nixon visit and subsequent cultural exchanges, the establishment of liaison offices in Washington and Peking—all these are manifestations of the most recent phase of Chinese development. In the United States, China has become "in," and the pendulum that Harold Isaacs has written about has begun to swing in the direction of favorable and positive images of the Chinese. In China, Americans—businessmen, educators, observers of all sorts—are welcomed and permitted to see more than ever before. Evidently the 1970's promise to be a new era in Sino-American relations.

Exactly why this reversal has taken place remains a subject of historical controversy. Yet it is important to recognize that no matter how drastic these changes may appear to be, to understand them from the Chinese point of view, one must place them within the context of Chinese history and thought. To repeat: "The China of today is vastly different, but not unrecognizable from the China of the past."

• 1 •

China Joins the World Community

On October 25, 1971, the People's Republic of China was admitted to membership in the United Nations and the Republic of China (Taiwan) was expelled. This historic event was in direct opposition to what had been a key part of American foreign policy since the Korean War. Support among member nations for the U.S. position had been dwindling and perhaps eventual admission of China was inevitable. But the Nixon administration, in the summer of 1971, took the initiative by reversing the traditional American position. In August, Secretary of State William Rogers announced that the U.S. would support the seating of China while opposing any attempt to expel Taiwan. Rogers argued that this was in accord with the Nixon policy of building for a stable peace, opening avenues of communication, and accommodating to the realities of a changing world. The official U.S. position on "two Chinas" was defeated in the General Assembly, but the U.S. had made it clear it would not oppose the seating of the People's Republic.

The first selection presents the roll call vote on the resolution calling for the seating of Peking and the expulsion of Taiwan. Can you detect any discernible pattern of alliances and/or interests in the voting? Can this vote be considered a major defeat for the United States? The second reading contains excerpts from the maiden speech to the U.N. by Chiao Kuan-hua, Chairman of China's delegation. Does he present an accurate view of the history of modern China? How would you evaluate his general assumptions for maintenance of world peace?

U.N. ROLL CALL ON CHINA

On Seating Peking

Resolution to seat Communist China and expel Nationalist China.

IN FAVOR—76

Afghanistan
Albania
Algeria
Austria
Belgium
Bhutan
Botswana
Britain
Bulgaria
Burma
Burundi
Byelorussia
Cameroon
Canada
Ceylon
Chile
Congo (Brazza.)
Cuba
Czechoslovakia
Denmark
Ecuador
Egypt
Eq. Guinea
Ethiopia
Finland
France
Ghana
Guinea
Guyana
Hungary
Iceland
India
Iran
Iraq
Ireland
Israel
Italy
Kenya
Kuwait
Laos
Libya
Malaysia
Mali
Mauritania
Mexico
Mongolia
Morocco
Nepal
Netherlands
Nigeria
Norway
Pakistan
Peru
Poland
Portugal
Rumania
Rwanda
Senegal
Sierra Leone
Singapore
Somalia
So. Yemen
Soviet Union
Sudan
Sweden
Syria
Tanzania
Togo
Trinidad-Tobago
Tunisia
Turkey
Uganda
Ukraine
Yemen
Yugoslavia
Zambia

OPPOSED—35

Australia
Bolivia
Brazil
Cambodia
Cent. Afr. Rep.
Chad
Congo (Kinsh.)
Costa Rica
Dahomey
Dominican Rep.
El Salvador
Gabon
Gambia
Guatemala
Haiti
Honduras
Ivory Coast
Japan
Lesotho
Liberia
Madagascar
Malawi
Malta
New Zealand
Nicaragua
Niger
Paraguay
Philippines
Saudi Arabia
South Africa
Swaziland
United States
Upper Volta
Uruguay
Venezuela

ABSTENTIONS——17

Argentina	Greece	Mauritius
Bahrain	Indonesia	Panama
Barbados	Jamaica	Qatar
Colombia	Jordan	Spain
Cyprus	Lebanon	Thailand
Fiji	Luxembourg	

Absent—China, Maldives, Oman.

CHIAO KUAN-HUA

Speech at the U.N. General Assembly

Mr. President,
Fellow Representatives,

As is known to all, China is one of the founding members of the United Nations. In 1949, the Chinese people overthrew the reactionary rule of the Chiang Kai-shek clique and founded the People's Republic of China. Since then, the legitimate rights of China in the United Nations should have gone to the People's Republic of China as a matter of course. It was only because of the obstruction by the United States Government that the legitimate rights of the People's Republic of China in the United Nations were deprived of for a long time and that the Chiang Kai-shek clique long repudiated by the Chinese people was able to usurp China's lawful seat in the United Nations. This was a gross interference in China's internal affairs as well as a wilful trampling on the Charter of the United Nations. Now such an unjustifiable state of affairs has finally been put right. . . .

Human society invariably makes constant progress, and such progress is always achieved through innumerable revolutions and transformations. Take the United States, where the United Nations headquarters is situated. It was owing to the victory of the revolutionary war of 1776 led by Washington that the American people won independence. And it was owing to the great revolution of 1789 that the French people

Reprinted with permission, from "Speech of Chiao Kuan-hua, Chairman of the Delegation of People's Republic of China, at U.N. General Assembly," *Peking Review*, November 19, 1971.

rid themselves of the yoke of feudalism. After mankind entered the 20th century, the victory of the 1917 Russian October Socialist Revolution led by the great Lenin opened up a broad path to freedom and liberation for the oppressed nations and peoples of the world. The advance of history and social progress gladden the hearts of and inspire the peoples of the world and throw into a panic a handful of decadent reactionary forces who do their utmost to put up desperate struggles. . . .

Mr. President and fellow representatives,

The Chinese people have experienced untold sufferings under imperialist oppression. For one century and more, imperialism repeatedly launched wars of aggression against China and forced her to sign many unequal treaties. They divided China into their spheres of influence, plundered China's resources and exploited the Chinese people. The degree of poverty and lack of freedom suffered by the Chinese people in the past are known to all. In order to win national independence, freedom and liberation, the Chinese people, advancing wave upon wave in a dauntless spirit, waged protracted heroic struggles against imperialism and its lackeys and finally won the revolution under the leadership of their great leader Chairman Mao Tse-tung and the Chinese Communist Party. Since the founding of the People's Republic of China, we, the Chinese people, defying the tight imperialist blockades and withstanding the terrific pressure from without, have built our country into a socialist state with initial prosperity by maintaining independence and keeping the initiative in our own hands and through self-reliance. . . .

Taiwan is a province of China and the 14 million people who live in Taiwan are our fellow countrymen by flesh and blood. . . . On behalf of the Government of the People's Republic of China, I hereby reiterate that Taiwan is an inalienable part of China's territory and the U.S. armed invasion and occupation of China's Taiwan and the Taiwan Strait cannot in the least alter the sovereignty of the People's Republic of China over Taiwan, that all the armed forces of the United States definitely should be withdrawn from Taiwan and the Taiwan Straits and that we are firmly opposed to any design to separate Taiwan from the motherland. The Chinese people are determined to liberate Taiwan and no force on earth can stop us from doing so.

Mr. President and fellow representatives,

The Chinese people who suffered for a long time from imperialist aggression and oppression have consistently opposed the imperialist policies of aggression and war and supported all the oppressed peoples and nations in their just struggles to win freedom and liberation, oppose foreign interference and become masters of their own destiny. . . .

The continued existence of colonialism in all its manifestations is a provocation against the peoples of the world. . . .

The independence of a country is incomplete without economic independence. The economic backwardness of the Asian, African and Latin American countries is the result of imperialist plunder. Opposition to economic plunder and protection of national resources are the inalienable sovereign rights of an independent state. China is still an economically backward country as well as a developing country. Like the overwhelming majority of the Asian, African and Latin American countries, China belongs to the third world. . . .

The one or two superpowers are stepping up their arms expansion and war preparations and vigorously developing nuclear weapons, thus seriously threatening international peace. It is understandable that the people of the world long for disarmament and particularly for nuclear disarmament. . . . However, the superpowers, while talking about disarmament every day, are actually engaged in arms expansion daily. The so-called nuclear disarmament which they are supposed to seek is entirely for the purpose of monopolizing nuclear weapons in order to carry out nuclear threats and blackmail. China will never participate in the so-called nuclear disarmament talks between the nuclear powers behind the backs of the non-nuclear countries. China's nuclear weapons are still in the experimental stage. China develops nuclear weapons solely for the purpose of defense and for breaking the nuclear monopoly and ultimately eliminating nuclear weapons and nuclear war. The Chinese Government has consistently stood for the complete prohibition and thorough destruction of nuclear weapons and proposed to convene a summit conference of all countries of the world to discuss this question and, as the first step, to reach an agreement on the non-use of nuclear weapons. The Chinese Government has on many occasions declared, and now on behalf of the Chinese Government, I once again solemnly declare that at no time and under no circumstances will China be the first to use nuclear weapons. . . .

We have always held that the just struggles of the people of all countries support each other. China has always had the sympathy and support of the people of various countries in her socialist revolution and socialist construction. It is our bounden duty to support the just struggles of the people of various countries. For this purpose, we have provided aid to some friendly countries to help them develop their national economy independently. In providing aid, we always strictly respect the sovereignty of the recipient countries, and never attach any conditions or ask for any privileges. We provide free military aid to countries and peoples who are fighting against aggression. . . .

Mr. President and fellow representatives,

In accordance with the purposes of the United Nations Charter, the United Nations should play its due role in maintaining international peace, opposing aggression and interference and developing friendly relations and cooperation among nations. However, for a long period the one or two superpowers have utilized the United Nations and have done many things in contravention of the United Nations Charter against the will of the people of various countries. This situation should not continue. We hope that the spirit of the United Nations Charter will be really and truly followed out. We will stand together with all the countries and peoples that love peace and uphold justice and work together with them for the defense of the national independence and state sovereignty of various countries and for the cause of safeguarding international peace and promoting human progress.

• 2 •

President Nixon Journeys to the Middle Kingdom

On July 15, 1971, President Nixon announced that he had accepted an invitation from Premier Chou En-lai to visit the People's Republic of China for the purpose of beginning to normalize relations between the two countries and to exchange views on questions of mutual concern. The President departed for Peking on February 17th being careful to caution the American people and the world against any myopia but stressing the need for the two nations to coexist and communicate in spite of present and future differences. It is perhaps an exaggeration to view the President as following the well-trodden path of other foreigners who came to pay tribute to the Middle Kingdom. The desire for the meeting was quite obviously born from mutual interests. But it was the Americans who went to China, and not the Chinese who came to America first. Given the tremendous efforts the U.S. had been making toward a Vietnam settlement, and the major domestic considerations that the administration had to deal with, this analogy may not be entirely without meaning. It was the Nixon visit to China, with all its ritual meaning, that became the symbol for all subsequent developments in Sino-American relations.

This group of readings includes the toasts given by Premier Chou and President Nixon at the banquet in Peking in honor of the Nixon entourage, as well as the text of the joint communique issued at Shanghai just prior to the President's return to the United States. Do the words of the toasts symbolize significant changes or empty rhetoric? Can you detect any differences between the words of Chou and the words of Nixon? Can the joint communique be considered a charter for future Sino-American relations? Will Taiwan continue to be the major stumbling block between the U.S. and China?

BANQUET HONORING PRESIDENT NIXON, PEKING, FEBRUARY 21, 1972

Toast by Premier Chou En-lai

Mr. President and Mrs. Nixon, ladies and gentlemen, comrades and friends: First of all, I have the pleasure on behalf of Chairman Mao Tse-tung and the Chinese Government to extend our welcome to Mr. President and Mrs. Nixon and to our other American guests.

I also wish to take this opportunity to extend on behalf of the Chinese people cordial greetings to the American people on the other side of the great ocean. . . .

The American people are a great people. The Chinese people are a great people. The peoples of our two countries have always been friendly to each other. But owing to reasons known to all, contacts between the two peoples were suspended for over twenty years. Now, through the common efforts of China and the United States, the gate to friendly contacts has finally been opened. At the present time it has become a strong desire of the Chinese and American peoples to promote the normalization of relations between the two countries and work for the relaxation of tension. The people, and the people alone, are the motive force in the making of world history. We are confident that the day will surely come when this common desire of our two peoples will be realized.

The social systems of China and the United States are fundamentally different, and there exist great differences between the Chinese Government and the United States Government. However, these differences should not hinder China and the United States from establishing normal state relations on the basis of the Five Principles of mutual respect for sovereignty and territorial integrity, mutual non-aggression, non-interference in each other's internal affairs, equality and mutual benefit, and peaceful coexistence; still less should they lead to war. As early as 1955 the Chinese Government publicly stated that the Chinese people do not want to have

---

Reprinted with permission, from "President Nixon's Visit to the People's Republic of China," *The Department of State Bulletin*, vol. 56, March 20, 1972.

a war with the United States and that the Chinese Government is willing to sit down and enter into negotiations with the United States Government.

This is a policy which we have pursued consistently. We have taken note of the fact that in his speech before setting out for China President Nixon on his part said that "what we must do is to find a way to see that we can have differences without being enemies in war." We hope that, through a frank exchange of views between our two sides to gain a clearer notion of our differences and make efforts to find common ground, a new start can be made in the relations between our two countries. . . .

Toast by President Nixon

. . . Mr. Prime Minister, I wish to thank you for your very gracious and eloquent remarks. . . .

In the spirit of frankness which I hope will characterize our talks this week, let us recognize at the outset these points: We have at times in the past been enemies. We have great differences today. What brings us together is that we have common interests which transcend those differences. As we discuss our differences, neither of us will compromise our principles. But while we cannot close the gulf between us, we can try to bridge it so that we may be able to talk across it.

So, let us, in these next five days, start a long march together, not in lockstep, but on different roads leading to the same goal: the goal of building a world structure of peace and justice in which all may stand together with equal dignity and in which each nation, large or small, has a right to determine its own form of government, free of outside interference or domination. The world watches. . . .

What legacy shall we leave our children? Are they destined to die for the hatreds which have plagued the old world, or are they destined to live because we had the vision to build a new world?

There is no reason for us to be enemies. Neither of us seeks the territory of the other; neither of us seeks domination over the other; neither of us seeks to stretch out our hands and rule the world.

Chairman Mao has written: "So many deeds cry out to be done, and always urgently. The world rolls on. Time passes.

Ten thousand years are too long. Seize the day, seize the hour."

This is the hour. This is the day for our two peoples to rise to the heights of greatness which can build a new and a better world.

In that spirit, I ask all of you present to join me in raising your glasses to Chairman Mao, to Prime Minister Chou, and to the friendship of the Chinese and American people, which can lead to friendship and peace for all people in the world.

TEXT OF JOINT COMMUNIQUE, ISSUED AT SHANGHAI, FEBRUARY 27, 1972

President Richard Nixon of the United States of America visited the People's Republic of China at the invitation of Premier Chou En-lai of the People's Republic of China from February 21 to February 28, 1972. . . .

President Nixon met with Chairman Mao Tse-tung of the Communist Party of China on February 21. The two leaders had a serious and frank exchange of views on Sino-U.S. relations and world affairs.

During the visit, extensive, earnest and frank discussions were held between President Nixon and Premier Chou En-lai on the normalization of relations between the United States of America and the People's Republic of China, as well as on other matters of interest to both sides. . . .

There are essential differences between China and the United States in their social systems and foreign policies. However, the two sides agreed that countries, regardless of their social systems, should conduct their relations on the principles of respect for the sovereignty and territorial integrity of all states, non-aggression against other states, non-interference in the internal affairs of other states, equality and mutual benefit, and peaceful coexistence. International disputes should be settled on this basis, without resorting to the use or threat of force. The United States and the People's Republic of China are prepared to apply these principles to their mutual relations.

With these principles of international relations in mind the two sides stated that:

—progress toward the normalization of relations between China and the United States is in the interests of all countries;

—both wish to reduce the danger of international military conflict;

—neither should seek hegemony in the Asia-Pacific region and each is opposed to efforts by any other country or group of countries to establish such hegemony; and

—neither is prepared to negotiate on behalf of any third party or to enter into agreements or understandings with the other directed at other states.

Both sides are of the view that it would be against the interests of the peoples of the world for any major country to collude with another against other countries, or for major countries to divide up the world into spheres of interest.

The two sides reviewed the long-standing serious disputes between China and the United States. The Chinese side reaffirmed its position: The Taiwan question is the crucial question obstructing the normalization of relations between China and the United States; the Government of the People's Republic of China is the sole legal government of China; Taiwan is a province of China which has long been returned to the motherland; the liberation of Taiwan is China's internal affair in which no other country has the right to interfere; and all U.S. forces and military installations must be withdrawn from Taiwan. The Chinese Government firmly opposes any activities which aim at the creation of "one China, one Taiwan," "one China, two governments," "two Chinas," and "independent Taiwan" or advocate that "the status of Taiwan remains to be determined."

The U.S. side declared: The United States acknowledges that all Chinese on either side of the Taiwan Strait maintain there is but one China and that Taiwan is a part of China. The United States Government does not challenge that position. It reaffirms its interest in a peaceful settlement of the Taiwan question by the Chinese themselves. With this prospect in mind, it affirms the ultimate objective of the withdrawal of all U.S. forces and military installations from Taiwan. In the meantime, it will progressively reduce its forces and military installations on Taiwan as the tension in the area diminishes.

The two sides agreed that it is desirable to broaden the understanding between the two peoples. To this end, they discussed specific areas in such fields as science, technology, culture, sports and journalism, in which people-to-people contacts and exchanges would be mutually beneficial. Each side undertakes to facilitate the further development of such contacts and exchanges.

Both sides view bilateral trade as another area from which mutual benefit can be derived, and agreed that economic relations based on equality and mutual benefit are in the interest of the peoples of the two countries. They agree to facilitate the progressive development of trade between their two countries. . . .

The two sides expressed the hope that the gains achieved during this visit would open up new prospects for the relations between the two countries. They believe that the normalization of relations between the two countries is not only in the interest of the Chinese and American peoples but also contributes to the relaxation of tension in Asia and the world.

• 3 •

A Recent View of China

More Americans have visited China since Henry Kissinger's secret visit in 1971 than in the previous two decades. Many of these itinerants have published their thoughts, impressions and photographs in articles and books. The general consensus of these travelers seems to be in direct contrast to the image of China put forth during the 1950's and 1960's—instead of China being seen as a totalitarian giant reducing its population to ants and threatening to overrun the rest of Asia, China appears to be on the verge of creating a model society and achieving superpower status. This euphoria has been reflected in the way that things Chinese have become the rage in such diverse places as department stores and schools. It almost seems that the Americans and Chinese have conducted a love-hate relationship over the years, and this year it's love. This is not to say that there is not much to admire about contemporary China, or that increased intensification of study about China is not essential. What is necessary, perhaps above all, is perspective and proportion.

A. Doak Barnett, an eminent Chinese scholar, made the journey with a delegation from the National Committee on U.S.-China Relations. The group visited eight cities, many rural areas and had the opportunity to observe factories, communes and schools. They were treated in the grand and courteous Chinese manner, but were given much latitude and freedom to view proletarian China. Following are some of Mr. Barnett's perceptions of the new China. What are the major insights Barnett provides? Do you think his impressions are too positive, too negative, or well balanced?

A. DOAK BARNETT

. . . China today is a country in transition, cautiously adjusting, experimenting and changing in an interim between two great events. In the aftermath of the Cultural Revolution, its leadership and institutions are still being rebuilt. At the same time, the country is poised in anticipation of the post-Mao succession. . . .

After the derailments of the 1960's, the country is back on the track of development and growth, but the process of development, which faces great problems and obstacles, is relatively gradual. Broad modernization of the society is clearly still at a fairly early stage, and though the country has undergone many significant changes it has certainly not been suddenly "transformed." One of my most striking impressions, in fact, was of continuity with the past. There is a timeless quality, still, about China and the Chinese despite all of the factories that have been built, the many signs of creeping modernization in the countryside and the far-reaching political and social changes that have occurred. . . .

Mao remains the country's one and only ideological sage, constantly quoted and universally glorified. Yet, one senses

---

Reprinted with permission, from A. Doak Barnett, "There Are Warts There, Too," *The New York Times*, April 8, 1972.

that from the perspective of working-level cadres, he is remote, and his cult has been muted. The most ubiquitous symbols of Mao are no longer the "little red books"; they are reproductions of Mao's inimitable calligraphy, which seems to symbolize Chinese culture and nationalism more than Marxist-Leninist ideology. In general, despite continuing strong ideological pressures on China's intellectuals, the prevailing mood affecting most people seems to be one of political relaxation. China is still plastered with Maoist slogans, but only a few appear new, and the oldest are beginning to fade. . . .

The succession poses great and unanswerable questions about the future. Surprisingly, cadres at almost all levels in China are quite willing to discuss it; it seems to be on their minds. They acknowledge that it will constitute a milestone in Chinese Communist history, and will involve continuing "struggle between two lines," but they assert that what will emerge will be a new and stable collective leadership—doubtless with Chou En-lai in a key position if he is still around—that will define a "correct line" for the future. One senses, however, that in reality they are quite uncertain about what the process will be, precisely who will emerge and what shape the "correct line" will take.

Another major imponderable is the role of the military in politics. At the height of the Cultural Revolution, the assaults on the Party and Government created a temporary breakdown of authority and a political vacuum that the military filled. Subsequently, as Party and Government structures were reconstructed, there appeared to be a steady process of "recivilianization." However, although the military has withdrawn from many political and economic posts, it has retained far-reaching influence. . . .

The overwhelming bulk of the facts and impressions one obtains on a short trip relate to what the society looks like, how people seem to live, what the state of the economy appears to be, how "basic-level" institutions are organized and function. One major surprise was my initial impression that so much seems so similar to what I had remembered from twenty-three years before. I was always acutely aware of important changes, and as the trip progressed I saw more and more evidence of them, but, as I suggested earlier, the strong sense of continuity with the past persisted. I was greatly struck by how much the people we encountered at all levels seemed to behave much as Chinese generally have, in other times and other places. Despite two decades of revolution, many old patterns of thought and behavior—some admirable, others less so—clearly persist. The majority of Chinese one meets today still show the same civility, politeness and preoccupation with personal relationships, as well as the matter-of-fact practicality, which have long been admired by foreigners, including me. The Chinese still impress one as able, proud and hard-working, as they always have. They also still show deep-rooted traditional predispositions to think in terms of status and hierarchy, stress protocol, submit to authority, conform to orthodoxy and fit into the social roles required of them—despite the efforts that China's revolutionary leaders have made over the years to change many of these patterns.

A feeling of the past lingers, too, because despite all the economic accomplishments of the regime—many of which are impressive—there are fewer visible signs of dramatic modernization in either the cities or countryside than I had expected. Visually, the Chinese landscape looks much the same as before. The changes of social organization that have revolutionized rural life in many respects and the modern technology that has gradually reached the villages have altered but they have certainly not yet "transformed" the countryside. New factories have mushroomed and are impressive, but the core areas of the cities that I knew well in the past have undergone much less change than I expected. Because so much of the product of industrial growth is reinvested in more industrial growth, the fruits of modernization have only just begun to permeate the society as they have in many other developing societies where mass consumption receives higher immediate priority.

Industry has been the sector in which the greatest progress has been made, and this progress is visible. One sees the new factories, large, medium-sized and small, not only in cities like Shanghai, Shenyang and Anshan—which were major industrial centers before 1949—but also in towns that had little or no modern industry previously, and in scattered rural sites paralleling the major railways. . . .

Overall the Chinese economy struck me as being one of a great developing nation struggling with problems of almost unique dimensions, making progress—but at a relatively moderate rate, in part because of the sheer size of the country and its population, the intractability of its basic problems and the tenacious hold of traditions. . . . Its greatest progress has been in expanding its productive base and in slowly building the sinews of national power. It has only begun the task of transforming the material base of Chinese life.

One of the highest-ranking Chinese leaders we met said to us: "You have been to other Asian nations. You know we are saying the truth when we say that we are a developing nation. We have a very long way to go." In years past I had tended to view such statements as examples of calculated modesty, designed to elicit compliments. I now view them as accurate statements, made by realistic men who, while proud of what China has accomplished since 1949, are under no illusions about all that must be done before China becomes a fully modernized society.

In China's major cities large numbers of buildings now have a seedy, run-down appearance. Apart from the new factories, which are largely in the fringe areas, the most notable new construction has been that of new worker apartments. Many of these, while simple, are quite attractive; but most are in the suburbs next to new factories (except in Peking where a substantial number are in the old city, near new Government office buildings). The great development in China's cities, therefore, has been outward, into suburban or fringe areas, and the core cities have changed relatively little. In the older part of these areas, the most visible changes have been for the worse. . . .

The streets of China's cities today are much cleaner than in the past, and new trees along many roads are a plus, but air pollution has become a serious problem, and the prevailing atmosphere of austerity is illustrated by the decline of urban modern transport. The basic transport system in the cities depends above all on the bicycle, and one of the most striking sights for a visitor is the endless phalanxes of workers pedaling to work in the pre-dawn hours and returning home at dusk. Motorized vehicles are notable by their scarcity; there are many fewer than in China's cities before 1949, or in most other Asian metropolises today. The explanation, clearly, is the regime's determination to economize; leg-power is much cheaper than gasoline or electricity. Also dictated by motives of economy is the general cutback on the use of heat and light. There are no bright lights; everywhere, light bulbs are used sparingly, giving the cities a dim and dreary look at night. . . .

One of the major goals—and most striking accomplishments—of the regime has been the elimination of the worst poverty and the raising of living standards of the lowest strata of society to an acceptable minimum, at least in the areas we visited. Nowhere (and this applied to suburban and rural areas as well as to the cities) did we see the kind of grinding poverty, or the miserable beggars and shanty town slums, that one used to encounter not infrequently (though some writers exaggerate how prevalent they were in the past). The mass of ordinary Chinese that one sees today appear to be reasonably healthy, well-fed, and well-clothed.

Yet to put this accomplishment in perspective, it should be recognized that the minimal subsistence standard that has been guaranteed for everyone is very low—Spartan in fact—and has been achieved in part by a leveling downward of living standards for many. . . .

The setting of a minimal floor under living standards has not meant, however, the disappearance of surprising and significant income differentials, despite the extraordinary stress that the regime has placed on egalitarianism. Incomes at the top are as much as 15 or 20 times those at the bottom. . . .

It is more difficult for a visitor to China to form even impressionistic judgments about rural areas. But again I got a sense of continuity with the past. I was struck by timeless images of centuries-old sculptured terraces, traditional village housing, peasants working as always by hand in the fields—and a general feeling that the deep-rooted ancient harmony between man and nature continues. It soon becomes clear, however, that there have been some very significant changes. Wherever one goes one sees evidence of a tremendous amount of work on new canals, ditches, ponds and reservoirs. This effort—which has an ancient tradition in China—has had a major positive effect on agricultural stability and growth. Rural electrification has also been greatly expanded; new power lines now penetrate deep into rural areas. One major consequence has been a great increase in the use of electric pumps for irrigation. Small pumping stations dot the countryside. Rural electrification has also permitted a steady expansion of the small-scale rural industries. Other changes: fields consolidated and enlarged (with the old grave mounds removed); men and women working in the fields in sizable groups instead of individually or in small clusters; a great many young new trees on hillsides and along roads (for lumber, protection against erosion, and shade). . . .

Of all the critical fields of growth in China, the one in which the regime appears to have had not only some of its greatest successes but also some of its greatest failures is education. Many of the successes are measurable in quantitative terms. Statistics given to us by a key member of the State Council's Scientific and Educational Group in Peking indicated that overall school enrollments have grown enormously since 1949, rising by 1972 to 127 million in primary schools and 36 million in middle schools. It is claimed that at present 80 per cent of China's children of primary school age attend school. The growth has been particularly impressive in rural areas. A Western visitor to primary and middle schools is impressed by the extent to which order, discipline and rote learning prevail (one sees no traces of the student activism and independence of the Cultural Revolution period), and also the degree to which ideology and politics are injected in fairly extreme and overt ways into every conceivable course. Nevertheless, expansion of basic education in China is rapidly raising the society's general level of knowledge and skills in a way that will support national development in the future. . . .

The picture in higher education, however, is very different. Of all basic institutions in China, the universities have been among those most hard-hit, and most seriously damaged, by events during and since the Cultural Revolution. One entire generation of students—those who as Red Guards were in the forefront of the struggles of 1966 to 1968—has been sent to rural areas and remote provinces, and there is no sign that they will be allowed to complete their education. . . .

More important, the Cultural Revolution was succeeded in the universities by a new movement, the so-called "educational revolution." Today ideology and politics continue to dominate the universities' atmosphere, and the process of restoring normal educational activity has been an extremely slow and difficult one. The purpose of the "educational revolution" is to carry out a radical restructuring of higher education, eliminate all traces of élitism (the alleged tendency to produce "spiritual aristocrats"), purge the universities of all "revisionist tendencies" and enshrine Maoist values as the ultimate repository of truth. Decision-making power in China's universities today rests in the hands of political cadres (many of them in their 30's or 40's), not educators, and in the background the role of the military—exercised through so-called Mao Tse-tung Thought Propaganda Teams—continues to be very great. . . .

All of this adds up to a very mixed picture. The China with which the United States is now restoring ties is a proud nation pulling itself up by its own bootstraps, determined to solve its own problems its own way and moving steadily toward playing a major role in world affairs, but it also is a country wrestling with great difficulties and facing many uncertainties. The re-establishment of normalized relations between the two countries is a historic task, essential for the creation of a viable balance in international relations and peace in Asia. The progress already achieved is cause for optimism. To create a significant, lasting and increasingly friendly relationship, however, we must approach China in a spirit not only of hope but also of realism, without illusions and without unrealistic images.

China — Bibliography

A. General

*Bell, Oliver. *The Two Chinas.* New York: Scholastic Books, 1952.

An introduction intended for the high school student. Well balanced but superficial.

*Bodde, Derk. *China's Cultural Tradition: What and Whither?.* New York: Holt, Rinehart, and Winston, 1963.

Highly recommended as the best short introduction to major ideas, features, institutions, and characteristics of Chinese civilization.

*Creel, H.G. *The Birth of China.* New York: Ungar, 1964.

A scholarly survey of the origins and formative period of Chinese civilization that is intended for the general reader. An excellent book that is a pleasure to read.

*de Bary, Wm. Theodore, et al (eds.). *Sources of Chinese Tradition.* 2 vols., New York: Columbia Univ. Press, 1964.

Collection of source materials revealing the way Chinese have thought about themselves and the world. Includes excellent explanatory notes introducing each general topic and specific selection.

*Ewing, Ethel E. *Far Eastern Society.* Chicago: Rand McNally, 1966.

Intended to introduce the high school student to the civilizations of China, Korea, and Japan. One of the better efforts of this kind.

*Fairbank, John K. *The United States and China.* New York: Viking, 1964.

This is an excellent one-volume history of Chinese civilization with special emphasis given to China's cultural tradition as studied through its institutions. The latter part of the book deals with China's relations with the

* Indicates paperback edition.

U.S. as part of China's response to the West in modern times. The author seeks to explain how the Chinese cultural tradition still influences modern China in spite of great changes.

———, and Edwin O. Reischauer. *A History of East Asian Civilization*. 2 vols. Boston: Houghton Mifflin, 1960, 1965.

The most complete and authoritative text on the histories of China and Japan. Though often dry reading, these two volumes can be used as excellent reference works.

*Fitzgerald, C.P. *China: A Short Cultural History*. New York: Praeger, 1966.

Detailed and lengthy but readable study of China's cultural history and tradition. Excellent plates.

*Goodrich, L. Carrington. *A Short History of the Chinese People*. New York: Harper & Row, 1961.

One of the best short studies of Chinese history with some attention given to cultural achievements and influence.

*Griswold, A. Whitney. *The Far Eastern Policy of the United States*. New Haven, Conn: Yale Univ. Press, 1962.

Though limited to the period before World War II, this scholarly volume analyzes the shifting currents of U.S. policy, and helps to place today's policies in perspective.

*Grousset, René. *The Rise and Splendor of the Chinese Empire*. Berkeley: Univ. of California Press, 1963.

A good survey of the history of China through the eighteenth century that gives major attention to political aspects and cultural achievements.

*Hudson, G.F. *Europe and China*. Boston: Beacon Press, 1961.

A survey of relations between China and Europe through the eighteenth century. Particularly revealing is how the author shows that many aspects of Western culture, including the ideas of natural rights and revolution, may have their origins in Confucian thought.

*Kuo, Ping-chia. *China*. New York: Oxford Univ. Press, 1965.

A small but excellent introductory survey of past and present China. Good maps and chronology charts.

*Latham, R.E. (tr.). *The Travels of Marco Polo*. Baltimore: Penguin, 1958.

Easy-to-read version of the work that formed the traditional Western view of China till modern times. Available in other translations.

*Latourette, Kenneth Scott. *China*. Englewood Cliffs, N.J.: Prentice-Hall, 1965.

Brief, but compact history of China. Author, like others, points out the continuity of Chinese history.

———. *A Short History of the Far East*. New York: Macmillan, 1957.

A lengthy but useful historical survey of the peoples and civilizations of Asia, with special emphasis on China and Japan.

*Lattimore, Owen. *Inner Asian Frontiers of China*. Boston: Beacon Press, 1962.

A scholarly study of relations between China and her central Asian neighbors. Difficult.

*Menzel, Johanna M. (ed.). *The Chinese Civil Service. Career Open to Talent*. Boston: D.C. Heath, 1965.

A collection of essays that argue about the effectiveness of the Civil Service as a means of advancing social mobility.

*Meskill, John (ed.). *The Pattern of Chinese History: Cycles, Development, or Stagnation*. Boston: D.C. Heath, 1965.

Series of essays offering various views on the nature of Chinese history.

B. PHILOSOPHY AND RELIGION

*Arvon, Henri. *Buddhism*. New York: Walker, 1962.

A summary of Buddhist principles with special emphasis on its development in China and Japan.

*Burtt, E.A. (ed.). *The Teachings of the Compassionate Buddha*. New York: Mentor, 1958.

An anthology of basic Buddhist teachings.

*Chai, Ch'u and Winberg. *The Story of Chinese Philosophy*. New York: Washington Square Press, 1961.

An introduction for the general reader that describes the lives and thoughts of eight philosophers including excerpts from their works.

Creel, H.G. *Chinese Thought from Confucius to Mao Tse-tung*. New York: Mentor, 1963.

An excellent and lucid introduction to Chinese philosophy that is easy to read. Though not much emphasis is given to modern thought, the author's treatment of the evolution of Chinese thought suggests that traditional thinking is still of major importance.

*de Bary, et al (eds.). *Sources of Chinese Tradition.* (See above.)

*Fung Yu-lan. *A Short History of Chinese Philosophy.* Derk Bodde (ed.). New York: Free Press, 1966.

An excellent and readable study of Chinese philosophy with emphasis on the evolution of Confucianism and Taoism. Particularly valuable is the opening chapter in which the author explains how Chinese systems of thought differ from those of the West.

*Gard, Richard A. (ed.). *Buddhism.* New York: Washington Square Press, 1963.

An analysis of the principles and teachings of Buddhism with selections from Buddhist sources.

*Lutz, Jesse G. (ed.). *Christian Missions in China: Evangelists of What?* Boston: D.C. Heath, 1965.

A collection of essays that seeks to analyze and evaluate the effects of the missionary movement from both the Chinese and Western view.

Ross, Nancy Wilson. *Three Ways of Asian Wisdom: Hinduism, Buddhism, Zen.* New York: Simon and Schuster, 1966.

An excellent introduction for the beginner to the study of Hinduism, Buddhism, and Zen. Contains excellent plates showing relationship between art and philosophy.

*Waley, Arthur. (tr.). *The Analects of Confucius.* New York: Vintage, 1960.

Contains the essence of Confucian thought on government, morality, and harmony in society. Highly recommended as an introduction to Chinese thought.

*———. *Three Ways of Thought in Ancient China.* New York: Anchor, 1956.

Contains excerpts from the works of Chuang Tzu (Taoism), Mencius (Confucianism), and Han Fei Tzu (Legalism). Excellent introduction for studying these aspects of Chinese thought—all of which helped to form the Chinese cultural tradition.

*——— (ed.). *The Way and Its Power: A Study of the Tao Tê Ching and Its Place in Chinese Thought.* New York: Grove Press, 1961.

A translation of the major book of Taoism.

*Wright, Arthur F. *Buddhism in Chinese History*. New York: Atheneum, 1965.

A series of essays on the rise and fall of Buddhism in China, and an assessment of its permanent influence.

*——— (ed.). *Confucianism and Chinese Civilization*. New York: Atheneum, 1964.

A collection of essays that analyzes the effects of the Confucian world view on Chinese civilization.

*Yang, C.K. *Religion in Chinese Society*. Berkeley: Univ. of California Press, 1961.

A study of Chinese religious systems and cults and how they influenced the past and present.

C. Village, Clan, Family, and Class

*Fairbank, John K. *The United States and China*. (See above.)

Lang, Olga. *Chinese Family and Society*. Hamden, Conn.: Shoe String, 1968.

Good study of structure of the traditional family and its importance in Chinese society.

*Mace, David and Vera. *Marriage: East and West*. New York: Dolphin, 1960.

A study of attitudes toward marriage and of the role of the female in both cultures. Interesting reading, though somewhat simplified.

*Myrdal, Jan. *Report from a Chinese Village*. New York: Signet, 1966.

Fascinating first-person study of changes in a Chinese village. Myrdal was granted permission to reside in a village for a period of time and the bulk of the text is his report of interviews with the many and diverse members of this village. A record of the meaning of the Chinese village.

*Yang, C.K. *Chinese Communist Society: The Family and the Village*. Cambridge, Mass.: M.I.T. Press, 1959.

Originally two separate volumes. A sociological analysis of the changes that have taken place in these two important Chinese institutions since 1949. Though no longer up to date, this book is still extremely valuable for a study of modern China.

*Yang, Martin C. *A Chinese Village*. New York: Columbia Univ. Press, 1945.

A study of a village before the Communists came to power. Good material on daily life—work, family relations, leisure—of the Chinese peasant.

D. MODERN CHINA: CHINA'S RESPONSE TO THE WEST

Chiang Kai-shek. *China's Destiny*. New York: Macmillan, 1947.

Written during the war, this book reveals the thinking of Chiang and suggests he is much closer to Chinese ways of thinking than to the West.

*Clubb, Edmund O. *Twentieth Century China*. New York: Columbia Univ. Press, 1964.

Excellent history of the major events in the twentieth-century Chinese revolution. Particularly valuable is the analysis of the strengths and weaknesses of the Kuomingtang written by the last American consulate-general in Peking.

*Fairbank, John K. *The United States and China* (See above.)

*Feis, Herbert. *The China Tangle*. New York: Atheneum, 1965.

A detailed study of American policy toward China from Pearl Harbor to the Marshall Mission.

*Fitzgerald, C.P. *The Birth of Communist China*. Baltimore: Penguin, 1964.

A provocative study of the entire spectrum of the twentieth-century revolution. The last chapters attempt to show how Communist China continues many traditional patterns of Chinese culture and institutions despite the great changes.

*Isaacs, Harold R. *The Tragedy of the Chinese Revolution*. New York: Atheneum, 1966.

This fascinating work was originally written in the late 1930s within a Trotskyite political perspective. Subsequently revised, the author, often convincingly, argues that Stalin and the Comintern sacrificed the true interests of the Chinese Communist Party and the Chinese people during the 1920s in order to consolidate Stalin's power after the death of Lenin. Highly recommended.

*Loh, Pichon P. (ed.). *The Kuomintang Debacle of 1949: Conquest or Collapse?* Boston: D.C. Heath, 1965.

Excellent collection of essays revealing a variety of

interpretations of the failures of the Nationalist government.

Schwartz, Benjamin D. *Chinese Communism and the Rise of Mao.* Cambridge, Mass: Harvard Univ. Press, 1951.

A history of the Chinese Communist Party, and how it changed under the leadership and strategy of Mao.

*Snow, Edgar. *Red Star Over China.* New York: Grove Press, 1961

The classic eye-witness account by the American journalist in which the origins of Chinese Communism are described. Contains one of the earliest interviews with Mao and a brilliant description of the Long March. Also discusses the strategy and appeal of the CCP.

*Teng, Ssu-yü and John K. Fairbank. *China's Response to the West: A Documentary Survey, 1839-1923.* New York: Atheneum, 1963.

An excellent collection of sources that documents how China reacted to the impact and force of the West.

*White, Theodore H. and Annalee Jacoby. *Thunder Out of China.* New York: William Morrow, 1961.

An eyewitness account of China during the war years which helps to explain the eventual collapse of the Nationalist regime.

E. Modern China: Communism in China

*Barnett, A. Doak. *China After Mao: With Selected Documents.* New Jersey: Princeton Univ. Press, 1967.

A study of the present crisis in China with relevant documents.

*———. *Communist China and Asia: A Challenge to American Policy.* New York: Vintage, 1961.

An analysis of the differences between China and the U.S. with special emphasis on Asia. In conclusion the author discusses the alternatives facing the U.S.

*———. *Communist China in Perspective.* New York: Praeger, 1962.

A short book in which the author takes stock of the Revolution and its place in Chinese history.

*Boyd, R.G. *Communist China's Foreign Policy.* New York: Praeger, 1962.

Special attention is given to relations between China and the USSR.

*Buss, Claude A. *The People's Republic of China.* Princeton, N.J.: Van Nostrand, 1962.

A short but well-balanced survey of Communism in China.

*Cartier-Bresson, Henri and Barbara B. Miller. *China.* New York: Bantam Books, 1964.

A superb photographic record of China since 1949 which contrasts the old and new China.

*Feuerwerker, Albert (ed.). *Modern China.* Englewood Cliffs, N.J.: Prentice-Hall, 1964.

Excellent group of essays on today's China dealing with such topics as population, family, agriculture, KMT, economic policy. Recommended.

*Fitzgerald, C.P. *The Birth of Communist China.* (See above.)

*Floyd, David. *Mao Against Khrushchev.* New York: Praeger, 1964.

A study of the origins of the conflict, with relevant documents.

*Greene, Felix. *China.* New York: Ballantine, 1962.

An eye-witness report of present-day China by an English journalist sympathetic to the Revolution. Very valuable but should be read with a critical eye.

*Jacobs, Dan N. and Hans H. Baerwald (eds.). *Chinese Communism: Selected Documents.* New York: Harper & Row, 1963.

Excellent source book on the history of Communism in China and relations between China and the USSR.

Karol, K.S. *China: The Other Communism.* T. Baistow (tr.). New York: Hill & Wang, 1967.

A recent—and one of the best—eye-witness accounts of developments in contemporary China. Written by a perceptive journalist.

*Lamb, Alastair. *The China-India Border.* New York: Oxford Univ. Press, 1964.

Traces the factors that led to the current border dispute.

*Levenson, Joseph R. *Modern China and Its Confucian Past.* New York: Anchor, 1964.

A study of the attempt of modern Chinese intellectuals to assess the continuity of their own history. The author stresses the great appeal that Confucian thinking still has for many Chinese.

*Mao Tse-tung. *Quotations From the Chairman.* New York: Bantam, 1967.

This is the famous (or infamous) red book. Interesting, but not a very good introduction to Mao's thought.

*Myrdal, Jan. *Report from a Chinese Village.* (See above.)

*North, Robert C. *Chinese Communism.* New York: World Univ. Library, 1966.

Brief, well-balanced account of the Chinese civil war and of China today. Excellent photographs.

Riboud, Marc. *The Three Banners of China.* New York: Macmillan, 1966.

Superb photographic record (with good notes) of three aspects of contemporary Chinese life: The People's Communes, the Great Leap Forward, and the new General Party Line.

*Schram, Stuart R. *The Political Thought of Mao Tse-tung.* New York: Praeger, 1969.

Excellent introduction to Maoism with ample selections from his works.

*Schurmann, Franz and Orville Schell. *The China Reader.* 3 vols. New York: Vintage, 1967.

Excellent documentary record of three stages of modern Chinese history—imperial, republican, communist. Valuable commentary.

Snow, Edgar. *The Other Side of the River: Red China Today.* New York: Random House, 1962.

One of the best accounts of China since 1949 written by the only American journalist permitted to enter China. Snow is generally sympathetic to the efforts of the regime but tries not to let himself be fooled. His conclusions suggest that the Great Leap Forward may not have been as total a disaster as usually assumed. Recommended.

Tang, Shêng-hao. *Communist China Today.* New York: Praeger, 1957.

Though somewhat out of date, this scholarly study of the rise of Chinese communism and the policies of the Communist state in China is still a valuable reference work. Generally unsympathetic, the author poses the problems that China holds for the world.

*Wu, Yuan-Li. *The Economy of Communist China.* New York: Praeger, 1965.

Good, recent study of the achievements, failures, and costs of Chinese economic policy.

*Yang, C.K. *Chinese Communist Society: The Family and the Village.* (See above)

F. BIOGRAPHY

*Buck, Pearl. *My Several Worlds.* New York: Pocket Books, 1969.

The autobiography of the daughter of a missionary in China.

*Creel, H.G. *Confucius and the Chinese Way.* New York: Harper & Row, 1960.

A superb study of Confucius and Confucianism that attempts to divorce the man from the myth. Deals extensively with the influence of Confucianism not only in China and Asia, but also in the West.

Cronin, Vincent. *The Wise Man from the West.* New York: Dutton, 1955.

A biography of Matthew Ricci, a Jesuit who served the Ming emperor in sixteenth century and influenced China and the West's ideas of China.

Sharman, Lyon. *Sun Yat-sen; His Life and Its Meaning, a Critical Biography.* Calif: Stanford Univ. Press, 1968.

A good, but limited biography of China's first nationalist leader.

G. LITERATURE AND THE ARTS

*Binyon, Laurence. *Painting in the Far East.* New York: Dover, 1959.

An introduction to the history of painting in China and Japan through the nineteenth century. Excellent plates.

Birch, Cyril and Donald Keene (eds.). *Anthology of Chinese Literature.* New York: Grove Press, 1965.

Includes excellent samples of prose and poetry throughout the nineteenth century.

*Buck, Pearl. *The Good Earth.* New York: Pocket Books, 1968.

If you have not already read this classic, you should.

Though the book has produced a new set of stereotypes (Pearl Buck's "Chinese") it still presents a remarkable picture of the human tragedy in a decaying social order.

*Bynner, Witter. (tr.) and Kiang Kang-Hu (comp.). *The Jade Mountain*. New York: Anchor, 1964.

Excellent anthology of poems from the T'ang dynasty including works of the masters Tu Fu, Li Po, P. Chu-yi. Good notes.

Dawson, Raymond (ed.). *The Legacy of China*. New York: Oxford Univ. Press, 1964.

A series of essays on Chinese achievements in the arts and sciences.

*Hersey, John. *A Single Pebble*. New York: Bantam, 1956.

More of a parable than a novel, this short work portrays the conflict in life and thought between East and West. The setting is a junk on the Yangtze during the 1920s and the protagonists are a young idealistic American engineer and the Chinese navigator of the boat.

Hsia, C.T. *History of Modern Chinese Fiction: 1917-1957*. New Haven, Conn.: Yale Univ. Press, 1961.

A critical analysis of how Chinese fiction was influenced by contact with the West.

*Lin Yu-tang (ed.). *Famous Chinese Short Stories*. New York: Washington Square Press, 1961.

Good, readable anthology.

Malraux, André. *Man's Fate*. New York: Modern Library, 1934.

One of the great novels of the twentieth century. The plot deals with the revolutionary movement in China during the 1920s and the main protagonist is a follower of the Communists.

*Payne, Robert (ed.). *The White Pony: An Anthology of Chinese Poetry*. New York: New American Library, 1957.

Good anthology.

Scott, A.C. *An Introduction to the Chinese Theatre*. New York: Theatre Arts, 1958.

Good introduction that discusses the origins and the techniques of Chinese drama and gives plot summaries of important plays.

*Tsao Hsueh-Ch'in. *Dream of the Red Chamber*. Wang Chi-chen (tr.). New York: Anchor, 1958.

An abridgement of what is generally considered to be

the greatest novel written in China. The book deals with the lives of a gentry family during the Manchu dynasty revealing a cross-section of Chinese life and presenting a superb picture of the decay of the traditional social order.

*Wu Ch'eng-en. *Monkey*. Arthur Waley (tr.). New York: Grove Press, 1958.

"Folk" novel of China that uses humor and satire to poke fun at many ideas and institutions. Probably developed as part of the tradition of oral storytelling, till written down and polished in the eighteenth century.

Waley, Arthur (tr.). *Chinese Poems*. London: Allen & Unwin, 1946.

The best anthology of traditional Chinese poetry.

H. RECENT BOOKS ON CHINA

Barnett, A. Doak. *A New U.S. Policy Toward China*. Washington, D.C.: The Brookings Institution, 1971.

Baum, Richard. *China in Ferment: Perspectives on the Cultural Revolution*. Englewood Cliffs, N.J.: Prentice-Hall, 1971.

Bulletin of the Atomic Scientists. *China After the Cultural Revolution*. New York: Random House, 1970.

Clubb, C. Edmund. *China and Russia: The "Great Game."* New York: Columbia Univ. Press, 1971.

*Committee of Concerned Asian Scholars. *China: Inside the People's Republic*. New York: Bantam, 1972.

Friedman, Edward, and Selden, Mark (eds.). *America's Asia: Dissenting Essays on Asian American Relations*. New York: Random House, 1971.

Hinton, William. *Fanshen: A Documentary of Revolution in a Chinese Village*. New York: Random House, 1968.

Iriye, Akira. *Across the Pacific*. New York: Harcourt Brace Jovanovich, 1970.

Maxwell, Neville. *India's China War*. New York: Pantheon, 1970.

Salisbury, Harrison. *To Peking and Beyond*. New York: Quadrangle Books, 1973.

Stoessinger, John G. *Nations in Darkness: China, Russia, America*. New York: Random House, 1971.

*Terrill, Ross. *800,000,000: The Real Chinese*. New York: Delta, 1972.

*Ting, John C. *An American in China*. New York: Paperback Library, 1972.

*Wilson, Dick. *Anatomy of China: An Introduction to One Quarter of Mankind*. New York: Mentor, 1969.

Index

Lisa Rosner